# Least Restrictive Environment: The Paradox of Inclusion

## Lawrence M. Siegel

LRP Publications
Horsham, Pennsylvania

LRP Publications
An Axon Group Company
Horsham, Pennsylvania   19044

The story of Janet Morrison is a universal one and reflects real experiences of children with disabilities. While the story represents a composite of those children and the other individuals involved in the process, it does not, nor is it intended to represent any real person, living or deceased.

### Library of Congress Cataloging-in-Publication Data

Siegel, Lawrence M., 1946-
   Least restrictive environment : the paradox of inclusion /
Lawrence M. Siegel. -- 1st ed.
      p.      cm.
   Includes bibliographical references and index.
   ISBN 0-934753-79-2 (acid-free paper) : $27.50
   1. Mainstreaming in education--United States.   2. Educational law
and legislation--United States.   3. Mainstreaming in education-
-Political aspects--United States.   4. Handicapped children-
-Education--United States.   5. Deaf children--Education--United
States--Case studies.   I. Title
LC4013.S54   1994
371.9'046'0973--dc20                    94-26941
                                          CIP

Printed on acid-free paper in the United States of America.
First Edition
99   98   97   96   95   94              6   5   4   3   2   1

To my daughters, Catherine and Elisabeth, and to my wife, Gail.

# About the Author

Lawrence M. Siegel is an attorney at law and Commissioner of the California Advisory Commission on Special Education. He earned his A.B. and M.A. from the University of California at Berkeley, and his J.D. from Hastings College of the Law. He is the co-founder and co-chair of the California Deaf Education Coalition and is a member of the National Association of the Deaf Commission on Equal Educational Opportunities for Deaf Children. Mr. Siegel has assisted state organizations in Texas, Indiana, Nebraska, California, and South Dakota in the formulation of special education legislation, and has testified before various state legislatures and Congress regarding the Individuals with Disabilities Education Act and placement rights.

Mr. Siegel has published many articles dealing with special education law and policy, and was the author of the nation's first educational bill of rights for deaf children, passed in South Dakota in March of 1993.

# Table of Contents

I want to thank Ken Kresse and Jack Levesque, for their support and ongoing commitment to creating an educational system that serves all the needs of a child; Sandy Harvey and Ann Kinkor, for their passionate understanding of those principles; Henry Klopping and Jacob Arcanin, for their friendship and support; and Gertie Galloway, for her kindness and leadership. By all I am constantly reminded of the beauty and variety of communication.

My appreciation to Erana Bumbardatore and Stacey Ann Cortese, and to Elaine Gruenfeld Goldberg for her patience and support.

Finally, in appreciation to my family: Nancy, Steve, Natalie, Noah, Jerry and Russell, and to my parents, who believed that fairness should be applied with the broadest of brushes.

# Introduction

Some years ago, a family sought to place their six-year-old daughter in a state school for the deaf. The school was many hundreds of miles away from the child's home; she would see her family only on weekends and during holidays. The child's school district opposed such a placement because it was, to them, a "segregated" program. A lengthy, and at times acrimonious, dispute followed. Attorneys were engaged, mediation was tried (but failed), and finally a five-day administrative hearing was held, during which witnesses testified under oath. At the heart of the dispute over one child's placement were significant, emotional, and often paradoxical issues regarding the right and importance of integrating children with disabilities into mainstream education.

Since Congress passed the Individuals with Disabilities Education Act in 1975, the inclusion of previously excluded children has become a daunting and even controversial matter.[1] One might suppose that the effort to include children with disabilities would have none of the rancor or uncertainty that racial integration has engendered. The story of this one family illuminates, however, the complexity of inclusion, for there is no consensus about the efficacy of including children with disabilities into the educational mainstream. Almost 20 years after the passage of the historic mainstreaming law, there is, in fact, a growing and divisive dispute about integrating children with disabilities. This argument not only divides educators from parents, but also parents from other parents.

Even as the full inclusion movement, which in one variation calls for the integration of all children with disabilities into regular classrooms, has galvanized the educational community, countermovements have been spawned, and so the full inclusion debate reveals the complexities of educating children with disabilities.

Part One of this book analyzes the ways in which the law and educational practices encourage inclusion and attempt to bring children with disabilities into the educational mainstream. Part Two assesses how the same law and practices send an entirely different message. The analysis will also consider the consequences of a law that simultaneously calls for inclusion and separation; the educational and political attitudes regarding the placement of children with disabilities; the concurrent movements to strengthen the integration of disabled children and to preserve separate educational programs; and, ultimately, the story of one child among the five million children with disabilities in this nation.

## Endnotes

1.    Pub. L. 94-142; 20 U.S.C. § 1400 (1975).

# Prologue

Separate but equal is not acceptable. . . . [segregated special education is] immoral.[1]

Judith Heumann, Undersecretary of Education

My son was the victim of the failed approach to main-streaming. Five years have been literally wasted for him. The damage [from integration] is done and irreparable.[2]

Ginger Greaves, parent and Chair of IMPACT-HI

Outside the school administration building, a man marched methodically up and down the street. He carried a sign, a marker for his child's history, a single statement of his discontent. He was tall and bearded. He appeared stoic, certainly quiet, but there was little doubt that he meant to affect a change through his demonstration. There is a kind of unintended redundancy or what may appear to be self-indulgence to the activity. Perhaps we have seen too many television re-creations. The traditions of Walden Pond, John Brown, and Martin Luther King have been watered down until it appears that every malcontent, visionary, or angry taxpayer has taken to the pavement. Civil disobedience has lost its drama. At least that is what some inside the building must have thought.

All of which was fully irrelevant to the man; he gave no thought to whether this had been done once or one thousand times. His adversary was his daughter's school district, and now

3

he could either go into court and face an expensive and lengthy battle there or he could do this simpler thing.

He said nothing, at least conventionally, pacing up and down the street, until the local paper took his picture, until people inside the building pushed back the blinds and watched him, some tired of his inexhaustive attitude, others merely disgusted.

His lawyer had explained the options. Court would take time, a lot of time, and resources that the family could not amass even if they had years to do so. How long would it take? the father had asked; his daughter had missed a great deal of school and it was March.

The lawyer had explained that since there had been an administrative decision, the court would not take up the matter for some time, absent proof of some emergency. It would be difficult to convince the court that there were compelling reasons to change her school now.

Compelling? The father asked the attorney why his daughter's educational needs were not compelling enough. I am not asking for more books and different tests. Compelling? He was incredulous. She has no one in that school to communicate with. Isn't it compelling enough that she is a good child who wants a teacher she can talk to? They don't know her language.

He walked in front of the school building for days. His daughter, Janet, was deaf. He was deaf. His wife was deaf. His four other children were deaf. He and his wife wanted his daughter to go to the state school for the deaf, several hundred miles away. His daughter was six years old and would come home only on the weekends if she attended the state school. He had pleaded with his school district to allow her to go away from home. He had hoped that one person inside the building could look beyond the laws, regulations, policies, statements of intent, generic philosophies and attitudes, and merely see one man wanting one thing for his child.

4

He lived north of Sacramento in California's flat San Joaquin Valley. On clear days, Mount Shasta, snow-covered and rising to 14,000 feet, was visible if one looked toward Oregon. Not far to the east and 78 years earlier, the last "wild" Yahi Indian had walked out of those foothills emaciated and ill, and had surrendered. Janet's father was not threadbare like Ishi had been, and he was not yet ready to defer to those he thought of as his daughter's captors.

The school district believed its county hearing-impaired program was appropriate for Janet, and thought it unwise for a six-year-old to be separated from her family to go to a school with 500 other deaf children—sooner or later she would live in a hearing world and she needed to adjust to that world now, not later. Janet's father thought it the other way around.

And so he marched back and forth, never fully convinced that the school district wanted to harm his daughter, and never fully trusting those who ostensibly had the training and knowledge to make educational decisions for his child.

They watched through the windows; some who had been involved in the case were angered at the man's persistence. They had fought this battle through informal meetings, too many phone calls between lawyers and educators and lawyers and lawyers, lengthy encounters with school personnel, through a mediation and a formal administrative hearing. They had paid for private counsel, at private rates, to fly all too frequently from Southern California. They understood the case had implications beyond Janet and had hired one of the best-known education law firms in the state. They had won; Janet's father had lost. The United States Congress had required them to bring this child into the mainstream or certainly closer to it.

The law was clear, or so it seemed. Children with disabilities, a class of students who had been historically excluded from mainstreamed education, would be integrated to the maximum extent appropriate with non-disabled children. How could this man want, in his rational mind, to remove his child from her home? The local program was not perfect, but it met legal standards, was appropriate for the child, and it brought her closer to, rather than farther from, society's mainstream. That the child was educated almost exclusively with other students with some hearing loss was merely a variation on the law's demands. The law said she must be educated in a regular classroom or, in the alternative, as close to home as possible. The county's program was 25, not hundreds of miles from Janet's home. The courts of the United States had agreed with the law's core sentiment: there is a legal preference for "serving disabled individuals in the setting which [sic] is least restrictive to their liberty and which is near the community in which their families live."[3] Raymond Morrison viewed liberty in terms particular to his daughter's needs; her freedom was further from, rather than closer to, home—her freedom was in a school where there were only children who could not hear.

Liberty is a difficult concept to qualify without looking like you're undermining the Constitution. He knew he would not see Janet every night or hug her every morning as she left for school if she went away. This was acceptable. The district said she would be isolated and segregated if placed in the state school. He marched on this notion. How could she be isolated when she was with children who were like her, who could communicate with her? How could she be "segregated," when language and people opened up to her at the state school like the morning sun filling the San Joaquin Valley to the west? Someone from the local paper asked why he didn't want his child mainstreamed. He marched, the sign said, to free her from the mainstream.

The school's personnel watched him and wondered whether there might be reasons to change their point of view. They had made their stand for integration. It was he who would choose to isolate his child. If he wanted his daughter to be "segregated," why not let him do it? History, in this small matter, would be turned on its head by the individual, not the institution. They watched him for another moment and then went back to work. His pace never slowed.

––––––––––

In 1975 the United States Congress passed the Education for All Handicapped Children's Act, a national commitment to end the isolation of children with disabilities.* By 1993 IDEA served five million students with disabilities, 10 percent of the total student population in the United States.[4] It was not the first "disability" law, but was, and remains, *the* congressional statement on the educational rights of children with disabilities.

At its heart, IDEA is an integrating law. Because of its passage Janet Morrison and her peers were to enjoy, finally, the same educational experience as non-disabled children. Before the passage of IDEA in 1975, one million children with disabilities were excluded entirely from the public school system, while approximately four million other "handicapped" children received inappropriate educational services.[5] These children were ignored, isolated, and often placed at the periphery of the school property or beyond with other "retarded" children. The new law sought to include children with disabilities in the mainstream of American education. Fairness alone would seem to argue as much; integration should be a simple proposition.

Yet the heart of IDEA—its inclusionary spirit—is controversial and inherently paradoxical. Raymond Morrison's protest was no anomaly; IDEA is dangerously at odds with itself. More than that, it is viewed as having failed children both by those who consider it too exclusionary and "segregationistic" and by those who consider its integration purpose too broad and too frequently applied in a generic way. Almost 20 years after the

––––––––––

* In 1991, the Act's name was changed to Individuals with Disabilities Education Act (IDEA). It will be referred to in this book as IDEA. At times various commentators, judges and others may refer to IDEA as EHCA, the Act, EHA or Pub. L. 94-142.

passage of IDEA, it is considered, by some, to have hurt more students than it helped and to have established a funding structure that encouraged, rather than reduced, separation. And with the rapid growth of reform movements seeking to greatly modify IDEA or even eliminate separate education altogether, a counter-revolution formed, with concerns as well articulated and reasoned as those who seek an end to separate special education. The dichotomy between the two camps is marked by a good deal of anger and fear; the U.S. Undersecretary of Education calls separate education "immoral," while others characterize those who would bring all children with disabilities into regular education as "advozealots."[6]

The great conflict of IDEA is initially reflected in its dual purpose: to maximize integrative opportunities while mandating comprehensive programs to meet individual needs. This may require the removal of children from regular classes and the creation of separate educational programs. While IDEA requires that children with disabilities be mainstreamed to the "maximum extent possible" in the schools they would attend if not disabled, it also requires a "continuum of placement alternatives," including *separate* classes, schools, institutions, and hospitals.[7]

The American educational system has been both decent and recalcitrant in its efforts to fulfill IDEA's requirements. To the extent that IDEA was perceived as a vehicle for bringing most, if not all, children with disabilities into the mainstream, statistics suggest very mixed results. During the 1989-90 school year, for example, 31.5 percent of all children with disabilities were in regular classrooms. In 1977 special education cost $7 billion; by 1993 the cost for special education programs that were described as still significantly "separate and unequal" was $30 billion.[8] The evolution of the "full inclusion" reform movement is the direct result of a real failure of IDEA's promise.

IDEA is an integrating law that cannot make up its mind about its core purpose. As a result there is a deep, ironic, and acrimonious split within the large special education community.

The first paradox of IDEA is reflected in the lineup of proponents and opponents of educational mainstreaming. The debate is not merely between parents and administrators—historic antagonists—but between parents and parents, advocates of one group against advocates of another, with the lines between "inclusionists" and "separatists" sometimes harshly drawn. The former believe that IDEA requires more than major legal fine tuning, but rather look for the eradication of any separate educational system. For the "separatists," the provision of nonregular placement options for children with disabilities is not only consistent with the law, but educationally, linguistically, psychologically, and culturally sound. Therefore, these options must be protected against the full inclusion onslaught.

Proponents of full inclusion view the "continuum" of placement alternatives as an admission of the system's failed "segregating" philosophy. Some argue that there is a direct relationship between "segregation" and the abuse of children with disabilities.[9] Some parents and educators who oppose full inclusion meet in emergency sessions to develop strategies for the integration battle while others testify passionately before Congress about the tragically isolating experiences their children had in *mainstreamed* programs.

Appearing before the House of Representatives Subcommittee on Select Education, the late Dr. Larry Stewart, a well-respected deaf psychologist, called integration "arbitrary . . . unprofessional [and] abusive to the constitutional and human rights of many deaf children. . . ." Dr. Stewart further stated that integration, in relation to deaf children, defeated rather than encouraged and invigorated the historically excluded child.[10]

The array of full inclusion proponents includes some interesting converts. Recently a national association of special education administrators published its call for inclusion, particularly extolling the movement's effort to eliminate the entire special education system. Parenthetically in the same publication, adjacent to the call for inclusion, the association described action taken by one of its member school districts *appealing* a court decision ordering the inclusion of a child with disabilities, and calling inclusionists "ideologues."[11]

State departments of education, considered by some to be directly responsible for "segregated" programs, create task forces that call for across-the-board integration. In August 1993, the Nebraska Special Education Advisory Council issued a 40-page report on the integration of children with disabilities, stressing its "vision" that "[a]ll students will attend their neighborhood school."[12] Two months later a coalition of parents, teachers and deaf people formed the Nebraska Coalition for Deaf Children, specifically to stem the "full inclusion" tide, preserve the state school for the deaf, and articulate why integration of some children increases, rather than reduces, student isolation.

In January 1993 the Learning Disabilities Association of America, representing two million children with learning disabilities, issued a position paper strongly opposing the full-scale integration of children with disabilities, stressing that the "placement of *ALL* with disabilities in the regular education classroom is as great a violation of IDEA as is the placement of *ALL* children in separate classrooms on the basis of their type of disability."[13] Two months earlier the National Association of School Boards of Education—representing those individual school boards that often found themselves in court as defendants in integration cases—had issued its "Winners All: A Call for Inclusive Schools," a plan for broad-based integration of children with disabilities.[14]

And so the first and perhaps most surprising paradox of IDEA and the integration of children with disabilities is that an ostensibly noble effort to end the exclusion of children has created a deep and perhaps irreparable rift among the very communities the law was intended to serve.

There is a second paradox that particularly affects the divergent camps of the special education community. Despite its inherent uncertainties, IDEA is an "integrating" statute—even a cursory examination of its legislative history reveals Congress's recognition of, and concern about, long-standing exclusionary practices regarding children with disabilities. But IDEA does not mandate absolute integration and in fact sets out, as noted, viable alternative placement options. This duality creates real problems for those who seek to change IDEA.

Many who favor full inclusion, or at least greater integration opportunities for children with disabilities, view IDEA as being essentially too exclusionary, but they still recognize IDEA as an important civil rights law. Those who oppose any kind of generic full inclusion believe that IDEA already requires too much system-wide integration, even as it provides certain important options that also must be protected. Not surprisingly, both camps walk the difficult line between reforming and protecting the legal status quo. This is particularly complex when different groups want to retain different sections of the law, and these groups recognize that by opening such a debate a third group—perhaps composed of some in the regular education community who believe special education is too powerful and too expensive—will have their day and IDEA will be irrevocably weakened.*

The third paradox of this integrating law—its internal uncertainty—is found deeply wedged between the two core components of IDEA: the requirement to educate children with disabilities in the "least restrictive environment" (LRE) and the requirement to provide them with a "free *appropriate* public education" (FAPE).[15] In many ways this paradox mirrors the differing opinions within the special education community. Full inclusionists consider LRE to be the trump card of special education law, while those who believe there is a need for separate placement options see "need" as superior to "placement."

---

* After one court decision in which a school district was required to more fully integrate a child with disabilities, the local newspaper called for the abolition of IDEA. *See* Chapter 1 discussion of the *Holland* case.

11

This paradox is further complicated by the language of IDEA. It is a mainstreaming law that never uses the terms "mainstreaming," "inclusion," or "integration." LRE, as statutorily defined, is the right and requirement to educate children with disabilities "to the maximum extent appropriate" in classrooms with non-disabled children. A FAPE provides for the unique needs of the child. The LRE and FAPE mandates have frequently been in conflict and reveal the potential incompatibility between placement-integration and service-program factors.

A child with disabilities may need significant support services, such as occupational and physical therapy, language development help, or a behavioral modification program. A child may need specialized physical components, a special curriculum or methodology, placement in a program in which there are no children who act out, or specially trained teachers. Those items make up the FAPE for that child. Whether that program can be provided in a regular classroom or even the neighborhood school has been, and continues to be, at the heart of "the war" between "seasoned combatants" over the "future welfare, education and happiness of" children with disabilities.[16] The irony of this third paradox is that IDEA insists on two laudable goals—appropriateness and least restrictiveness—and, in so doing, creates the basis for conflict.

The placement-need question touches other significant matters, including the fundamental query of how far a school district has to go to provide an appropriate education. School districts are required to provide comprehensive programs, but what constitutes such a program? The United States Supreme Court ruled in its first analysis of IDEA that the school system need only ensure that a child with disabilities progress from grade to grade.[17] Other courts have ruled, however, that social opportunities, linguistic development, and other nonacademic items may be part of a child's appropriate education.

The fourth paradox involves what appears to be the limited range of the integration-segregation choice (a child is either included or excluded, there is no such thing as a little "segregation"), and the actual fluid quality of the LRE requirement of the law. In passing "mainstreaming" legislation, Congress included statutory direction both to mainstream children and to "remove" them from the regular educational environment. The law prefers mainstreaming, even as it backs away from it—there is about IDEA a kind of $\frac{3}{4}$ or $\frac{7}{8}$ or $\frac{15}{16}$ commitment to inclusion; no matter how close one gets to a full right to mainstreaming, it is never absolute. Therefore, as the boundaries blur, difficulties arise with the uncertainty of the charge.

By its very nature LRE involves placement relativity. Not only are there regular classrooms at one end of the spectrum and completely separate ones at the other, there are a good number of options in between. Some children are mainstreamed part of the day. Others, as they progress, are moved from residential programs to fully separate classes, but within a regular school setting.

In many special education disputes, there is no question that the child should not be in a regular classroom; the fight is over two nonregular options. The school district in Janet Morrison's case never offered a regular classroom, but rather offered a special classroom for deaf children in a regular school. Her district could take the moral high ground since it offered a program closer to her home than that sought by her parents. Pragmatic integration.

There are, of course, many variations on this theme. For example, a parent of a child with a serious emotional disturbance seeks to place her child in a 24-hour residential program, and the school, for financial and/or philosophical reasons, offers a therapeutic day program in which there are fewer services. Or the school seeks to place the child in a state institution, while the parent fights for a less "segregated," closer placement. The only issue is how much separation is appropriate, or what the degree of non-mainstreaming will be. So it was in the Morrison case.

The roles taken by parents and schools in these disputes are further evidence of the paradoxical nature of the 20-year effort to integrate children with disabilities. Parents frequently wage long battles to integrate a child, while school districts spend in attorneys' fees many times the cost of the service that would allow for mainstreaming. But roles are often reversed. Parents fight for exclusion; schools take a stand on "principle" and fight to integrate a child. School districts wear the unwelcome mantle of obstructionists, or educational Neanderthals. Parents fight to place their children in distant programs and are seen by some as traitors to the cause.

Ultimately, a fifth paradox emerges. While there is a tendency to view those placements that move away from the regular classroom as more restrictive (for example, the special class in a regular school is less restrictive than a special class in a special school, which in turn is less restrictive than a residential school), human beings may define such options quite differently. The Morrisons believed the residential state school for the deaf, with its hundreds of peers and deaf teachers and language-rich environment, was fundamentally least restrictive. What is legally "least restrictive" may in fact be an educational prison. What is legally "most restrictive" may be, for the child, a marvelous educational oasis. This paradox may be the most difficult one for the inclusion movement to accommodate, because it requires recognition that a regular classroom may be inherently inappropriate.

Some would argue that the only reason some parents seek less integrated settings is because the school has not put the resources into the regular program to make it work. While the provision of unlimited funding might suggest an end to the conflict (based on the idea that given enough money, any regular class could be made to accommodate any child), the Morrison case is just one of many in which the availability or lack of resources did not trigger the dispute. Unlimited funding could not provide an appropriate language environment for Janet. No amount of resources could give Janet the chance to "chat" with peers during recess. There weren't any peers there, and there was no way the school system could provide them.

What of the psychotic child who has lost touch with reality? How would additional resources make a regular classroom of 35 students appropriate for a child who is terrified of crowds and open spaces? Or the behaviorally disturbed child who, despite a full-time one-to-one aide, will cause significant chaos in any class of more than eight children? What of the blind child who requires specialized programs and material that cannot be replicated in a regular class? What of the child with profound and life-threatening medical conditions that require the presence of a trained doctor for emergencies?

A final paradox plays about the effort to include children with disabilities into mainstreamed educational programs. IDEA, above all, is a law that requires careful assessment of the individual needs of each child. Unlike "regular education," where a third-grader would be generically assigned to one of several third grades, all of which provide the same or generally the same curriculum and methodology, special education prohibits such generic decisionmaking. The development of an "individualized education program" (IEP) is required for each child, and the child's parent must agree to the IEP before it can be put into action.[18] Should a parent disagree with a school district over any element of the child's IEP, the parent has the unilateral right to bring evidence before an impartial administrative law judge and, if necessary, appeal that administrative ruling to court.[19] But even as this individual determination is the core procedure of IDEA, some in the "full inclusion" movement seek a system in which there is only one choice for all children, and so the individual nature of IDEA is damaged, if not destroyed, in the name of full integration. In late 1993 the secretary of the United States

Office of Special Education and Rehabilitative Services remarked that when it came to including all children, "all means all."[20]

IDEA was passed because children with disabilities had been historically channeled into one program, usually off campus. Now the de-individualization of children is stood on its head, albeit for emotionally appealing reasons. But those who propose that all children with disabilities be integrated must contend with Janet Morrison and, to the extent that they ignore her needs, become educational fundamentalists. There is no little irony here—some who struggle against historic "segration" are ultimately viewed as reactionaries.

It is tempting to compare racial desegregation with disability desegregation in American schools. An analysis of IDEA touches the broader American issue of inclusion and, in fact, the way children with disabilities have been integrated may have its genesis in earlier desegregation efforts. In both cases the effort, whether badly or effectively done, tells us much about our national values. There are similarities, not the least of which are certain historic stereotypes and institutional opposition to efforts to open up the process to previously excluded individuals.

It would be easy, one supposes, if the analogy held fully or if the disputes about the desegregation of children with disabilities pitted only institutions against individuals or the wealthy against the poor. Then the analysis would be broad-based and succinct, the lines of dispute clearly illuminated.* That in fact the disputes

---

* Where is the moral high ground? Some years ago the author met with a representative of a national organization working for the placement of all children with disabilities in regular programs. When the issue of a "Janet Morrison" came up, the representative stated that she understood why it made sense for some children to be placed in state schools where there were a sufficient number of peers. Nonetheless, she would still fight for full inclusion, she said, because it represented an educational "utopia" for *all* children, a goal well worth fighting for. The next day a parent of a deaf child would go before a congressional committee and testify in tears why the mainstreaming of her deaf son had been a disaster. This parent changed jobs and moved her family several times before a school district was found that would allow her son to go to a so-called more restrictive, non-utopian environment.

are not so well drawn, not so distinctively divided, makes for a more complex problem to assess, but also perhaps a more revealing and rich account of our systems and attitudes. School administrators study reform, issue reports calling for full inclusion, and use resources to contest the mainstreaming of children with disabilities. Full of passion, parents call for the end to any exclusion. Full of fear, parents fight the full inclusion movement. They are asked: How can you oppose bringing children into the mainstream? They respond with a question of their own: Who will explain to my children why they have to sit alone in a regular classroom? It appears that the analogy with racial desegregation is, for many, a shaky one.

IDEA was and still is an effort to remedy old attitudes and policies. It may have been more carefully drafted so as to avoid its inherent conflict, but there is no proof yet that given a thousand lawmakers, a thousand legislative sessions, and a thousand problems, the policies and laws would be any different. The paradoxes of IDEA reflect the uncertainties in society about bringing children with disabilities into the mainstream of American life, and thus underscores the difficulty of generalizing for *all* what may apply to *many*. To some, IDEA is a process through which the inclusion of children is to be accelerated. In north central California it was, to the parents of one child, an obstacle to her growth and well-being. It is because of Janet Morrison and others like her that the law must fairly and fully accommodate all children with disabilities. The changes that must come require that the special education community make peace with itself and accept many, if not all, of the paradoxes of educational inclusion.

## Endnotes

1.  *Heumann: Oberti Decision Is Core of the ED's Inclusion Position,* THE SPECIAL EDUCATOR 85, 86 (1993).

2.  *Hearing on EHA Discretionary Programs Reauthorization: Hearing Before the Subcomm. on Select Education of the House Comm. on Education*

*and Labor,* 101st Cong., 1st Sess., 101-3 (1989) (statement of Ginger Greaves, Chair of the Federal Legislative Committee, IMPACT-HI).

3.     Sherri A.D. v. Kirby, 975 F.2d 193, 206, 19 IDELR 339, 344 (5th Cir. 1992).

4.     Joseph P. Shapiro et al., *Separate and Unequal,* U.S. NEWS & WORLD REP., Dec. 13, 1993, at 47 [hereinafter *Separate and Unequal*].

5.     20 U.S.C § 1400(b) (1990).

6.     Bernard Rimland, *Beware the Advozealots,* 7 AUTISM RESEARCH REVIEW INTERNATIONAL 3 (1993).

7.     34 C.F.R. § 300.551(b) (1993).

8.     *Separate and Unequal, supra* note 6, at 46.

9.     *DREDF cases force sweeping changes in special education,* DISABILITY RIGHTS AND EDUCATION DEFENSE FUND [DREDF] NEWS, Nov. 1993, at 1.

10.     *Hearing on EHA Discretionary Programs Reauthorization: Hearing Before the Subcomm. on Select Education of the House Comm. on Education and Labor,* 101st Cong., 1st Sess., 101-3 (1989) (testimony of Dr. Larry Stewart, Psychologist/Educator).

11.     COUNTERPOINT, (published by the National Association of Directors of Special Education) (Winter 1992) at 6.

12.     NEBRASKA SPECIAL EDUC. ADVISORY COUNCIL, AD HOC COMMITTEE ON NEIGHBORHOOD SCHOOLS AND INCLUSION IN NEBRASKA, FINAL REPORT, at 1 (Aug. 6, 1993).

13.     LEARNING DISABILITIES ASSOCIATION OF AMERICA, POSITION PAPER ON FULL INCLUSION, Jan. 1993 (emphasis in original).

14.     *Winners All: A Call for Inclusive Schools,* EDUCATIONAL DAILY, National Association of School Boards of Education, Oct. 30, 1992.

15.     20 U.S.C. §§ 1401(18), 1412(B)(5) (1990) (emphasis added).

16.     Sherri A.D. v. Kirby, 975 F.2d 193, 196 (5th Cir. 1992), 19 IDELR 339, 340.

17.     Board of Educ. v. Rowley, 102 S. Ct. 3034, 3049 (1982), 1981-82 EHLR 553:656.

18.     20 U.S.C. § 1401(9)(20) (West Supp. 1994).

19.     20 U.S.C. § 1415 (1990).

20.  *ED supports continuum, OSERS chief tells NASDSE audience,* INCLUSIVE EDUCATION PROGRAMS, Jan. 1994, at 3.

# Part One

The Inclusive Nature of
Special Education Law

# 1

---

# The Law's Preference for a Mainstreamed Education

---

The Morrisons lived in an older house on a windy and barren street on the outskirts of town. The city thinned out there, and while there was a sense of space because the houses were not close together, the area was worn down and bleak. The Morrison house was stucco, the paint faded, and the small lawn patchy and brown. Without much green to the neighborhood, the flat and austere nature of the area was intensified. The Morrisons' street was on the east-west axis of the town. Cars drove by quickly.

The Morrisons' house was filled with the smell of near poverty and their furniture was sparse and worn, but the warmth of this family was stronger than the surrounding environment. There were several dogs and a television. The youngest child toddled about with his nose running and diaper sagging. Two children sat in front of the television set. On top of the set was a decoder, providing access to those programs captioned for the deaf.

Months before Raymond Morrison would march and gain temporary notoriety in the local paper, he sat with his attorney at the small kitchen table. Beers were offered around as they discussed Janet's case against the school district. The attorney's sign-language skills were rudimentary, so communication was awkward. Complex matters were reduced to the simplest of language. Later an interpreter was brought to the house, making it easier for the attorney to communicate. Although the Morrisons were used to hearing people assuming that a few signs would suffice for communication, they preferred to know what was going on.

They discussed the strategy of Janet's case. Given the mainstreaming preference of the law and the relativity of the integration mandate, they would probably have to show that Janet was having difficulties, and that in order to meet her increasingly more complex needs she required a more restrictive environment. Janet was in fact a stable and strong child, who was experiencing considerable stress because of the dispute. She wanted to attend the state school and could not understand why that was not possible.

The school district had other plans, and the law appeared to be on its side. The district saw its legal duty as narrow in scope—Janet must attend a school closer to home than the state school. And although the law provided grounds for more distant placements, the district disfavored them. In short, the Morrisons would have to show that six-year-old Janet was exhibiting signs of linguistic and cognitive deterioration in order to prove her need for peers and teachers with whom she could communicate. The Morrisons had already taken Janet to the University of California Center on Deafness in San Francisco, where she was found to be cognitively and linguistically intact, with some inchoate signs of emotional turmoil related to the arid communication environment offered by the school district.

Raymond Morrison signed slowly, almost painfully, "My daughter either is not screwed up enough to win the case or is screwed up enough for us to worry?" The attorney paused, his own signing inadequate to convey clearly that because Janet was not sufficiently troubled, they were at a disadvantage. How was he to communicate that with such a small signing vocabulary?

24

Although Raymond and Betty Morrison were in their thirties, they were fatigued and appeared older. Raymond, an intense and animated man whose single-mindedness flew from him like visible waves, dressed in khaki pants and a plaid shirt. He had thin blond hair and a long, disheveled beard. He would appear to others who did not know him to be slightly ajar. He was partially beaten by larger frustrations, but they were not of his making. He would see that his daughter had what she needed.

Betty Morrison was a pale, thin woman, who wore a plain cotton dress. She reminded the attorney of one of the women photographed for *Now Let Us Praise Famous Men*: almost fully broken. She was bright and kind and felt the frustration of this difficulty. She knew that those who did not understand her or her daughter nonetheless had all the authority, but she did not have the anger or energy of her husband.

They discussed the upcoming administrative hearing, the witnesses to be called by both sides, the strategies, and the documents. Their only other option was to move and hope that a different school district would be more flexible. Other families had undertaken such journeys; one had moved three different times before they found a school district that allowed a state school placement. In another case, the school administrator would not approve of placement in the residential program at the state school, so the family drove the child to the state school every morning and picked her up every evening—100 miles each way, two round-trips each day.

Betty Morrison described her visit to the district's "hearing-impaired" class in the middle of the county, 25 miles from the Morrison home. She signed slowly for the attorney.

"The class is filled with other children who know no signs or only a few signs, like 'hello' and 'goodbye.' The teacher has good skills in English, but not American Sign Language.* Janet

---

* There are different kinds of sign languages in America: English-based sign languages and American Sign Language (ASL), which is wholly unrelated to English. The differences are significant. English-based sign languages most

is by herself. She does not sign much with the other children. They are very oral."

Raymond Morrison watched his wife intently. Both were oblivious to the noise and youthful uproar of the house. Betty Morrison turned to check something on the stove and finished her story.

"The aide is bad. She has very little skill."

"Like me." The attorney signed slowly.

"No, you are not the teacher, and anyway you sign better than she does. It is worse. I visited the classroom and I watched her. She works with Janet and the other children throughout the day. She talks a lot and does not use signs for many of her words. When she does sign, many of her signs are wrong. The children sit and watch her and are confused. One day when she was at the blackboard, she turned her back on Janet and was talking as she wrote. I could not tell what she was saying. How can Janet be educated like that?"

Raymond sipped from his beer and signed, "Why should Janet be in that class?!"

"At one point she was telling the story of a child who moved to a new school. She kept using the sign for 'book' when she was actually referring to the school. She also referred to the teacher as a boy rather than a girl."

---

frequently use a sign-for-word structure, so that the signs are direct visual representations of the spoken words. ASL, on the other hand, has an entirely different syntax and is conceptually unrelated to English or any aurally based languages. For example, if one were to sign "she looked at the book again and again" in an English-based sign language, there would be a corresponding sign for each of the eight words, and the word order of the signs would be similar to that of the spoken words.

In ASL "she" and "the book" would be placed in space. The sign for "look" would be repeated using a circular motion. Repetition is thus entirely visual. The differences between the languages are significant, both in terms of how they are conveyed and how they are learned. While there is much debate about early language development, a growing number of linguists argue that a deaf child, like all children, requires a native language, in this case a true visual language such as ASL. ASL was Janet's native language and as such further complicated the dispute. *See* OLIVER SACKS, SEEING VOICES (1989).

Raymond grimaced and signed rapidly to his wife.

"Tell him about her bad language."

Betty smiled and hesitated.

"Hmmm. Yes the signs for 'both' and 'shit' are similar. 'Both' is signed by pulling the two index fingers of the right hand from the fist of the left hand. 'Shit' is signed with the same motion and same hand shapes, but the thumb is pulled from the fist of the left hand. She used the sign for 'shit' many times. Janet laughed at that."

They talked on as the day darkened and dinner simmered on the stove. They shared another beer as the children roared about the house, chasing one another, tattling on offending siblings, jumping on their father. Janet sailed through the kitchen. There was no containing her. Any depressions she felt about being isolated at school or frustrations she felt at not being able to attend the state school were not apparent. She was, after all, only six, and on this day she was a jubilant soldier at the head of a homecoming parade.

She sprinted through the kitchen, made a U-turn, and piled into her father, who took her into the air. He put her down and they rapidly and effortlessly signed something that the attorney did not fully understand. Betty Morrison looked over from the stove and signed for them to come to dinner. Janet ran out of the kitchen, bringing a smile to her father's face and chagrin to her mother, who knew that dinner would be later rather than sooner. Janet's small suitcase had been packed and stood, as it had for weeks, by the door of her bedroom.

———

Whether or not children with disabilities ought to be placed in regular educational settings might appear to be beyond debate or rancor, but at the heart of the integration-segregation paradox of IDEA and the very different ways in which parents, educators, and advocates see the law's tilt is an issue of national concern. American society appears to have moved in great fits and starts toward integration. It is a widely debated issue that has roused the deepest passions and hatred and given rise to the most profound and rabid of oratory. It is a complicated matter, as evident as the packed suitcase of Janet Morrison .

There is a temptation to compare "segregated" and "integrated" educational settings based on race with those of children with disabilities. In both cases children have encountered longstanding shibboleths, disproportionate use of funds, stereotypical thinking, and institutional opposition. Not infrequently critics of IDEA refer to separate placements as "segregated," raising powerful images.

Some in the field of special education point to a "direct relationship between segregation and abuse," citing lawsuits in which children with disabilities were tied to potty chairs and wheelchairs, placed on urine-soaked floors, hosed off, had hot pepper sauce put on their tongues, and experienced other verbal and psychological abuses.[1]

In 1992, for example, the Association for Retarded Citizens of the United States (ARC) issued its "Report Card to the Nation on Inclusion in Education of Students with Mental Retardation."[2] They found, as others have, a compelling point of reference in *Brown v. Board of Education,* and confirmed Dr. Kenneth Clarke's finding that "[s]egregation is the way in which society tells a group of human beings that they are inferior to other groups of human beings in that society."[3]

The concept, and ultimately the policy, of integration has impacted American society in unique, disharmonious, and even touching ways. Insofar as the struggle focused on education, *Brown* represented a historic shift in the national vision. In a relatively short opinion, the Supreme Court ruled that in "the field of public education the doctrine of 'separate but equal' has no place. Separate educational facilities are inherently unequal."[4] The case resolved a major social issue, perhaps the most important in American legal history: separate facilities were a clear violation of the United States Constitution. In a sense the war ended with that case, but pacification goes on 40 years later.

Ironically, there is evidence that the special education system in the United States is overrepresented by nonwhite students. According to the U.S. Department of Civil Rights 1990 Survey of Schools, 39 states enrolled African-American students in special education at a higher rate than their percentage of the population.[5] In addition, race appears to play a role in the labeling of children with disabilities. In 1990, 47 percent of African-American students in Alabama were labeled "retarded," in Ohio 41 percent, and in Indiana 37 percent.[6] In the "black belt" county of Perry, Alabama, where African-Americans represented 96 percent of the population, 236 students were labeled "retarded," while 14 were "learning-disabled." In a wealthier county to the north, where whites made up 99 percent of the population, only 15 were determined to be "retarded," while 271 students were labeled "learning-disabled."[7]

In their piece entitled "The Yoke of Special Education—How to Break It," Alan Gartner and Dorothy Kerzner Lipsky argued for full integration of children with disabilities, noting the analogy with racial segregation-integration and the underlying moral imperative:

> Speaking of turmoil created in a school characterized by the "wrongs of racial discrimination and segregation and the treatment of the handicapped" and its effort to reform, Albert Shanker (1988) points out that a "school is...a moral community...[which cannot] be 'good' for only a small, privileged handful at the expense of discriminating against or excluding many others."

> A community, indeed a "moral community," is the result of human choice. Persons with disabilities can be full participants in a community as friends, neighbors, workers, citizens, and family members.

> What can be done to shape an educational system that includes *all* students, one that is both consonant with and

builds an inclusive society? Clearly it is not done by taking students from the regular education setting, labeling them "deficient" and placing them in a separate, second-class program....

The ultimate rationale for quality education in an integrated setting is based not just on economics, law or pedagogy, but on values. What values do we honor? What kind of people are we? What kind of society do we wish to be build for ourselves and for all of our children? The current failure to provide quality education to all students and the perpetuation of segregated settings is not only morally unsound and educationally unnecessary, but says  much about the answers to these questions.[8]

It is beyond argument that a significant moral tenet underscores the whole placement debate in special education. As a result there is deeper resonance to the discussion, making it more difficult to question the reasons for mainstreaming children with disabilities. After all, "[i]ntegration in the schools is just the beginning of full integration in society," and is necessary to prepare children for life, to encourage normal experiences, to change attitudes, and to teach democracy.[9]

Although the need for different members of society to interact in a positive way may be self-evident, it may not be as simple as that. The civil rights movement of the 1950s and 1960s understandably had separatist sentiment. Marcus Garvey predated *Brown*. Abraham Lincoln at least considered "resettlement" once the slaves had become freedmen. Garvey and Lincoln had, to be sure, significantly different reasons for looking to Africa, but what is of note is that integration has been viewed even by the historically excluded as a complex and not always acceptable remedy.

Because groups need to retain their separate identities and cultures the issue of inclusion remains unsettled. The issue is further unsettled because some of the "excluded" actively resist inclusion. At first glance the inclusion movement seems to be on the higher moral ground, but the call for one placement for all children, albeit a cherished one in American society, complicates the moral imperative.

Opposition to racial integration in the schools has come from both the larger community and, to some extent, the institutions themselves. Opposition to the integration of disabled children has come from educational institutions, but also from significant portions of the community for which the mainstreaming mandate was created. Unlike parents of Caucasian children in the South and elsewhere, the parents of non-disabled children have not broadly opposed mainstreaming. And while there may be some counterpart to racism among school personnel (for example, ignorance, fear, or misconceptions about children with disabilities), institutional opposition often reflects concerns about cost and administrative convenience.

Ultimately one might argue that to suggest distinctions between one kind of separation and another is to justify intellectual bigotry. Yet cases like the Morrison dispute make the issue of comparing racial and disability separation more complex than that and may expose it to more than one moral template. In December 1993 U.S. Undersecretary Judith Heumann met with a number of organizations that opposed generic full inclusion. She had previously referred to separate education as "segregated" and "immoral." The use of a pejorative term to describe programs that had provided extraordinary opportunities for some children outraged numerous parents and educators. They understood the undersecretary's concerns about the historic exclusion of children with disabilities, but to them a "regular" classroom was inappropriate and even immoral, while an appropriate "separate" one was moral and necessary. The distinction was crucial and the apparent failure to see the differences hit a nerve.[10]

\*     \*     \*

To the extent that IDEA was passed to accelerate the full integration of children with disabilities, it has not accomplished

31

that goal. As of 1991 approximately 1,592,000 students with disabilities were in regular classes, while 3,159,000 were in alternative programs.[11] It is not difficult to see why the full inclusion movement has grown to be a potent force. By late 1993, inclusion programs initiated by parents, teachers, school administrators, state departments of education and college faculty were flourishing in Vermont, Oregon, Kentucky, North Dakota, Louisiana, New Mexico, Utah, Pennsylvania, and Washington.[12]

The full inclusion movement is not the first organized effort to make IDEA's integration goal fully operative. The "regular education initiative" of the 1980s called for the merging of regular and special education.[13] In the mid-1980s Madeleine Will, Assistant Secretary of the Office of Special Education and Rehabilitative Services, U.S. Department of Education, recognized the historic separation and alienation of regular education from special education and emphasized that the department was committed "to increasing the educational success of children with learning problems and challenges states to renew their commitment to serve...as many of these children as possible in the regular classroom...."[14] Will added that "[e]ducation in the...LRE is what I envision as the last barrier to full implementation of Public Law 94-142....In my own mind all [my beliefs] have evolved with the concept of least restrictive environment as the core concept."[15]

Under Will's administration, states were monitored to determine whether they were meeting the law's mainstreaming requirements. In California, for example, a Least Restrictive Environment Task Force was formed as an advisory committee to the State Department of Education. Among other things it concluded that

> [t]here is a recognizable movement toward the integration of students with severe handicaps onto general education campuses and away from separate facilities designed only for students with handicaps....the [State Department of Education] should be prepared to support new models and methods for offering students a quality integrated program.[16]

The task force identified barriers to systemwide integration and called for modifications to the special education funding model to encourage movement of pupils with severe disabilities to less restrictive settings.[17]*

Increasingly the academic community has analyzed special education and found it wanting. With the growth of special education systems and budgets and the evolution of a separate system which, according to some, made a "mockery" of a "noble intent to differentiate and enhance instruction for students with disabilities," the chorus grew more critical.[18]

In May 1991 Schools Are For Everyone (SAFE) initiated a campaign to compel the federal Department of Education to move more quickly toward systemwide mainstreaming and to fully include all children in regular education classes. The provision of educational services for all students at the school they would attend if they did not have a disability is "the underlying philosophy by which we educate all students. . . . Educational preparation should emphasize the elimination of traditional separations between 'regular' and 'special' education. . . ."[19]

In October 1992 the National Association of State Boards of Education (NASBE) reported that it wanted to help state officials create education systems in which *all* children with disabilities would be placed in regular classrooms. NASBE wanted "to move special education and regular education into a new arena," and recommended that "states change funding systems that reward schools for identifying children as disabled and retrain regular and special educators to teach children from all ability levels."[20]

By late 1992 the full inclusion model called for thoroughly remaking special education with a focus on student outcome, not separate programs. The National Center on Educational Restructuring and Inclusion defined an inclusive education as one

---

* Six years later the California LRE Task Force reconvened. Many of the meetings, which the author attended, were marked by acrimonious and unresolved debates about inclusion and LRE.

in which "all students, including those with severe handicaps," would have "equitable opportunities" to be placed in "age-appropriate classes in their neighborhood schools, in order to prepare [them to be] full members of society."[21] In its report, "Winners All: A Call for Inclusive Schools," NASBE decried the unnecessary "segregation" and labeling of children and further noted that even the heart of IDEA—mainstreaming—splintered "the academic and social lives of many students."[22] NASBE believed that fully inclusive education would mean blended funding and would lead to a full breakdown of the barriers between special and regular education.[23]

Whether the daily activities of school administrators match their philosophies is less clear than printed manifestos like *Winners All*. The National Association of State Directors of Special Education (NASDE) reported its goal to radically alter the special education system in the Winter 1992 edition of *Counterpoint* at the same time it ran a headline, "School system appeals ruling on inclusion."[24]

The Board of Education of the Borough of Clementon School District in New Jersey opposed the inclusion of a severely retarded and behaviorally troubled eight-year-old boy into regular classes. It argued before the Third Circuit Court of Appeals that full inclusion was "educationally bankrupt" and served only as an "ideological vehicle to advance mainstreaming in inappropriate cases."[25] The board concluded that replicating special education programs in regular classes ("parallelism") was like "saying class could be 'conducted in the main aisle of a church during services without distracting the congregation from their prayers.'"[26]

In fall 1993 the *Inclusion Times* began publication and defined "inclusion" as a "unitary educational program," which meant eliminating the current process whereby students with disabilities had to prove they could partake in the "dominant" regular education system.[27] *Inclusion Times* listed a number of applicable books and videos, including one that called for comprehensive local school models for which no student was so severely disabled that he or she could not receive a free appropriate education at the local school.[28]

But opposition to the movement soon formed. Three months after the first issue of *Inclusion Times* was published, organizations representing blind, autistic, learning disabled, deaf, and severely disabled children formed Action for Children to Insure Options Now (ACTION), a national coalition specifically opposed to systematic full inclusion and the generic integration of children with disabilities. A matter that seemed beyond dispute—who would oppose those who sought to include children?—had become controversial.

What does this integrating law, which has created so much debate, stand for? Does it or does it not give children with disabilities the right to access regular classrooms? A passionate and vigorous argument is being made to eliminate special education, to educate all children with disabilities in the classrooms they would attend if they were not "disabled." Does the law as written and implemented by educators and courts allow as much? Is there an absolute right to a mainstreamed program and does the law support a melding of regular and special education systems?

The immediate answer is no, resoundingly so when the statutory and regulatory language is analyzed. In addition, court decisions regarding IDEA placement disputes are so diverse that they dampen hopes for generic full inclusion. Even recent decisions that are fully inclusionistic in spirit and which alter the national debate have not changed the legal mandate of IDEA or the requirement that the child's right to be included must be weighed against other important factors, including cost and the impact on other children.

While the law and its reading do not quite match the fervor of those who contend that there is no room for any exceptions to a fully inclusive educational experience, IDEA is inherently a law of placement. And though it does not provide an unmistakable right to placement in a regular classroom, there is a great deal of statutory phrasing that would seem to imply as much.

Section 1401 of the Act defines a child's "individualized education program" as a written statement that must include, among other things "a statement of the specific educational services to be provided to such [a] child, and *the extent to which* such [a] child will be able to *participate* in *regular* educational programs...."[29] This philosophy is more thoroughly crafted in Section 1412(5), which creates eligibility requirements for states receiving federal financial assistance under the Act, notably

> (A) procedural safeguards...and (B) procedures to assure that, to the *maximum* extent appropriate, children with disabilities, including children in public or private institutions or other care facilities, are educated with children who are not disabled[.][30]

There is some shakiness to the law's underlying inclusionary charge because the language changes throughout the legislation. IDEA uses the phrase "the extent" to which a child "*will participate*," then shifts to the "maximum extent *appropriate*," and finally, in Section 1414, turns "to the maximum extent *practicable*."

The regulations promulgated pursuant to the Act are generally parallel to the statutes, but here and there they add some different and provocative language, ultimately reinforcing the mainstreaming preference of the law while carving out more explicit exceptions to that preference.[31] Sections 300.550-.552 provide, among other things, that children with disabilities are entitled to placement in the schools they would attend "if not handicapped" and, in any case, "as close to home as possible" unless other arrangements are necessary.[32]

What does this extensive statutory discourse mean? Nowhere does Congress say that children with disabilities will be placed in specific programs or schools. The terms "mainstreaming," "integration," and "full inclusion" are not employed. The concept of "least restrictive environment," a term of evident relativity, provides the impetus for placement considerations. On the other hand, Congress is not so vague as to hide its preference. Perhaps it understood the multitude of children and the variation of circumstances that affect each of them. Perhaps it understood what ironclad requirements would mean. Congress seemed to be saying in all of its language that it would like for children with disabilities to have opportunities like all other children, but that it understood that that might be difficult indeed.

Such ambivalence may be no more clearly reflected than in the use of the terms "practicable" and "appropriate." "Practicable" speaks to the needs of the provider (the school district), while "possible and appropriate" suggests greater concern with the child. What is practicable may very well be less than appropriate for the child, and what is appropriate may very well be impracticable for the district. Practicable gives the administrator leeway, appropriate nudges the balance toward the child, and "possible" narrows the school's flexibility.*

At the very least the varying and at times contradictory language of the law suggests a congressional imprecision that may have either been lassitude—perhaps one of the drafters of the IDEA selected "practicable" late one night without thinking of how it might be juxtaposed with "appropriate"—or purposeful crafting.

What else do the regulations say about a disabled child's right to be educated in a regular classroom? Section 300.550(2) provides

> [t]hat special classes, separate schooling or other removal
> of handicapped children from the regular educational envi-
> ronment occurs only when the nature or severity of the
> handicap is such that education in regular classes with the

---

* Courts have used still other phrases. One court referred to LRE as placement with non-disabled children, "'to the maximum extent *possible*.'" Springdale v. Grace, 494 F. Supp. 267, 273 (W.D. Ark. 1980), 1980-81 EHLR 552:191.

use of supplementary aids and services cannot be achieved satisfactorily.[33]

The child can then be removed from regular education when his or her disability warrants removal and when, even with the use of additional services, the child cannot demonstrate satisfactory results in the classroom. There is a real burden here. Although a good deal must be proven before the child is removed, it is statutorily permissible.

The law further requires that school districts provide a continuum of placement options, alternatives including special classes, special schools, home instruction, and instruction in hospitals and institutions.[34] If IDEA required placement in regular education at all times for all children, then a continuum would be wholly unnecessary.

One may conclude that least restrictive environment, not mainstreaming or full inclusion, is the coin of the realm. Since the least restrictive environment may not be a regular classroom, LRE and mainstreaming as extrapolated from the law are not the same thing. Mainstreaming is an easier concept to master—it is a particular place. LRE, on the other hand, is a more fluid term and suggests less a specific placement than a process for determining what works for a particular child.

Finally and perhaps most fundamentally, the law integrating children with disabilities requires that the child's needs be met, and that the child be provided a "free appropriate public education.[35] There is no precise method for determining how and when particular needs trump placement considerations or whether it is a school district's responsibility to provide for all needs in a mainstreamed environment. Not infrequently courts, if not school districts, view the provision of an appropriate education as incompatible with LRE. The concepts, if not mutually exclusive, have a good deal of tension between them.

\*     \*     \*

For all the qualifications of LRE, the law has at its core the hope, if not the absolute requirement, that children with disabilities will be placed in regular educational environments. The "preference" for regular education is clear even as the tension in the law is evident—it has been judged to be fundamental to the scheme and purpose of the law.[36]

In *Thornack v. Boise Independent School District No. 1*,[37] the Idaho court ruled that "the preference for mainstreaming was so strong that it must be considered as a *presumptive requirement* of a free appropriate public education and not merely as a balancing factor."[38] Gabriel Thornack was a 12-year-old multiply disabled child with epilepsy, cerebral palsy and moderate mental retardation. Gabriel had an IQ of 37 and the mental capacity of a two- or three-year-old. In 1981 his school district unilaterally removed him from public school and placed him in a private day-care facility. Finally, in 1983 the school district offered placement in a segregated classroom with ten other disabled students, a special education teacher, and one aide. Gabriel's parents preferred to keep him mainstreamed in the private school, with the services of a full-time, one-to-one aide. After three years of litigation, through two separate lawsuits against two different school districts, the court finally ruled that Gabriel was entitled to placement in the private, mainstreamed program with the use of a one-to-one aide.

The *Thornack* court found that when a physically disabled student participates in the regular curriculum with non-disabled students and achieves passing grades, there is a strong presumption that the provided education is adequate. The *Thornack* court found that Congress did not intend to restrict mainstreaming to students who could progress from grade to grade in a regular academic program. Gabriel had made "remarkable progress" in his mainstreamed program, thus the "presumptive" nature of the mainstreaming requirement. The court stated that unless the child could not meet the academic requirements of his IEP in a mainstreamed environment, a nonmainstreamed placement is not legally sufficient and does not constitute a free appropriate public education.

The burden of proof* falls squarely on those charged with the responsibility of integrating children with disabilities:

> One probable reason for the lack of mainstreaming in [the public school offering] is the district's policy of placing the burden of proving the appropriateness on the child. Ms. Hobdey testified that mainstreaming is provided '[i]f the child is able to handle [it] and it's appropriate [for] him.[39]

Noting that this policy contravened the congressional intent that mainstreaming takes place whenever possible, the court questioned the perfunctory mainstreaming opportunities offered by the school district, specifically that Gabriel would be with regular children during lunch, for an hour of recess, and would be exposed to fourth grade children once a week and a fifth grade boy every day in the afternoons. The burden, therefore, is on the school district to justify the inappropriateness of a mainstreaming placement before "segregating" disabled children.

The *Thornack* court acknowledged the district's comparison of mainstreaming benefits with those gained by "precision" teaching in a more restrictive environment (a quality-of-education versus quality-of-placement balancing act repeated through many LRE disputes), but found that Congress had clearly intended mainstreaming as the *critical* ingredient in an appropriate education. And because acceptance of federal funding legally obligates the district to "accept mainstreaming as a presumptive requirement of an appropriate education," it cannot "attempt to now argue against the policy."[40]

In 1988 the Idaho Supreme Court affirmed the lower court decision, stating that the mainstreaming mandate "is a major

---

* Other disputes and other courts suggest, however, that the burden is on those who would "challenge" a nonmainstreamed program to prove its inappropriateness. In Lachman v. Illinois State Board of Education, 852 F.2d 290 (7th Cir. 1988), the court ruled that parents who oppose a nonregular classroom must go forward and disprove the school's decision to "segregate."

and important factor [along with the child's emotional and intellectual make-up] to be balanced in assessing an appropriate placement."[41] A "segregated" placement might be perceived to be academically superior, but in reality may only reflect a disagreement with the mainstreaming "concept."

By using terms like "presumptive requirement" and indicating that a nonmainstreamed placement might be "legally insufficient," the *Thornack* court comes clearly down on the side of an inherent, "almost" unchallengeable right to integration. Other courts have viewed the placement segment of IDEA in similar ways:

> Although defendants' experts dispute the soundness of the mainstreaming approach to the education of the handicapped, Congress has made a clear choice among competing educational philosophies. In electing to receive federal funds, the state of Alabama has bound itself to act in accordance with that philosophy.[42]

Joseph Campbell was an 18-year-old, severely retarded student for whom the school district was unable to obtain a measurable testing response. His mental age was approximately two-and-one-half, and he was almost entirely nonverbal. He did learn some self-help skills, including toileting and eating. He enjoyed the company of others, but often displayed inappropriate behavior, including touching, hair pulling and throwing food to the ground. Accordingly the school district offered only "custodial care," which the parents rejected. Joseph was enrolled in a learning center which required his mother to drive him 24 miles to the county line where a bus picked him up and took him to and from the center.

This continued for two years, after which the school district offered home instruction for one hour per day. There was evidence that Joseph was capable of functioning at higher levels, that he had the desire to communicate, had all the prerequisites for symbolic communication, and could benefit from peer interaction.

The district's final placement offer was at the Munford Center, a renovated wood-framed house some distance from the high school and separated by a high fence. There were no non-disabled children at Munford. Joseph was taken to the high school for lunch, where his contacts with non-disabled children were minimal.

The court found this placement failed in "design and execution," merely filling up Joseph's time with activities without offering him any real educational benefit. The program was "ill-suited to impart to Joseph any functional or communicative skills which might, to whatever degree, increase his independence."[43] As to Joseph's specific need to be with non-disabled children, the *Campbell* court found, consistent with *Thornack,* that Joseph would be able to benefit from increased contact with non-disabled students provided he received proper supervision.

Interestingly, the court suggested a number of ways to remedy the problem, notably that the district could move Joseph's class into the main high school building or move non-disabled children into the Munford center. If the district chose neither of these options, they had the "heavy burden of insuring that Joseph's interactions with non-handicapped students will be substantially equal to that he would enjoy were his classroom located in the main school building."[44]

Daniel R. was a six-year-old boy with Down's syndrome who had a speech impairment, was mentally retarded with a developmental age of between two and three, and had communication skills "slightly less than those of a two year old."[45] In 1985 Daniel's parents enrolled him in the El Paso School District's Early Childhood Program, a half-day special education program. For the 1986-87 school year, the parties agreed that Daniel would be placed in a regular pre-kindergarten class for half of each day and in the Early Childhood Program for the other half of each day. The pre-kindergarten instructor soon felt the placement was unwise since Daniel did not participate without "constant, individual attention from the teacher or her aide" and "failed to master any of the skills" taught to the students.[46]

Modifying the curriculum and teaching methods to "reach" Daniel would have changed them, according to staff members, "beyond recognition." The school district decided that Daniel would only attend the Early Childhood Program, but would eat lunch in the school cafeteria with non-disabled children three times a week only if his mother would be present to supervise him. He would also have contact with non-disabled peers during recess. Daniel's parents rejected this plan. After a five-day hearing which produced over 2,500 pages of testimony, the hearing officer concluded that Daniel could not participate in the regular pre-kindergarten class without constant attention since the curriculum was "beyond his abilities." The officer also concluded that Daniel was receiving "little educational benefit" and was disrupting the class because he absorbed so much of the teacher's time. Finally, the officer found that 90 to 100 percent of the pre-kindergarten curriculum would have to be downgraded to bring it to Daniel's level. The district court affirmed the hearing officer's findings.

Two years later the matter reached the Fifth Circuit, which addressed the underlying mainstreaming issue stating that "the decision whether to mainstream a child must include an inquiry into whether the student will gain *any* educational benefit from regular education. Our analysis *cannot* stop here, however, for educational benefits are *not* mainstreaming's only virtue."[47] Instead, mainstreaming has a less tangible value, an inherent benefit "in and of itself," including the language and behavior models available from non-handicapped children."[48] Although a child with disabilities might not absorb all of the regular education curriculum, he or she might benefit from *nonacademic* experiences in the regular classroom. The child belongs, a priori, in a regular classroom.

The court spoke of educational benefits, noneducational benefits inherent in the mainstreaming experience, and nonacademic

43

values, and in so doing raised the questions of what constitutes an education and to what degree certain nontraditional and academic factors must be factored into the mainstreaming equation. Once purely academic matters are left behind, the rationale for mainstreaming grows. Daniel R. had a right, then, to learn his three Rs and to benefit from the "intangibility" of mainstreaming. The *Daniel R.* court had created a mainstreaming gestalt.*

Approximately three years after *Daniel R.*, the "in and of itself" purpose of mainstreaming took on a decidedly inclusionistic tone as numerous courts began to look more critically at IDEA's integration record, reflecting both growing dissatisfaction with mainstreaming statistics and, coincidentally, the Clinton administration's interest in "inclusion."

In *Oberti v. Board of Education*,[49] an eight-year-old boy with severe linguistic, intellectual, and behavioral problems (toileting accidents, temper tantrums, crawling and hiding under the furniture, touching, hitting, and spitting) was ordered into a mainstreamed program. The court acknowledged its reticence to use the term mainstreaming because it "suggests, in [the full inclusion movement's] view, the shuttling of a child with disabilities in and out of a regular classroom."[50] While the court did not endorse generic full inclusion and declined to substitute that term for mainstreaming, it did call for a "more precise" term that put greater emphasis on using supplementary aides to insure more mainstreaming.

According to the *Oberti* court, the mainstreaming/inclusion requirement of the law prohibited removal from regular classrooms and even when a separate placement would be "necessary for the child to receive educational benefit, the school may still be violating IDEA if it has not made sufficient efforts to include

---

* Despite this reasoning, the *Daniel R.* court affirmed the lower court decision to remove Daniel R. from a regular classroom. While the court of appeals focused forcefully on what steps must be taken by a school district in order to encourage mainstreaming—mere "token gestures" will not do—it also concluded that the requirement is "broad" but not "limitless."

the child in school programs with non-disabled children *whenever possible.*"[51]* The decision was described in headlines as an "Order for Full Inclusion."[52]

The sense of a full inclusion mandate took on additional meaning in *Board of Education v. Holland.*[53] Rachel Holland was a nine-year-old child with an IQ of 44 who functioned academically at a four-year-old level. After several years in self-contained, nonmainstreamed special education classes, Rachel was unilaterally placed in a "regular" private kindergarten class. With the assistance of a part-time aide, Rachel made academic and social progress. Her public school district offered placement in a program that would provide mainstreaming for nonacademic subjects—art, music, lunch and recess—and placement in a special education class for academic classes. This plan would have required Rachel to move six times each day. A hearing officer ruled that the district failed to integrate Rachel to the maximum extent appropriate and ordered the district to place her in a regular classroom with support services, including a part-time special education consultant and part-time classroom aide. The federal court affirmed the administrative decision, noting that a mainstreaming decision must be based on an analysis of: (1) the academic and non-academic benefits to the child; (2) the effect the child with disabilities would have on the teacher and other children, and; (3) the cost of the supplementary aids and services needed to facilitate the mainstreaming.

The court ruled that Rachel Holland had received academic and nonacademic benefits—her IEP goals and objectives could be met in the regular classroom and she had demonstrated

---

* Seven years earlier Madeleine Will had written that the "pullout approach"—removing disabled students from regular classrooms—was "driven by a conceptual fallacy," namely that poor performance (by learning disabled children) was due to the student's deficiencies, not those of the learning environment. Will recommended changes in the dual system to more effectively and frequently encourage retention of children with disabilities in regular classrooms. *See* endnote 14.

growth in communication skills and self-confidence and had developed friendships. The court also found that the school district had not proven that the use of public funds for Rachel's inclusion adversely impacted on services for other children. Further, the court found that with the use of an aide there was no disruption to the teacher or to other children.

The law's presumption in favor of mainstreaming required that a disabled child be educated in a regular classroom even if it is not the best academic setting for that child. The "fundamental purpose" of the mainstreaming portion of IDEA involved "significant non-academic benefits," including exposure to non-disabled peers. The *Holland* court found that nonacademic benefits related closely to academic progress. The school district contended that the cost of placing Rachel in a mainstreamed program would be $109,000 by the time teacher training and other costs were included. The court called the figure "exaggerated" and "hyperbolic," and further noted that the district should factor into the cost equation benefits that would redound to other children in the class.

The *Holland* court re-affirmed the core mainstreaming portion of the law and the heavy burden on schools to justify alternative placements and provide the resources for mainstreaming. At the same time it did not rule that the law required full inclusion for all children with disabilities; even for the individual child, full inclusion did not mean that the child had to be placed in the regular classroom 100 percent of the time. There is an "explicit" presumption in favor of mainstreaming, but the extent of mainstreaming that is appropriate for each child will vary.

Clearly though, according to the *Holland* court, "mainstreaming is the starting point....[a] placement in other than a regular class is a fall-back choice made only after it is determined that placement in regular classes will be unsuccessful."[54] The court acknowledged a full inclusion philosophy, but like many others, it found the law's preference for inclusion to be strong but not absolute.

In early 1994, the United States Court of Appeals for the Ninth Circuit affirmed the district court decision in *Holland*.[55] In April 1994, the Sacramento City Unifed School District voted to appeal the case to the United States Supreme Court, because, as one district trustee noted, the "professionals ought to be in charge of the education system."[56] Potential cost to the district just for the Hollands' legal fees was anticipated to be between $800,000 and $1,000,000. When the district voted to appeal, two trustees sought to have their names disassociated from the case, citing that such effort would only "dirty" the district's name in the "eyes of the nation."[57] Soon thereafter the Sacramento *Bee* called for the repeal of IDEA, noting that mainstreaming was both expensive and, after all, merely desirable.[58] In June 1994 the United States Supreme Court refused to hear the district's appeal, ending the *Holland* litigation.

The Clinton administration, in a departure from its predecessors, filed an amicus ("friend of the court") brief on behalf of Rachel Holland. Judith Heumann, the U.S. Department of Education's Assistant Secretary for Special Education publicly supported the department's "belief in inclusion for children with disabilities" and its desire to look for cases "where we can be supportive."[59] The Department's involvement in *Holland* was an important sign, particularly since the *Holland* case was viewed, correctly or not, as a full inclusion decision. At the very least it illuminated the Clinton administration's willingness to take an active role in a dispute that occurred in a state where only 3.1 percent of mentally retarded children were taught in regular classrooms.[60]

While the *Holland* and *Oberti* cases are interesting because they were viewed as the first "inclusionistic" decisions and therefore represented a break from past judicial analyses, they did not establish any new legal requirements. The four-point *Holland* "rule" was fully consistent with Sections 300.550-.552, that is, removal only if it were demonstrated that the child could not function in a regular classroom even with the use of supplemental aides.

That is not to say that the perception of these cases as inclusionistic was not significant, that the rulings did not suggest a more forceful focus on the inclusion mandate of the law, or that public perception (as opposed to the actual rulings) did not impact on policy. But *Holland* and *Oberti* followed a long line of mainstreaming cases, and by emphasizing a test for (as opposed to an absolute right to) inclusion, they implicitly sanctioned inclusion *and* removal. For every Rachel Holland, there will be a child whose education in a regular classroom may prove to be too costly, too disruptive, or too educationally inappropriate.

*       *       *

If *Oberti, Thornack*, and *Holland* did not represent a significant step toward judicial approval of generic full inclusion, they did suggest the courts' willingness to frame the debate in full inclusion language. A late 1993 case from New York took the full inclusion philosophy a step closer to a generic application.

In *J.G. v. Rochester*,[61] the federal district court monitored the school district's compliance with earlier consent decrees, in particular its need to remedy past mainstreaming failures. In Appendix E of the order—labeled "Inclusion"—the court noted these stipulations:

1. To ensure that most of the defendant's students will receive special education in their *home* schools...the School District will redefine catchment areas...and provide sufficient space for students with disabilities at each site....

3. The defendant will expand its school based support...to facilitate the placement of students with disabilities in their home schools or schools of choice.

4. To provide for a more even distribution and space for

students with disabilities, newly formed magnet programs shall be located in schools traditionally of low
general education enrollment.

5. All new schools as well as schools undergoing a major
redesigning...will be opened or re-opened with an *inclusion* model in place....

7. To provide incentives to schools, monies will be made
available to schools willing to implement an approved
plan for educating home school students with disabilities
in their site beginning in September, 1994.

8. Resources shall be made available to assure sufficient
support staff...to implement the inclusion model....[62]

These stipulations, including the monetary incentives, reveal
a willingness to set up an inclusive structure that may have
affected most, if not all children in the school district, and therefore raised questions about the individual nature of special education decisionmaking. Ultimately *J.G.* represented, as of 1994,
the strongest legal endorsment of generic full inclusion.*

*        *        *

There is clear case law that underscores the mainstreaming
preference of IDEA. Some, like *Thornack,* come as close as possible
to identifying the mandate as absolute. But even as courts use
terms like "presumptive requirement," none have concluded that
one child has an absolute right to a fully mainstreamed education
under any circumstances, or that all children should be mainstreamed.

The *Daniel R.* and *Holland* courts acknowledged the multifac-
eted needs of a child, and academic and nonacademic factors

---

* In May 1994 the author spoke with one teacher in the Rochester area. She
indicated that the *J.G.* decision was not being generically applied and that
nonregular classroom placements were still available.

are now included in the exclusion/inclusion debate. As a result, the debate broadens. Some have suggested, for example, a kind of bifurcated approach to special education, showing the need for a clear division between children with disabilities who need access and those who need remediation. The child in the wheelchair needs to get into the regular classroom. Janet Morrison was academically on target, needed no remedial assistance, but required access to a language-appropriate environment.

Other children with disabilities need significant help in learning basic academic or independent living skills, or need intense programs to be able to function adequately in the classroom.* The more complex the child's needs, the more likely a placement decision will bend to the weight of the special needs. The more "disabled" the child is, so it is argued, the greater the need for homogenous and comprehensive programs.

A simple educational profile becomes the exception, not the rule. There are children with AIDS, children with significant psychiatric needs, and children with complicated medical conditions that directly impact the daily educational experience. How far must a school go to address factors that have not traditionally been within the purview of teachers and school administrators? How far must the school go to ensure a least restrictive environment?

A child needs psychotherapy to contain his rage. A child needs a nurse to ensure that her tracheostomy is functioning. A child is hospitalized for schizophrenia. A child has hepatitis B. In all of these situations, the underlying condition will surely impact on the child's educational experience. What is required

---

* Some members of the deaf community will argue, for example, that deaf children should be "removed" entirely from special education, that these children are not "disabled" but merely use a different communication mode. There is "nothing wrong" with the children but they still suffer the stigma of special education identification and therefore a special education placement is detrimental to them. Ironically, the issue of stigmatization is at the heart of the full inclusion argument against separate placement.

to ensure the provision of an appropriate education and what is required to ensure placement in the LRE? The schizophrenic child is entitled to psychotherapy in order to benefit from special education. Must a psychiatrist be provided to increase the chance of mainstreaming? Is mainstreaming the only way to define LRE?

A school district centralizes its program to serve students throughout its jurisdiction. Is the district required to establish single programs in a regular class or school for each of its children with severe disabilities? Current policies, attitudes, and programs for the placement of children with disabilities vary greatly, reflecting uncertainty about these questions and inclusion. In North Dakota, 72 percent of the special education population is in a regular classroom. In South Dakota, geographically and demographically similar to its neighbor to the north, 8 percent of children with disabilities is in a regular classroom.[63]

These questions shake the mainstreaming preference, push it a little further from any possible absolute reading. The presumptive requirement is in fact rebuttable. Full inclusion proponents view existing law and policy as inadequate and are forced to critique a law that is inclusionary in spirit if not in terms of absolute reach. But the pressure, as evidenced by *Holland, J.G.,* and other decisions to create generically inclusive programs grows, and with it is the increased likelihood of a lengthy and rancorous debate that is potentially as divisive as any matter in the 20-year history of IDEA. Unfortunately, the focus on generic inclusion may obscure the unacceptable failure of the system to include the many children who should be in regular, neighborhood schools.

## Endnotes

1. *DREDF cases force sweeping changes in special education,* DISABILITY RIGHTS AND EDUCATION DEFENSE FUND [DREDF] NEWS, Nov. 1993, at 1.

2. Sharon Davis, Ph.D., Association for Retarded Citizens of the United States, REPORT CARD TO THE NATION ON INCLUSION IN EDUCATION OF STUDENTS WITH MENTAL RETARDATION (1992), at 4.

3.   Brown v. Bd. of Educ., 347 U.S. 483, 494 (1954).

4.   *Id.* at 495.

5.   Joseph P. Shapiro et al., *Separate and Unequal*, U.S. NEWS & WORLD REP., Dec. 13, 1993, at 48 [hereinafter *Separate and Unequal*].

6.   *Id.*

7.   *Id.* at 55.

8.   ALAN GARTNER & DOROTHY KERZNER LIPSKY, NATIONAL CENTER ON EDUCATION AND THE ECONOMY, THE YOKE OF SPECIAL EDUCATION — HOW TO BREAK IT 32-33 (1989).

9.   DOUGLAS BIKLEN ET AL., TECHNICAL ASSISTANCE FOR PARENT PROGRAMS (TAPP), PURPOSEFUL INTEGRATION...INHERENTLY EQUAL 49, 15-17 (1987).

10.   U.S. Undersecretary Judith Heumann, Meeting of ACTION (Action for Children to Insure Options Now), Alexandria, Va. (Dec. 12, 1993) (attended by author).

11.   U.S. DEPARTMENT OF EDUCATION, STATISTICS FOR THE 1990-1991 SCHOOL YEAR, Table AB1 (1992).

12.   Dorothy Kerzner Lipsky, *National Survey Gives Insight into Inclusive Movement*, INCLUSIVE EDUCATION PROGRAMS, Mar. 1994, at 5 [hereinafter *National Survey*].

13.   Douglas Fuchs and Lynn S. Fuchs, *Inclusive Schools Movement and the Radicalization of Special Education Reform*, 60 EXCEPTIONAL CHILDREN 297 (Feb. 1994) [hereinafter *Inclusive Schools Movement*].

14.   U.S. DEP'T OF EDUC., EDUCATING STUDENTS WITH LEARNING PROBLEMS — A SHARED RESPONSIBILITY, at 20 (1986).

15.   *Id.*

16.   CALIFORNIA LEAST RESTRICTIVE ENVIRONMENT TASK FORCE, THE REPORT OF THE LEAST RESTRICTIVE ENVIRONMENT TASK FORCE, AN ADVISORY TO THE CALIFORNIA STATE DEPARTMENT OF EDUCATION, at 10-11 (1988).

17.   *Id.*

18.   *Inclusive Schools Movement, supra* note 13, at 294 (this article provides a good overview of the history of special education reform movements that culminated in full inclusion).

19.   SAFE Philosophy Statement, adopted Dec. 1988, revised Dec. 1990.

20. *Special ed chiefs want states to revamp placement policies,* EDUCATIONAL DAILY, Nov. 9, 1992.

21. *National Survey, supra* note 12, at 7.

22. *Winners All: A Call for Inclusive Schools,* COUNTERPOINT, (publication of the National Association of State Directors of Special Education, NASDE) Winter 1992, at 1, 9.

23. *Id.* at 6.

24. *Id.*

25. *Id.*

26. *Id.*

27. *It means more than mainstreaming,* INCLUSION TIMES, Fall 1993, at 2.

28. *Id.* at 9-10.

29. 20 U.S.C. § 1401(a)(20) (West Supp. 1994) (emphasis added).

30. 20 U.S.C. § 1412(5) (West Supp. 1994).

31. 34 C.F.R. §§ 300.1-.754 (1993).

32. 34 C.F.R. § 330.552 (1993).

33. 34 C.F.R. § 300.550(2) (1993); 20 U.S.C. § 1412(5)(B).

34. 34 C.F.R. § 300.551 (1993).

35. 20 U.S.C. § 1401(a)(18) (1990).

36. Gladys J. v. Pearland Independent School District, 520 F. Supp. 869, 875 (S.D. Texas 1981) 1980-81 EHLR 552:480; Tokarcik v. Forest Hills, 665 F.2d 443, 458 (3d Cir. 1981), 1980-81 EHLR 552:513.

37. 115 Idaho at 466 (1984), 1984-85 EHLR 556:477.

38. 1984-85 EHLR at 482.

39. 1984-85 EHLR at 482.

40. *Id.*

41. 767 P.2d 1241, 1249 (Id. 1988).

42. Campbell v. Talladega County Bd. of Educ., 518 F. Supp. 47, 55 (N.D. Ala. 1981) 1980-81 EHLR 552:472, 477.

43. 518 F. Supp. at 54, 1980-81 EHLR at 477.

44. 518 F. Supp. at 56, 1980-81 EHLR at 478. *See also* Harmon v. Mead School District No. 354, No. CS-90-210-WFN (E.D. Wash. 1991), 17 EHLR 1029, 1031 (in which the court noted that reliance on "a more restrictive environment should only be used as a last resort.").

45. Daniel R. v. El Paso Independent School District, 874 F.2d 1036, 1039 (5th Cir. 1989).

46. *Id.*

47. *Id.* at 1047 (emphasis added).

48. *Id.* at 1047-48.

49. 995 F.2d 1204 (3d Cir. 1993), 19 IDELR 908.

50. 995 F.2d 1207, n.1

51. *Id.* at 1207.

52. INDIVIDUALS WITH DISABILITIES EDUCATION LAW REPORT, HIGHLIGHTS, July 29, 1993.

53. 786 F. Supp. 874 (E.D. Cal. 1992), 18 IDELR 761.

54. 786 F. Supp. at 883, n.9.

55. Sacramento City Unified School District v. Rachel H., No. 92-15608 (9th Cir. 1994).

56. Barry A. Zolotar, *In Rachel's case, loose ends about bias, funds,* Sacramento BEE, April 14, 1994.

57. *Id.*

58. *Id.* at B7. In this article, Barry A. Zolotar, deputy general counsel for the California Department of Education, wrote that while mainstreaming was a statutory mandate, it did not mean full inclusion for every child.

59. Debra Viadero, *Administration backs disabled child in 'inclusion' case* EDUCATION WEEK, Sept. 15, 1993, at 8.

60. *Id.*

61. 648 F. Supp. 1452 (W.D.N.Y. 1993), 20 IDELR 663.

62. *Id.* at 665.

63. *Separate and Unequal, supra* note 5, at 48.

# 2

# The Restrictions on Removing Children From Regular Education

To the west of the Morrison home were brilliantly green hills; to the north, Mount Shasta. The city was ringed with orchards and lots lined with slightly ragged trees that still bear fruit. It was still awaiting the necessary shift in property value and frustration with the money to be made from selling apples before bulldozing and the development of home divisions and malls would begin.

Far to the east and north are smaller towns and villages of the Sierra foothills. These were the hills Ishi came out of in 1911. His small band of remaining Yahis traveled at night, hopping from stone to stone so as to leave no footprints. He was integrated into the world, living at the University of California in San Francisco until he died of tuberculosis a few years later. Some thought it was exposure to the majority culture that enfeebled and ultimately doomed Ishi.

Janet's parents did not want Janet pulled from her hills. The dispute was long-standing, but became adversarial at a series of individualized education program (IEP) meetings. In passing IDEA Congress had required that before a child was placed in a program an IEP meeting of educators and parents must be held, at which time the parties would discuss the child's current levels of performance, would develop particular goals and objectives for the child, would decide on the right placement, including any support services required by the child's unique "disabling" condition, and would develop a written IEP. The parents and educators would be coequals in the process. No other parent-student community had such potential power. The IEP created enforceable duties for the school district.

While Congress wanted the parent and teacher at the IEP meeting and allowed for the parent and school district to invite any other appropriate individuals, it did not provide a precise decisionmaking mechanism for approval of the various IEP components. Subsequent federal department of education policy recommended that the IEP decision represent a consensus and that school districts should not intimidate parents by inviting a large number of school personnel to attend the IEP meetings.*

Not long after the passage of IDEA both parents and educators were, understandably, unsophisticated about such a method for program development. Educators had rarely, if ever, been required to share their authority with parents, and parents were certainly unaccustomed to asking for something based on existing rights.

Not surprisingly the results were varied—parents thought they could ask for the educational moon and felt confused and angry when it was not pulled from the sky; administrators thought they could write anything in the IEP (to please the parents) and then, to their horror, were told that if it was in the IEP, it had better be provided.

---

* In one local IEP meeting the author attended, the child's teacher was invited along with the local and county administrator, school nurse, school psychologist and program director. As the participants introduced themselves, one individual stated that she was the "teacher of the day." She was asked whether she knew the child. She did not. She had never seen and did not know anything about the child. When asked why she was there, the teacher of the day stated that she represented the teachers of the district.

By the time of the IEP meetings for Janet, the process had become more sophisticated. The parties already knew what the Morrisons wanted and what the district would offer, so the Morrison IEP meetings were reduced to a series of almost comical encounters. Unlike a dispute over the number of speech therapy sessions per week, where the parties have some room to give and take, the Morrisons and the school district could not bargain away miles.

The school district knew about IEPs and what should and should not be written on them. The Morrisons, clear in their intent, understood that the IEP had to be written to justify the distant and "segregated" placement. The struggle centered on goals and objectives (the heart of the IEP and the bane of special educators everywhere), and the foundation upon which a rationale for services and/or a placement is built.

Normally goals and objectives are narrow in scope, small but feisty animals with a short range of movement. For example—Goal: the child will improve reading comprehension. Objective: by the end of the next semester, the child will read a four paragraph story and understand 75 percent of the story.

IEP goals and objectives seem prototypically American—an earnestly conceived system to promote cooperation and growth, but also satisfying a need to quantify everything, to be able to concretely demonstrate movement from one point to another. As a result the IEP can lack flexibility and at times, notably in the Morrison case, ignore broader and more fundamentally important questions. The Morrison IEP meeting was held in the hearing-impaired program at Midvale School. Janet was then attending Midvale, the program the district had offered.

*   *   *

Midvale School was located in a hamlet about 25 miles and 40 minutes from Janet Morrison's home. There was no reason for the hearing-impaired program to be in Midvale, other than its location in the geographic center of a large county.* It was a bright day, the wind was up, the hills to the west were green but barely visible and the Sierras to the east were too far away for one to discern their color. Midvale was the color of yellow wheat.

Midvale was barely more than a quarter-mile square, a village deserted by freeways to the east and west, a grid of houses, and a store or two. A water tower was the only structure above one story. The school was in the center of the tiny town. The 11 hearing-impaired children came from all over the county. Since "deafness" is a low incidence "disability"—less than 2 percent of the population is profoundly deaf—school districts, particularly smaller ones, rarely have "enough" deaf students to form classes. This was so in Janet's case.

The school was a nondescript one-story American school built in the 1950s, with a large yard, some green grass, some brown. There was a ballfield and play structures and cyclone fencing. With the wind up and the sky clear, it was difficult, if one let go for just a second, to tell whether it was 1951 or 1991.

The yard was empty, but the recess bell rang and soon the playground was filled with elementary school children. Let loose, they did as all kids do; they ran and yelled and played various games and held important and private conversations and used the time to talk intimately with their teachers. They ate part of their lunch and they skipped rope and harassed one another.

---

* The term "hearing-impaired" is used to describe programs for deaf and hard-of-hearing children, but has a negative connotation. Since deaf people, whether "oral" or "manual" (those who use sign language) have a perfectly viable mode of communication, the term "hearing-impaired" is stereotypical, certainly as it relates to a communication impairment. The degree of hearing loss can vary greatly as reflected in the terms deaf and hard-of-hearing. The difference between an individual with a moderate hearing loss and residual hearing and a profoundly deaf individual is vast. In addition, the onset of the loss is important, particularly if the loss is pre- or postlingual (before or after the development of spoken language).

Some looked up as a jet raced across the clear sky toward San Francisco, contrails tracing its path from the east.

The members of the "hearing-impaired" class gathered in small groups. While all had a hearing loss, many were "oral," and even those who used sign language preferred an English-based sign language or had very rudimentary signing skills. Some of the "oral" children played with the "non-disabled" children. Several others played by themselves, several roamed about. The two older deaf girls went off to a corner to discuss some private matter. The teacher, Phillip Johnstone, watched from the shade of a building overhang.

Janet walked slowly out of her class, across the yard, past a four-square game and reached the climbing structure. She paused and then scrambled to the top, where she remained, by herself, for the rest of recess. This pattern rarely changed.

\*     \*     \*

The Morrisons and school personnel met in a small, unused classroom. The program administrator, Jean Francis, sat next to Phillip Johnstone, a precise, neat man. Between Johnstone and Francis was the Morrisons' interpreter. Francis was austere and rarely smiled. She was on guard—this family was asking for things she did not agree with. While there was a question of money—the district would pay 10 percent of the cost of the state school placement, approximately $3,000 and travel expenses—Francis would not concede that her program was not appropriate.

The Morrisons did not want to write technical goals and objectives; reading scores and math ability would come. There was no need to detail those hopes. Janet could already read and compute beyond her years. They wanted her to have classmates and teachers with whom she could communicate. They thought this was simple enough, and their attorney had advised them to be sure to include those as goals and objectives. But these were not the kinds of goals and objectives normally written at IEP meetings. Goals and objectives were narrow, technical, and academic in nature. They were not, as a general rule, about communicating with peers or socialization and they rarely touched upon the communication mode (manual or oral language) or particular language (American Sign Language or Signed Exact English) of a child.

But without these goals, what rationale would they have for the placement they wanted? Janet needed placement at the state school so she could effectively and directly communicate with her peers and teachers. Such goals and objectives were seen as unusual, probably because they were not subject to easy quantification. The district was savvy enough to know that any language goals and objectives might create a rationale for state school placement. The district (and the Morrisons) danced about the IEP much as boxers do in the early stages of a tactical fight.

Jean Francis was prepared.

"But I am not sure what you want here. Would you say that again?"

The Morrisons signed their intentions: "Janet shall improve her ability to relate to her peers. That is the long-range goal. The objective would be that she would relate to peers who are of her age and who use her language."

"But that is not a goal or objective."

"It is to us and Janet. It is the most important goal she should have."

"But we can't quantify that."

"What do you mean?" Janet's parents demanded.

"We must be able to determine whether a goal and objective has been met. How do we measure the success or failure of the goal? You want us to be able to determine whether it is working or not, don't you?"

"Of course, but we did not understand the law to require that a goal or objective be quantified in order to be a goal and objective."

"Well true, but these are not goals and objectives. Goals and objectives normally discuss reading or math or language or physical education concerns. All children need peers, all children should communicate with their classmates. But these are not goals and objectives. I simply don't see how this relates to Janet's IEP."

"Our daughter needs to communicate. What could be simpler?"

"All right. We can write goals regarding vocabulary growth, syntax development, that kind of thing."

"That would be good as well, but what use is that if she has no one to talk to?"

"But she does have ten peers in the class and also the opportunity to interact with non-disabled children."

"Those children in her class do not communicate at all like Janet. Many don't sign and those that do only know a few signs. And the regular children look at Janet like a freak. They can sign 'hi' but that isn't language. How would you like it if your child was in a school where the other kids could only say 'hi' to her?"

Francis frequently left the room to phone her attorney in Southern California. Frequently she would come back with new language, trying to walk the increasingly fine line between directly forbidding the parental request and agreeing to goals and objectives that might eventually cook the administrative goose at any due process hearing.

The Morrisons were stubbornly determined to include those goals and objectives. For one thing, their attorney pushed for them because they would make for a stronger case. For another, they were inherently significant.

"We also feel that Janet has a goal of being exposed to deaf role models and that she be able to play with her classmates after school," the Morrisons added.

"That is ridiculous. The school district cannot create role models and certainly has no responsibility for ensuring that Janet play with peers after school."

"She should come home and be able to communicate with her neighbors. She should have the chance to play with children who are in her school."

The Morrisons knew that none of the children in the district's proposed program lived near Janet. Most were 10 to 30 miles away. One child was 45 miles from their home.

"We understand your concern, but we cannot write goals about things we have no control over."

The district begrudgingly agreed to the most general communication goals: "Janet will be exposed to peers with whom she can communicate." Because Janet used American Sign Language (ASL) as her native language and because none of the other children or teachers used ASL, Francis knew she could not agree to any specific ASL goals. Although ASL is not frequently available in educational programs in the United States, it is a language "seen as fully comparable to speech . . . but with unique, additional powers of a spatial and cinematic sort."[1] ASL represents "at every level—lexical, grammatical, syntactic—a *linguistic* use of space . . . [it is] amazingly complex."[2]

Mr. Johnstone was particularly fluent in Signed Exact English, a manual form of English, but had only passing familiarity with ASL. Janet was fluent in ASL and communicated effectively and fluidly at a six-year-old level. Most of the other children in the class had only the most rudimentary signing skills. The two children who had communication skills close to Janet's were nine and ten years old. Johnstone's aide did not sign effectively in any language.

Francis determined that since ASL was not the coin of the realm in Johnstone's class, there could be no significant ASL goals or objectives. The Morrisons, on the other hand, believed Janet's ASL skills were essential to her educational well-being and the ongoing strength of the deaf community.*

---

* The issues of bilingualism and deaf education are complex. Deaf children, unlike hearing children who are learning English as a second language, will not "learn to hear." That is not to say, of course, that deaf children do not develop lipreading skills or develop a "voice." It is fallacious, however, to compare deaf children to Spanish-speaking or Chinese-speaking children who are in bilingual programs. The provision of educational opportunities in the

Ultimately, the Morrisons could not convince Francis to include anything more than very general communication goals and objectives. This would be increasingly frustrating for the Morrisons and would reveal some of the inherent weaknesses of IDEA. What use is an education if such fundamentals have no place on the IEP? Is communication access as or more important to Janet than reading and math development? Janet's parents wondered how the various needs of an individual child could be so easily compartmentalized.*

The language issues were equally complex for the school district. Would they have to provide particular language access for every child? Since there are many sign languages, would there need to be a program with full language access for each child? Should there be a qualified teacher who could communicate in ASL, Signed Exact English, Cued Speech, or pidgin Signed English, to name just some of the sign language and signing systems?

The discussion of placement was brief. Francis, frustrated with the lengthy debate over goals and objectives and sensing that it was all part of a larger strategy—which it was, because the Morrisons had no choice but to try to create an IEP rationale for state school placement—spoke briefly with her attorney and then returned to the IEP meeting.

"We are prepared to offer Janet placement in the hearing-impaired program at Midvale school. This program is appropriate for Janet and is the least restrictive environment for her."

The Morrisons waited for the interpreter to finish. Mr. Morrison signed slowly.

---

deaf child's sign language is not to prepare the child to "speak" in an English environment, but to provide basic communication development and access.

* Judge Harold H. Greene of the federal district court for the District of Columbia stated, in an early and oft-quoted IDEA case, that the "social, emotional, medical or educational" needs of a child can be "so intimately intertwined that realistically it is not possible for the Court to perform the Solomon-like task of separating them." North v. District of Columbia Bd. of Educ., 471 F. Supp. 136 (D.D.C. 1979), 1979-80 EHLR 551:157.

"We are part of the IEP team and we don't agree with that choice. We feel the state school is the only place that can provide for Janet's needs."

"Well that's fine, but you will have to go to fair hearing if you don't agree. There is a place on the IEP form for you to indicate your position. Our time is up."

The district had no other placement options; a truly mainstreamed program was never offered. In some ways Janet was exactly what IDEA had in mind when the "mainstreaming" preference was created. She was bright, at or above grade level in academic subjects, and eager to learn. The law required that a child be placed in a regular classroom "to the maximum extent appropriate" and removed only if it could be demonstrated that the child couldn't achieve satisfactorily even with the use of supplementary aids. The district never offered placement with the supplemental aide of an interpreter in a regular classroom at Midvale or at any school closer to Janet's home.

To the district, a special day class for the hearing impaired 25 miles from home was closer than a special day class for the hearing impaired in the state school 150 miles away. To the district, removal was a relative matter. If Midvale was not a mainstreamed class, it was the least restrictive environment. It said so on the map of California.

———

IDEA not only has mainstreaming as a core concept or "presumptive requirement," but it further requires that children with disabilities be "removed" from regular educational environments *only* under limited circumstances. It is a kind of back-up integration insurance policy.

The physical and psychological "removal" of individuals with disabilities has been part of American history. Individuals with disabilities have been the target of destructive stereotypes and ancient prejudices. The "disabled," from Quasimodo to the Rain Man, from Dr. Strangelove to Stephen W. Hawking, fill our literature. Plato wrote in his *Republic* that "[the children] of the inferior parents and any children of the rest that are born defective will be hidden away, in some appropriate manner that must be kept secret."[3] Earlier societies condemned the disabled to death. Until 1974, Chicago had an ordinance that established a $50 fine for any diseased, maimed, mutilated, or otherwise unsightly or "disgusting" person who appeared in public areas.

By 1937, 28 states had sterilization laws. The Mississippi law, which remains in effect, provides sterilization for those afflicted with "idiocy, imbecility, or feeblemindedness."[4] In various places, a deaf person was considered, prima facie, incapable of making a contract. A citizen of Kentucky who was of "unsound mind" was considered incapable of marrying. A blind person was considered unfit to travel. In 1927 Justice Oliver Wendall Holmes wrote in *Buck v. Bell* why sterilization of Carrie Bell, a retarded woman, was justified:

> We have seen more than once that the public welfare may call upon the best citizens for their lives. It would be strange indeed if it could not call upon those who already sapped the strengths of the state, for these lesser sacrifices, in order to prevent our being swamped by incompetence. It is better for all the world, if, instead of waiting to execute degenerate offspring for crime or to let them starve for their imbecility, society can prevent those who are manifestly unfit for continuing their kind. Three generations of imbeciles are enough.[5]

After Justice Holmes's death his Civil War uniform was found in his closet with a note affixed, confirming that the ancient stains were his own blood. How could Carrie Bell refuse to sacrifice in her own way for the good of society?

The passage of the Rehabilitation Act of 1973 (Section 504) was the first major national legal effort to address the policies, if not the attitudes, of removal and exclusion. Two years later Congress passed the Education for All Handicapped Children's Act (IDEA). The passage of IDEA was preceded and influenced by two landmark cases that addressed the practice of excluding individuals with disabilities. In *Pennsylvania Association for Retarded Children v. Commonwealth*,[6] a suit was brought on behalf of retarded children challenging the constitutionality of a Pennsylvania statute that was used to exclude those children from public education and training. The dispute ended in a consent decree that enjoined the state from denying access to free public programs of education and training to any mentally retarded child.

Subsequently in *Mills v. Board of Education*,[7] the court ordered that

> no [disabled] child eligible for a publicly supported education in the District of Columbia public schools shall be excluded from a regular school assignment . . . unless such child is provided (a) adequate alternative educational services suited to the child's needs, which may include special education or tuition grants, and (b) a constitutionally adequate prior hearing and periodic review of the child's status, progress, and the adequacy of any educational alternative.[8]

In passing IDEA, Congress was clearly aware of the removal psychology:

> This latter process known as 'mainstreaming,' has been gaining popularity in recent years and, in experimental tests, has been found extremely workable and beneficial to the children involved.
>
> . . . children ought to remain in a regular classroom until such time as it is determined, on the basis of sound testimony and joint consultation with parents and the child, that it is in the best interest of the student to be placed in a special class.[9]

There were many reasons for restricting removal. As Senator Stafford noted in the congressional debate on IDEA: "[i]t is an isolation for the handicapped child and for the 'normal' child as well. The sooner we are able to bring the two together, the more likely the attitudes of each toward one another will change for the better."[10]

Accordingly, Congress passed 20 U.S.C. § 1412(5)(B), which stated that: "special classes, separate schooling, or other *removal* of children with disabilities from the regular educational environment *occurs only when* the nature or severity of the disability is such that education in regular classes with the use of supplementary aids and services cannot be achieved satisfactorily. . . ."[11] A child with disabilities *starts* in a regular classroom, a strong statement about the inclusionary purpose of IDEA. Not surprisingly, though, there was no unanimity about the underlying integration nature of the law. The Ford administration had a different vision of the purpose and extent of removal options. Secretary of Health, Education, and Welfare Casper Weinberger reported to Congress that the administration was reluctant to "endorse the concept of mainstreaming" because "the assumption of mainstreaming children always represents the most effective means of educating handicapped children has not yet been shown."[12] Commissioner of Education T.H. Bell went further, concluding that there was no empirical data supporting mainstreaming:

> Despite large numbers of projects, however, it was difficult to find acceptable evidence that any given project had helped children to increase their achievement in the basic skills of reading and mathematics. It was still more difficult to find attempts to replicate a presumably effective project and, worse yet, virtually impossible to find a successful replication of an effective project.[13]

Congress understood, of course, the possibility and even the necessity of removal. As with the right to mainstreaming, the restrictions against "removal" were not unlimited. Congress recognized that a child's individual needs might require placement in various environments, including hospitals and other institutions, and specifically noted that while a regular classroom was optimal, it might not always be the most beneficial place of instruction.

IDEA added language to the "removal" section and in so doing, moved away from any absolute inclusion mandate: "[i]n selecting the LRE, consideration is given to any potential harmful effect on the child or on the quality of services that he or she needs."[14] But the "removal" language of the law, like the broader mainstreaming preference, is unmistakable if not absolute. LRE does not mean placement "to the maximum extent appropriate" with non-disabled students *and* other disabled students, but only with non-disabled children.[15]

In reality, the removal of many special education children happens long before an initial regular classroom placement is made. Parents and school staff meet and, as in the Morrison case, only discuss nonregular options. The psychological removal has taken place before the child enters the regular classroom. Few children with disabilities start in a regular classroom, fail to achieve satisfactorily, and are then "removed."* Not surprisingly, many have concluded, again using the race/disability comparison, that "Americans continue to pay for and send their children to classrooms that are often separate and unequal."[16]

There is both anecdotal and statistical evidence that removal is the rule and not the exception under IDEA. In the 1992 report issued by the Association for Retarded Citizens of the United States (ARC) entitled "Report Card to the Nation on Inclusion in Education of Students with Mental Retardation," the rate of "removal" was found to be disheartening.[17] The ARC determined that inclusion meant "the opportunity for all students to participate in the totality of the school experience . . . [which] includes integration into regular classrooms in neighborhood schools for both educational and social opportunities."[18]

The ARC defined an "inclusive school system" as one in which access to regular education is a self-evident requirement,

---

* In the Morrison case, the debate was over two nonregular programs; there was no "removal" issue since the law does not apply a removal test once the child is outside the regular classroom. One need not show, for example, a lack of achievement in order to move a child from one special class to another.

providing students with disabilities access to peer models, appropriate expectations, and diversity of experience. Moreover, according to ARC, "inclusion . . . is really a matter of human dignity and civil rights."[19]

The ARC report examined the 50 states, the District of Columbia, and Puerto Rico, and found that only two states educated more than 50 percent of their mentally retarded students in regular classes (Massachusetts, 59 percent, and Vermont, 54 percent).[20] Wyoming was next with 36 percent, then New Hampshire at 25 percent and only Idaho, Nebraska, Arkansas and North Carolina at more than 10 percent. Of the 52 jurisdictions, 44 had less than 10 percent of their students with mental retardation in regular classrooms. Thirty-two were under 6 percent and nine, including Florida, New Jersey, Illinois, Indiana and New York were under one percent.[21] Overall only "6.7 percent of children with mental retardation were educated in regular classrooms in the 1989-90 school year."[22] ARC gave grades to the 52 jurisdictions: only Massachusetts and Vermont received Cs with six states receiving Ds and the other 44 receiving Fs.[23]*

In its Fourteenth Annual Report to Congress on the Implementation of IDEA, the U.S. Department of Education reported that approximately two-thirds of state plans were *not* in compliance with the mainstreaming requirements of IDEA. Half of the

---

* At about the same time the ARC report was issued, a conference was held in Washington, D.C., titled "Full Inclusion of Children and Youth with Disabilities in Community Schools." In the description of the conference, the sponsors stated that:

> America 2000 and other education reform efforts promise a better
> system of schooling for *all* students. If such promise is to become
> a reality, then a renewed commitment to the full inclusion of chil-
> dren and youth with disabilities must be made.

Right before the 1992 presidential election, the Clinton-Gore campaign issued its plan "on Americans with Disabilities" which included its belief that "all persons with disabilities must be fully integrated into mainstream American society." The campaign further pledged to increase "efforts to *integrate children with disabilities into their schools,* instead of sectioning them off in special prostates removed children with disabilities before it was demon-strated that they had not achieved satisfactorily even with the use of supplementary aids and services.

These kinds of statistics have not gone unnoticed by an increasing number of courts. The Court of Appeals for the Eleventh Circuit recently indicated that

> school officials should consider the full range of supplemen-tal aids and services that may be provided in conjunction with regular classroom education, and they should share these considerations with the child's parents at the IEP meet-ing. It is not sufficient that school officials determine what they believe to be the appropriate placement for a handi-capped child and then attempt to justify this placement only after the proposed IEP is challenged by the child's parents.[24]

What must a school district do to prevent the "removal" that IDEA discourages? The list of supplementary aids that may be required is extensive as provided by law and judicial decree. Language habilitation, auditory training, speech reading, coun-seling, medical services, occupational and physical therapy, par-ent counseling and training, psychological services, recreation, social work services, speech and language services, and transpor-tation are listed in 34 C.F.R. § 300.16 as related services. Congress recognized, parenthetically, that the list was "not exhaustive."[25]

Supplementary services have been defined through court decisions and policy statements to include, among other things: one-to-one instructional aides, clean intermittent catheterization, sign language interpreters, parent sign language classes, psycho-therapy, after-school aides, cognitive therapy, escort services for retarded students, music therapy, note-takers, and sensory inte-gration therapy. The statistics of both private and governmental agencies belie the full effectiveness of these services, indicate

---

grams where they cannot socially integrate with other students." (Emphasis in the original.)

that they are not employed to satisfy the nonremoval requirement, and further suggest that removal is taking place in a preemptory manner. Law and practice, then, are quite different. The removal portion of IDEA has about it a kind of disfavored nation status—travel is discouraged, but interest is high.

\*    \*    \*

Of the hundreds of cases involving the mainstreaming of children with disabilities and the "removal" language of IDEA, a number have involved medical factors. These cases particularly reveal the services-removal conundrum as well as the complexity and nontraditional nature of the services required.

Seven-year-old Raul Espino had been in an auto accident that left him completely paralyzed in his lower extremities. He had limited muscle strength in his upper body, was considered quadriplegic, and used a wheelchair.[26] He was unable to dissipate or conserve body heat because he suffered severe damage to his sympathetic nervous system and had a malfunctioning hypothalamus. As a result he could not regulate his own body temperature and had to be maintained in a stable temperature-controlled environment between 68 and 78 degrees Fahrenheit. When subject to excess heat, Raul's skin turned red and he began to hyperventilate, his internal body temperature rose and he felt restless and weak and could not concentrate. If the external temperature fluctuated excessively, mucous would accumulate in Raul's lungs, thereby increasing respiratory difficulties.

As a young child Raul remained indoors and had little chance to interact with his peers. As he grew older he was somewhat better able to control his body temperature so that during the time of the legal dispute he could tolerate some temperature fluctuation. Raul had been enrolled in an air-conditioned kindergarten class at the Moody School for the Handicapped in Brownsville, Texas.

Because Raul was both pleasant and intelligent the school district recommended a regular first grade program in an air-conditioned class. However on the first day of school Raul was not assigned to an air-conditioned classroom but instead to a portable five-foot Plexiglas cubicle with a window air conditioning unit. The district had constructed the unit and contended that Raul did not need air-conditioning all the time, and certainly not when the external temperature was between 68 and 78 degrees. It also claimed that it could not afford to air-condition Raul's entire classroom. While the district did acknowledge that it was preferable for Raul not to be in the cubicle, it was concerned that if one classroom was air-conditioned, other children's parents would demand equal accommodations.

During September of this first year, Raul spent approximately 75 percent of his class time in the cubicle, but as the weather cooled he spent less time there—down to 25 percent in November. Yet by mid-April 1981 he was again spending a good percentage of his time in the cubicle.

Raul moved to and from the cubicle, which sometimes significantly interrupted his academic and social opportunities. Sometimes his teacher would go into the cubicle with him, but this proved to be a distraction to the rest of the children. The cubicle had a sound system, which occasionally malfunctioned.

Raul's grades during the school year were excellent—he received straight As. He was well liked by classmates and interacted well with them when given the opportunity. Testimony was introduced that the cubicle was inappropriate because it reduced Raul's ability to communicate effectively, interrupted his perception of nonverbal stimuli, brought undue attention to his disability, and reduced the positive reinforcement children get from direct peer interaction. In short, Raul's social, rather than his academic needs were affected by his placement in the cubicle.

The cost of air-conditioning Raul's room was $5,700. The school district had an annual budget of $39 million, of which $3 million was from federal funds. Approximately $250,000 was budgeted for students with disabilities.

The dispute reached federal court, which ruled against the use of the cubicle and in favor of classroom air-conditioning.

While the court focused on the monetary issues involved and was concerned with the cost ratio of air-conditioning the classroom to the total district budget, it also recognized the important mainstreaming issues, saying that "[f]ull social interaction is an important part of today's educational curriculum and is even more vital to a child like Raul who necessarily suffers a certain degree of isolation as a result of his handicap."[27]

The court found that Raul's academic progress and popularity with his classmates "attest[ed] to his courage and tenacity, and he should not be penalized for the fruits of his own efforts."[28] To deprive him of a "full educational opportunity" by placing him in a cubicle was contrary to his IEP and violated his right to an "appropriate" education. Financial considerations were not pertinent.[29]

There is no existing standard to determine the appropriate cost-to-value ratio.* For example, while the price of an air conditioner was $5,700 and therefore represented only .0001461 of the total budget for the school system, it did represent approximately .0228 of the total special education budget. Should that difference matter? Is there a budgetary line past which no special education cost can possibly go, thus justifying removal? Is there a price for integration and should it impact on placement decisions? The cost of air-conditioning was small, and thus the *Espino* court needed only to conclude that the ratio was acceptable. Without a financial barrier, the court could rule that the inclusion of Raul Espino was guaranteed by IDEA and that removal, even within the four walls of a regular classroom, would not meet the law's mandate. This court, like many others, recognized that nonacademic factors were part of an appropriate education and therefore part of the removal analysis.

---

* Thirteen years after the *Espino* decision courts have not yet determined any kind of exact cost/benefit equation. The *Holland* court (*see* Chapter 1) noted that cost was a factor in weighing the individual child's needs against the budgetary concerns of a school district, but did not provide specific direction for striking the appropriate balance.

The Third Circuit Court of Appeals affirmed the lower court. While noting the "tension" between the mainstreaming and provision-of-needs portions of IDEA, the court found that the key to resolving this issue appeared to lie in the proper use of supplementary aids and services by the school. A school must consider a "whole range" of aids to prevent unwarranted removal, and even proof that the child can make greater academic progress in a segregated setting will not justify exclusion of the child from a regular classroom.

\* \* \*

Katherine D. was a seven-year-old child who suffered from cystic fibrosis and tracheomalacia, which made her windpipes floppy instead of rigid.[30] Since the age of two, Katherine had used a tracheostomy tube, which allowed her to breathe. Periodically throughout the day, Katherine needed the tube removed, her lungs suctioned, and the tube reinserted. Claiming that the provision of such services was beyond its legal duty, Katherine's school district offered her homebound instruction.

The Ninth Circuit Court of Appeals ruled that such removal was contrary to the mandates of IDEA and that the provision of intermittent tracheostomy services in a regular classroom was appropriate: "The congressional preference for educating handicapped children in classrooms with their peers is made unmistakably clear in section 1412(5)(B) . . . it is fundamental to the scheme and purpose of [IDEA] that handicapped children be provided the same educational opportunity and exposure as those children who are not so disadvantaged."[31]

The *Katherine D.* court added that if a school district fails to offer a classroom for a disabled child who has clearly demonstrated their ability to function in a normal classroom the district would be responsible for paying for a private school until an appropriate public option is available.

\* \* \*

The weight of the mainstreaming-nonremoval mandate may be most clearly illuminated in those cases where the right to an "integrated" classroom is weighed against the health and safety needs of other children. In *New York State Association for Retarded Children v. Carey*,[32] a class of mentally retarded children who were hepatitis B carriers had been excluded from public school by order of the New York City Board of Education.

Hepatitis B affects the liver and, in acute cases, can cause jaundice and even lead to death. The incubation period is two to three months. At the time of the litigation no cure was known, although in many cases the consequences of the disease are mild, causing flu-like symptoms. The carriers of the disease may appear healthy, but they can transmit the disease to others by transfusions, by the use of contaminated needles, or through the carrier's saliva.

The board of education assessed the overall hygienic conditions in the school system and found that some of the "infected" children exhibited behavior that could lead to "communication" of the disease, including hand-to-mouth contact, scratching to the point of drawing blood, drooling, and bleeding from the gums. As a precaution the board decided to exclude the 48 "carrier" children from public education and place them in newly created special education classes, composed solely of hepatitis B carriers with mental retardation, and held in specified schools (one in each of the five boroughs). The board concluded that the children would not be harmed by the lack of contact with "normal" children, since there was so little contact in the first place.

In a February 1979 decision, the court rejected the proposal to "segregate . . . [all] mentally retarded children epidemiologically classified as hepatitis B carriers. . . ."[33] The court was particularly concerned about assigning children to programs different from the ones they had been attending, reducing the amount of contact with non-institutionalized children, grouping ("cohorting") carrier children with different developmental levels, and forcing these children to be placed in classes where there would be a reduction of nonacademic and extracurricular activity contact with non-disabled children. Ultimately such segregation would have increased the possibility of "devastating" stigmatization with a real impact on the children's opportunities for employment and community placement plans.

The court seemed especially concerned about peer interaction and modeling behavior. It found that the "relevant inquiry, therefore, is whether on balance the proposed segregation of carrier children, with its resultant educational disadvantages, is justified to protect the health and welfare of the non-carrier retarded children."[34] The court reviewed the scientific evidence and found it did not "demonstrate any causal relationship between the classroom setting and transmission of the virus."[35]

In *Community High School District 155 v. Denz*,[36] Ingrid Denz's school district recommended "homebound" placement based on concerns that her hepatitis B could be transmitted. Ingrid, like the students in *Carey*, was mentally retarded. She sought placement with non-disabled children. A hearing officer ruled that the "dangers posed by the health impairment for Ingrid and other children could be sufficiently minimized by appropriate, relatively inexpensive prophylactic procedures, and that Ingrid had an overriding right to an educational placement which affords her some degree of interaction with other children."[37]

Although there was testimony that the children—aged 3 to 21 at the particular center Ingrid would attend—often kissed, that there was physical proximity and common use of materials and sharing of food, and that the children frequently fell and cut themselves, "transmission of the disease [was] relatively difficult and that the mere presence of a carrier does not result in the disease's transmission."[38] There was also testimony that Ingrid was very aware of her condition, was very "meticulous" about washing, did not kiss people, and was not prone to drooling.

The court ruled that the district's desire to segregate Ingrid through home instruction "had the effect of infringing upon [her] right to be 'mainstreamed'" and restricting her "interaction with other children."[39] The provision of "supplementary" aids allowed

Ingrid to be in a less restrictive environment—the court (and hearing officer) in this matter recognized the generally simple cause-and-effect mandate of the least restrictive environment regulations. The cost of the aid was not prohibitive.

There have been a number of cases involving children with the AIDS virus. Most hearing officers or courts have found that the presence of the AIDS virus did not justify removal.

In November 1985 the Ryan W. matter, which gained national attention, came before an Indiana hearing officer.[40] Ryan, a hemophiliac, had contracted AIDS as a result of a blood transfusion. His school district recommended a special day class with *exclusive* homebound instruction by telephone, a tutor if needed, and video transmission if warranted. The school would look into transporting friends to Ryan's home for social interaction.

The hearing officer ruled that while Ryan had nosebleeds, he understood how the virus was transmitted and also how to prevent its transmission. She found that homebound instruction interfered with social interaction and ruled that Ryan was to be admitted to regular classrooms at such time as his health allowed him to do so. On appeal the Board of Special Education affirmed the ruling that Ryan had a right to attend a regular classroom.[41]*

---

* *See also* Thomas v. Atascadero Unified School District, CV-86-6609-AHS (C.D. Cal. 1987), 1987-88 EHLR 559:113, in which a child who was infected with AIDS had a fight with another child and bit the leg of his pant. The school district asked that Thomas remain at home. Ultimately the school board voted to keep him out of class.

In ruling that the school district could not bar the child from regular kindergarten solely on the grounds of his health condition, the court acknowledged his right to be in "the regular educational environment." Without proof that he could not achieve satisfactorily even with the use of supplementary aids and services he could not be removed, even with a serious and potentially infectious illness. *See also* Parents of Child, Code No. 870901W v. Group I Defendants, 676 F. Supp. 1072 (E.D. Okla. 1987) 1987-88 EHLR 559:315 (regarding an emotionally disturbed student with hemophilia who tested positive for the AIDS virus, and for whom it was ruled that he could not be denied educational rights under IDEA solely because of his illness) and District 27 Community School Board v. Board of Education of New York, 502 N.Y.S.2d 326 (Sup. Ct. N.Y. 1986), 1985-86 EHLR 557:241.

Eliana Martinez was a seven-year-old trainably mentally retarded child with the AIDS virus.[42] Eliana became infected as a result of early blood transfusions and although at the time of litigation she was in the "late stages" of the disease, her condition had stabilized. Eliana was not toilet-trained and suffered from thrush, a disease that produces blood in the saliva. Eliana frequently sucked her thumb and forefinger, which left saliva on her fingers. She also suffered from skin lesions.

Eliana's mother sought placement in the public school in a special classroom for trainably mentally retarded (TMH) children. The school district offered home instruction. A hearing officer ruled in favor of the district, but the federal district court found that there was "'remote theoretical possibility' of transmission of the AIDS virus through tears, saliva and urine."[43] It ruled that the most appropriate placement was in a separate room to be "constructed in the TMH classroom with a large glass window and sound system to allow Eliana to see and hear the students in the classroom."[44] Another student could enter Eliana's room only if the parent of the child signed a waiver absolving the school from liability. Eliana could be taught in the larger room once she was toilet-trained and no longer placed her fingers in her mouth. A full-time aide would ensure the necessary separation between Eliana and other students.

Eliana's mother appealed and the court of appeals ruled that the remote theoretical possibility of transmission through tears, saliva and urine did not rise to the "significant" risk level that was required for Eliana to be excluded from the regular TMH classroom. The court remanded the case to the district court to determine the overall risk of transmission in order to decide whether Eliana was otherwise qualified to attend classes in the TMH classroom.

The court of appeals noted no findings as to the "effect on Eliana of isolating her with an aide in a separate room in the TMH classroom"[45] and asked the lower court to hear "evidence concerning the effect of any accommodation that would be reasonable, based upon the risk of transmission."[46] This evidence "must, at the minimum, relate to the effect of the proposed remedy on her psychological and educational development."[47]

Ultimately the Eleventh Circuit ordered Eliana into the TMH class without any exclusionary bubble. Twenty-one days later she died.

*     *     *

Recently courts have more frequently looked to the provision of supplementary aids and services and their cost as they relate to the inclusive nature of IDEA. The *J.G.* court* used the full inclusion nomenclature and provided its imprimatur to a system-wide inclusive program, which included significant fiscal commitments to make the change work. Others have looked to the provision of supplementary services to prevent removal and therefore foster individual inclusion.

Emily Mavis was a mentally retarded thirteen-year-old whose school district would provide mainstreaming only in music, art and gym.[48] Her school district refused to provide supplementary aids and services to allow for additional mainstreaming. Ruling in accord with *Oberti* and *Daniel R.,*[49] the *Mavis* court concluded that IDEA clearly required services to facilitate mainstreaming and that even modification of the regular classroom curriculum might be justified to accommodate that placement for Emily.

The court was particularly concerned that Emily had been preemptively removed, that is, she was not given the "opportunity" (through the use of supplementary aids) to prove she could be successful in a regular classroom. The court directed the district to work with Emily's parents to develop and implement an IEP that met statutory requirements but did hedge its bet a bit, acknowledging that an appropriate LRE education for Emily

---

* *See* Chapter 1.

might not be one that provided "'everything that might be thought desirable'" by her "'loving'" parents.[50]

\*     \*     \*

IDEA provides both a presumption in favor of mainstreaming and a significant legal restriction against removing children with disabilities from regular class environments. Given the number of children who are actually removed—ARC reported that 92 percent of retarded children never enter the regular classroom, while the U.S. Department of Education reported in 1989-90 that only 6.76 percent of those children were in regular classrooms—it is not surprising that the full inclusion movement has evolved into a powerful force in special education.\* Its message, at least as it relates to the individual child, is an important one. The numbers are a direct indictment of the failure of the restriction on removal.

The antiremoval language of IDEA is strong, but the willingness to employ the exceptions exerts an equal, if not more substantial, force. In 1993, Anna Statum apparently became the first child with severe disabilities in the Birmingham, Alabama school system to be placed in a regular classroom.[51] Anna had an IQ of 25, was unable to walk, required a body suit to support her upper body, could not use her hands, and was able to make only a few sounds. The U.S. District Court for the Northern District of Alabama ruled that Anna was entitled to an aide, vocational and speech services, and other consultation and training services in order to remain in a regular classroom. When Anna entered a regular classroom in Birmingham, 18 years had passed since IDEA was promulgated by the United States Congress.

---

\* As of May 1994 legislation had been introduced in California (SB 1714) the core purpose of which was to prevent schools from removing children with disabilities from regular classrooms without specific IEP documentation of the reasons for such removal and proof that the use of supplementary aids did not work.

A difficult question, and one not proposed by ARC or those who look to systemic full inclusion, is whether removal is necessary for some children. Full inclusion proponents might respond that no child with disabilities is justifiably removed and that the failure of the existing separatist system to serve the child is revealed to the extent that the child is removed. The judge in the *Statum* case recognized that Anna may have been better served in a special environment where the teacher-to-pupil ratio was lower, but deferred to the wishes of Anna's mother.

Ironically, parents who seek to keep their child in regular classes experience a "double bind," having to stress their child's unique needs to justify related services, while at the same time proving his or her similarities with non-disabled children.[52]

Is there any room left for placement options? Should separate education be eliminated? Can "removal" of the Anna Statums be discouraged while it remains available to the Janet Morrisons? Can a unitary system serve them both and, if so, will it not inexorably fall back on some kind of dualistic model? These are the difficult question that must be addressed before the removal segments (and other mainstreaming qualifiers) of IDEA are replaced by something that is no less onerous for Janet Morrison and her peers in the blind, autistic, learning-disabled, and other special education communities.

# Endnotes

1.   OLIVER SACHS, SEEING VOICES 89 (1989).

2.   *Id.* at 87.

3.   THE REPUBLIC OF PLATO 6 (Francis MacDonald Cornford trans., Oxford University Press 1953).

4.   MISS. CODE ANN. § 41-45-1 (LEXIS 1993).

5.   Buck v. Bell, 274 U.S. 200, 207 (1927).

6.   334 F. Supp. 1257, 1258 (E.D. Pa. 1971).

7.   348 F. Supp. 866 (D.C. 1972).

8.   *Id.* at 878.

9.   121 CONG. REC. 25,539-40 (1975) (statement of Rep. Miller).

10.  121 CONG. REC. 19,483 (1975) (statement of Sen. Stafford).

11.  20 U.S.C. § 1412(5)(B) (West Supp. 1994)(emphasis added).

12.  121 CONG. REC. 25,540 (1975).

13.  *Id.*

14.  34 C.F.R. § 300.552(d).

15.  20 U.S.C. § 1412(5) (West Supp. 1993).

16.  Joseph P. Shapiro et al., *Separate and Unequal,* U.S. NEWS & WORLD REP., Dec. 13, 1993, at 46.

17.  Sharon Davis, Ph.D., ASSOC. FOR RETARDED CITIZENS, REPORT CARD TO THE NATION ON INCLUSION IN EDUCATION OF STUDENTS WITH MENTAL RETARDATION, (1992).

18.  *Id.* at 2.

19.  *Id.* at 1.

20.  *Id.* at 7.

21.  *Id.* at 8.

22.  *Id.* at 17.

23.  *Id.* at 20.

24.  Greer v. Rome City School Dist., 950 F.2d 688, 696 (11th Cir. 1991), 18 IDELR 412, 416.

25.  34 C.F.R. § 300.16 (note) (1993).

26.  Espino v. Besteiro, 508 F. Supp. 905 (S.D. Texas 1981), *aff'd,* 708 F.2d 1002 (5th Cir. 1983).

27.  *Id.* at 913.

28.  *Id.*

29.  *Id.*

30.  Department of Educ. v. Katherine D., 727 F.2d 809, 812 (9th Cir. 1983), 1983-84 EHLR 555:276, 277.

31. 727 F.2d at 817, 1983-84 EHLR at 281.

32. 466 F. Supp. 487 (E.D.N.Y. 1979), 1979-80 EHLR 551:138.

33. 466 F. Supp. at 489, 1979-80 EHLR at 139.

34. 466 F. Supp. at 496, 1979-80 EHLR at 143 (citing Hairston v. Drosick, 423 F. Supp. 180, 183 (S.D. W. Va. 1976), 1979-80 EHLR 551:143, the court noted that "a child has to learn to interact in a social way with its peers and the denial of this opportunity during his minor years imposes added lifetime burdens upon a handicapped individual.").

35. 466 F. Supp. at 499, 1979-80 EHLR at 144.

36. 463 N.E.2d 998 (Ill. App. Ct. 1984), 1983-84 EHLR 555:518.

37. 1983-84 EHLR at 519.

38. 463 N.E.2d at 1003, 1983-84 EHLR at 521.

39. 1983-84 EHLR at 522.

40. *In re* Ryan W., No. 225, 1985-86 EHLR 507:239 (Cal. State Ed. Agency Hearing Nov. 25, 1985).

41. *Id.* at 342.

42. Martinez v. School Board, 861 F.2d 1502 (11th Cir. 1988), 1988-89 EHLR 441:257.

43. 861 F.2d at 1504, 1988-89 EHLR at 258.

44. *Id.*

45. 861 F.2d at 1507, 1988-89 EHLR at 260.

46. *Id.*

47. *Id.*

48. Mavis v. Sobol, 839 F. Supp. 968 (N.D.N.Y. 1994), 20 IDELR 1125.

49. For a discussion of these cases, *see* Chapter 1.

50. 839 F. Supp. at 992, 20 IDELR at 1138.

51. Statum v. Birmingham Public Schools Board of Educ., No. CV92-P-2054-S (N.D. Ala. 1993), 20 IDELR 435.

52. *See* David M. Engel, *Law, Culture, and Children with Disabilities*, 1991 Duke L.J. 166, 187 (1991); *see also* Martha Minow, *Learning to Live with the Dilemma of Difference*, 48 Law & Contemp. Probs. 157, 181 (1985).

# 3

## The Neighborhood School

The Morrisons and school personnel met in mediation in the city library, a modern building with florescent lighting and low ceilings—efficient, but cold. The meeting was in a large room, perhaps 20 by 40 feet. There were the ubiquitous folding chairs and utility tables in the middle, but little else in the room save a few plaques on the walls. There was a bank of windows at the west end of the room, and as the meeting proceeded into early afternoon a harsh sunlight filled the room. It was January, and while the hills were wonderfully green and hopeful, a persistent wind came from the west. The sky was clear but almost harsh; a sense of trouble hung in the room.

IDEA provides for an elaborate due process mechanism to settle disputes about the substance of an educational program for a child with disabilities. The process, unavailable for the rest of the school population, allows parents and school personnel, like any other combatants in the American legal system, to present and argue evidence before a neutral party who determines who is right and who is wrong. In California, as with many states, there is a nonbinding mediation stage that precedes an evidentiary hearing.

Normally such mediations are attended by two or three school representatives, a teacher who knows the child, an administrator, and perhaps a psychologist or other specialists. Normally the parents appear without the child and may or may not have an attorney. There can be an odd kind of coziness even in these disputes. The parties know what they want and will fight for it, but there is an informal, almost friendly quality to the dispute.

The school district brought Janet's teacher, the immediate program manager, the school psychologist, the speech therapist, the school nurse, numerous other administrators, and their attorney, who had flown up from Southern California. Since Janet's local school district did not have its own program for deaf children and the special day class was a county program, administrators from both the school system and the county office of education were present.

The mediator sat at the west end of the large table, with the school personnel arrayed in double rows to her right. There was a somberness in the room that seemed to fit the austere nature of the library and the cold day itself.

Janet was not there. She and her family saw the dispute as a simple matter. She could not hear, but that was not so much a disability as a statement of reality. All the indices of growth and development were there. She was prepared to communicate with the world—it would not do so with her.

The way the Morrisons viewed themselves and their daughter went to the heart of the dispute and contrasted sharply with what was either a certain condescension or ignorance on the part of those who insisted that Janet not go to the state school.

Janet Morrison's struggle was more than a matter of an eductional disagreement; it touched our notions of "normalcy." How do we define a "disability," and is it enough to locate some physiological, developmental, or psychological condition that is unmistakably different from the "norm"?* Putting aside the

---

* Increasingly, the deaf community is telling the hearing world (or the latter is paying more attention) that deaf children and adults are not disabled. In "Deafness as Culture," Edward Dolnick wrote that "[d]eaf people, far from groaning under a heavy yoke, are not handicapped at all. Deafness is not a disability. Instead, many deaf people now proclaim, they are a subculture like

significant implication and feel that language carries—and the terms "disabled," "handicapped," and certainly "normal" carry very evident messages—the Morrison case questioned both stereotypical notions of children with disabilities and a prevailing kind of educational colonialism. It is, of course, not always that simple: sometimes parents are wrong and educators are right.* But the administrators in Janet's case viewed her as incomplete, rather than as a student for whom standards that applied to hearing children were irrelevant.

Janet's school district believed that placement in the state school would discourage adjustment to the hearing world. It did not understand that Janet would more likely be able to function in the hearing world if she developed her native language, created effective ties with her true language community, and therefore did the very things necessary to grow into a self-assured, literate, and communicationally sound individual.

Much like Ishi's Yahi tribe which did not seek out the newcomers from the east, the Morrisons did not choose involvement in special education. But IDEA included hearing loss as a disability, and so Janet was captured within its boundries. The law does not distinguish between those children who need additional assistance, whether it be particular services or special placements, and those who have disabilities, but need nothing more than to have educational doors opened. The difference between remediation and access is not an easy one, but Janet needed to be able to communicate with her teachers and peers. She could do so at the state school. She had communication opportunities in the

---

any other. . . . and are no more in need of a cure for their condition than are Haitians or Hispanics." (ATLANTIC MONTHLY, Sept. 1993, at 37.)

* The question of how to determine when the expert is right and the parent wrong is no easier when the preponderence of empirical data supports one position or the other. Whether they were right or wrong, should the Morrisons have had the final say because they were Janet's parents? Unless a child needs a life-saving medical procedure or medication, should all other decisions rest with the parents regardless of what the educational experts propose?

district's program, but the difference between the two options was the difference between a fluid, rich, and appropriate language world and a stagnant and very limited one. It was the difference between a six-year-old communicating with other six-year-olds and with adults who communicated as adults *and* a six-year-old communicating with peers who knew five or ten words and teachers who had the language skills of a six-year-old.

The mediator opened the meeting, explaining perfunctorily that she had no power to make the parties come to resolution. Her unstated power was that she understood the issues and the law and that she could assess the strengths and weaknesses of each side's case. The state mediator was pleasant and well-liked, but lacked the feistiness and determination necessary to make the mediation successful. Not infrequently a good mediator could convince parents and school districts to meet on some middle ground, neither fully happy, neither having lost.

Raymond Morrison addressed the meeting, begging the mediator, as he had begged the school personnel earlier, to allow his daughter to be removed from her home and placed in a state school for deaf children. Such was the nature of the dispute, and perhaps the school representatives saw intemperance or negligence in the family's position. Children with disabilities had been "segregated" or simply ignored for so long—now federal law would ensure that such children have the same opportunities as non-disabled children. The Morrisons sought to turn the law upside down.

The interpreter voiced Mr. Morrison's signs. The Morrisons ignored the interpreter when they were communicating expressively but watched her intently when she signed the spoken language of the hearing people in the room.

Mr. Morrison pleaded with the mediator, hoping that she had more power than she did and would respond to his plea as the school district had not. The mediator smiled and the interpreter, a few words behind Mr. Morrison's expressive signing, finished his sentence with a slight deflation in voice quality and pitch. She seemed embarrassed. Everyone to the left of the mediator seemed to sag. The Morrison's attorney told the mediator about Janet, about her abilities, about her needs, about the two placement options that were in dispute. Finally he asked the school personnel why a family would plead so passionately to have their child removed from their home.

"Either their parental abilities should be questioned or they know something that everyone else in this room does not. Unless these parents are negligent or unstable, you must ask why would they insist on something that seems, ostensibly anyway, contrary to common sense. Why? They are begging you, not for an extra hour of speech therapy, but to give their daughter what every hearing child in this county and state takes for granted—an environment in which she can communicate directly with peers and teachers. This is why they are so determined."

The school district's attorney spoke in a direct, dispassionate tone. She was generally direct, not given to overtly aggressive or unpleasant outbursts that sometimes characterize the profession. She was technically efficient in her approach to this particular dispute. Her job was to win the case for the district—there was no philosophical agenda. She had the resources of a large law firm and a client quite determined to draw the line in this matter.

"It may be that the state school has a better program," she began, "but the law requires only that we provide an appropriate education. Parents want the best for their children and it would be nice if that were always possible. But resources are limited, and the law does not require the best, only that which is appropriate *and* least restrictive.

"Here the local program will allow Janet to remain at home. It is the least restrictive environment, and that too is required by law. We would be breaking the law if we agreed to remove her from a program that is close to home and place her in one that is far away. The law gives this school district no choice and certainly does not give the Morrisons the right to unilaterally choose where she goes," the attorney finished.

The mediator met separately with each side, shuttling back and forth between the parties. Each session was lengthy, the absent party thinking, no doubt, that something substantial was happening in the other room, that the mediator would come in and tell of a breakthrough. Yet there was no change by either side and unlike many mediations, no viable alternatives were even suggested.

During the last private session with the Morrisons, the mediator asked whether the Morrisons felt that the law was wrong in seeking to place Janet in a more mainstreamed environment. "Wrong?" the Morrisons asked. Any law that prevented Janet from going to the state school was wrong. She was their daughter, not the school district's. They knew that integration was wrong for her. Why couldn't the district see this? She was not placed in a class of hearing children when she was in school. This law was wrong. The mediator studied the Morrisons, knowing that right or wrong, the law, particularly its LRE component, was too strong a force for this family to conquer. After three hours of this, the parties gathered in the library again. The day had faded and the lights were on. The mediation had failed and the issues were then set for the administrative hearing.

*      *      *

While the fair hearing makes use of such legal procedures as submission of evidence, examination and cross examination of witnesses, and determination of a "verdict" by an impartial hearing officer, there is a certain informality that sets the process apart from court confrontations. The Morrisons' fair hearing was held in the school administration building, a small, older structure, located in a pleasant, tree-lined neighborhood.

The hearing was in a very small conference room, no more than 15 by 8 or 10 feet. Each day the parties sat at the long, narrow table nodding to each other and exchanging perfunctory questions about each other's health and well-being. The smallness of the room had a kind of ameliorating affect. Although it was only February, the weather had turned unseasonably warm and the small room soon became distractingly hot. The lack of privacy was both a problem and a kind of comic relief.

Throughout the hearing private exchanges between attorney and client were difficult, and the school district's attorney relied on handwritten notes and whispers for discussion of important matters. Here the Morrisons were at some advantage; they merely signed with their attorney.

The case developed before the hearing officer in clear relief. The state school had approximately 500 deaf students, kindergarten through 12th grade. The variety among the children was vast. There were children who were profoundly deaf and could hear no more than the most intrusive environmental sounds. Others had substantial oral skills. Most of the students at the state school were residential students.

The school district attacked the placement issue directly by calling an expert witness from a nearby college. The professor had spent a career studying child development and its relationship to the family unit. He was opinionated and self-assured, an older man, carefully dressed, rail-thin, and impatient. His responses did not spare the Morrisons' attorney, the hearing officer, or the school's counsel.

"Tell me, professor, should children live with their parents?" The school's attorney studied her notes and did not look directly at the professor during direct examination.

"That seems obvious, doesn't it, counselor?"

"It does. Tell me, professor, might there be situations where a young child should be removed from home?"

"Certainly, if the child were in danger."

"What about when the child may not have enough language peers?"

"I do not want to dismiss the importance of such peers, but assuming a stable home environment there are only rare occasions when a child should be actively removed from home.

91

And I do understand that the removal here is sought by the parents and the child."

"Any other thoughts, professor?"

"Yes. Removal, no matter how noble the reason, may in fact retard educational growth, since the importance of the young child's relationship to his or her mother is so significant as to render any other factors questionable."

The Morrisons' attorney paused and then cross-examined.

"Professor, you have pretty strong opinions."

"Is that a question, counselor?"

"No. Tell me, do you know any deaf people?"

"No."

"Have you ever worked with deaf children?"

"No."

"Deaf adults?"

"No, but I've seen deaf students in school settings."

"Ever worked with them?"

"Observed."

"Ever studied deaf education or taken any classes in deaf education?"

"No."

"Know any sign language?"

"No."

"Ever been to the state school for the deaf?"

"No."

"Know anything about language development in deaf children?"

"No."

"Know any children or adults who attended the state school?"

"No, of course not, but let me tell you something. I know what you're trying to do with these questions. Deaf children are children and they need their parents."

"Ever met Janet Morrison?"

"No."

"Know anything about her?"

"No, but I will stand by my last statement regarding the basic needs of all children to be with their families."

"Do you believe in mainstreaming disabled children?"

"Yes, of course. It is an important method for helping these children realize their best."

"Assuming a disabled child is otherwise intact—that is, has normal intelligence, functions at an appropriate cognitive level—is there any reason he or she should not be mainstreamed?"

"No. No."

"Any reason he or she should not attend the neighborhood school?"

The professor paused, looking over the question for a trap or a potential confession that would hurt the party calling him or bring into doubt his initial findings.

"What is the point of your question?"

"Well, professor, the point of my question is not really relevant to the question. I want your opinion."

The hearing officer intervened and asked the witness to answer the question.

"Well, as a general rule, I would think no. Individual cases may vary, of course."

"All things being equal it is better for a child to attend his or her home school rather than a more distant school?"

"Depends on how distant."

"Let us say the home school and one 20 miles away."

"Well, common sense tells us the home school would be better. Assuming, of course, that the scholastic and other educational components are comparable."

"Thank you."

The school's attorney whispered something to the district administrator, looked at one of the many exhibits she had submitted and resumed her questioning of the professor.

"Tell me, professor, is it your testimony that children should attend a closer rather than distant school?"

"I just said that."

"I understand you did. Does that mean that all children should always attend the closer school?"

"I did not say that."

"Could you elaborate?"

"There are children who should, because of their special needs, attend special classes or special schools. Not all children can or should be mainstreamed."

"Thank you, professor."

The hearing officer looked over at the Morrisons' attorney.

"Any re-cross?"

"Yes. Professor, I assume then that there are children who should attend a state school?"

"Objection. That is not a question."

"Sure it is."

"No, it's not, and even if it is, it's a leading question."

"Objection sustained," the hearing officer decided.

"All right. Professor, you testified that some children can not be mainstreamed."

"You were paying attention, counselor."

"And you testified that some children can be mainstreamed."

"Right again."

"Are you aware that state law provides for a continuum of placement options?"

"Of course."

"Are you aware that one option on the state-mandated continuum of placement options is the state school?"

"Yes."

"Would this suggest to you that the state school might be an appropriate placement for some children?"

"For some."

"Having never seen, talked to, or read anything about Janet Morrison, are you testifying that the state school is not appropriate for her?"

"Objection."

"I'll answer that." The professor sat bolt upright.

"Just a minute please," the hearing officer said. "There is an objection before me."

The professor ignored the hearing officer. "I am testifying that there are certain basic notions about child-rearing which suggest that taking a young child and removing her from her parents is not a good idea. Does that answer your question, counselor?"

"Actually it doesn't, professor, but I'm not sure you're really qualified to testify about Janet Morrison."

"Objection!"

"I have no more questions for this witness."

The professor left the hearing. The school district had introduced evidence about the importance of children remaining at home, and the fact that the witness knew nothing about deaf children did not compromise the impact of his testimony. There was nothing more the Morrisons' attorney could do.

---

The neighborhood school retains an understandably powerful hold on our educational notions. This is no less so for children with disabilities. IDEA specifically recognizes a child's neighborhood school and it is about that section of the law that a final and persuasive "argument" in favor of inclusion hovers. Prior to 1975, eight million children with disabilities were "excluded entirely from the neighborhood school system. . . ."[1] IDEA was clearly intended to reverse the exclusionary attitudes and policies, but while the law called for mainstreaming, pull-out, non-home school options were and are a large part of the special education system. The American Association of Retarded Citizens (ARC) report provided evidence of the system's reliance on non-integrated placements.*

---

* See Chapter 2.

Noting the failure to place children in home schools, the critics of IDEA believe the system too frequently focuses on deficits, is "deviance-based" and, not surprisingly, perpetuates a "segregationistic" point of view. A kind of "fix-it" attitude prevails, one that the Morrisons rejected, as do many others. According to Alan Gartner and Dorothy Kerzner Lipsky, the current educational process "dichotomizes" students into regular and special, focuses on labels and category affiliation, creates artificial barriers, limits options, and relies on a "charity-like" philosophy toward children.[2]

The current dualistic system should be transformed, according to the full inclusion movement, into a unitary one; there should be no special education. Gartner and Lipsky, whose article provided academic impetus for the full inclusion movement, called for federal regulations mandating that all students be placed in regular settings, with the neighborhood school viewed as the appropriate place for all children.[3] The National Center on Educational Restructuring and Inclusion reported in early 1994 that a number of classroom practices are available to foster neighborhood inclusion, including: multi-level instruction (which allows for different types of learning but the same curriculum), cooperative learning (heterogeneous groupings with greater focus on group work), activity-based learning (emphasizing learning in natural settings), mastery learning (gaining mastery through focus on specific needs and a greater range of instructional modalities), and peer support and tutoring programs.[4]

By late 1993, the *Inclusion Times* reported that the move to integrate all students was a fait accompli, and that the theoretical basis for varied placements no longer existed. There would be a singular system in which there was "only one educational system from the beginning, encompassing all members equitably, without regard for variations in status. From such a perspective there is no need for integration because there is no initial separation to begin with. All degrees of variation in students' needs and performances will be accommodated."[5]

In early 1994, members of the National Council on Disability testified before the House Subcommittee on Select Education and Civil Rights that the provision of the continuum of placement options was wrong. Instead the council preferred an array of services which, according to the council, would be more freely accessible. The council, an independent federal agency whose members are appointed by the President and confirmed by the Senate, called for positive inclusion—a civil right—in "typical community schools." Finally, in underscoring its belief in home schools, the council noted the "massive" nature of segregation and the resulting "massive" violations of human and civil rights of students with disabilities.[6] The fervor of the council's concerns was matched by the fears these concerns created among members of the blind, deaf, learning-disabled, autistic, and other communities of the special education world.*

The academic push for full inclusion and a change in federal law regarding the right to placement in a home school setting has radiated out to state and local school systems. Many states have formed task forces to implement the transition to a full inclusion model. By late 1992, numerous states had received funding to plan, prepare, and implement full inclusion programs for all children.

The Statewide Programs Administrator for the California Department of Education stated that when a child "lives two doors down from the school, but receives his or her education in another district, and the neighborhood school doesn't know the child exists, that's sad."[7] Putting aside the complexities of school boundary lines, busing plans, commutes to distant private schools, and open enrollment, who would argue against a child's right to attend his or her neighborhood school? To even raise the

---

*  *See* Chapter 1 at 31, 35, for a description of Action for Children to Insure Options Now (ACTION).

97

question suggests a kind of retrogressive, if not "segregationist," attitude. Yet the program in Janet Morrison's neighborhood school might have been even more linguistically, socially, and emotionally isolating than placement in the partially "segregated" Midvale program, which itself was substantially more isolating than the state school. If there were only one Janet Morrison in the United States, she would still represent an exception to the rule that the National Council and other full inclusion proponents must address.

\*     \*     \*

The federal law, which seems to make proponents and opponents of full inclusion equally unhappy, provides through Section 300.552 of the federal regulations that: "Each public agency *shall* insure that (a) Each handicapped child's educational placement . . . (3) *Is as close as possible to the child's home* . . . [and] (c) Unless a handicapped child's individualized education program requires some other arrangement, the child *is educated in the school which he or she would attend if not handicapped*." The regulation is intriguing because it adds fuel to the generic full inclusion fire. There are, of course, important qualifiers—the "unless . . . some other arrangement" language is general enough to blunt some of Section 300.552—but the regulation's purpose is clear.\* Why this particular regulation has not been employed more frequently by parents and advocates is a bit of a mystery, but the Clinton administration recognized the degree to which it had been under-utilized. In late 1993 Tom Hehir, the Director of Special Education for the U.S. Department of Education, indicated the department's

---

\* This comment at the end of Section 300.552 works against those parents taking a "Morrison" position. The extent of the inclusionary spirit is evident here—the regulation does not provide for an opposite and equal "right" to *challenge* "close-in" programs. The assumption that no parent would place a child further away from home seems deeply rooted in IDEA.

desire to "bring services to kids, not kids to services as we do now."[8] Whether this will happen is another matter.

*　　*　　*

The U.S. District Court for New Jersey is one of the few courts to address the home school segment of IDEA.[9] Jennifer Remis was a 20-year-old autistic student with severe behavioral problems. Her mother sought to transfer her from the Au Clair school in Delaware to the Bancroft school in Haddonfield, New Jersey, the community in which the family resided.

The court, upholding placement in Bancroft, noted the LRE requirement of IDEA as well as the school's responsibility to place Jennifer "as close as possible to the child's home"; under Section 300.552 parents had a right to challenge more distant options, particularly residential programs. The court concluded that the education at Bancroft was comparable to that offered at Au Clair and thus Section 300.552 was applicable.

In *Manchester School District v. Williamson,*[10] the parents of Jeffrey Williamson sought placement for their son in West High School, Jeffrey's neighborhood school. Jeffrey had great difficulty in completing simple classroom tasks, such as hanging up his jacket, opening the correct door for the bathroom, and replacing his pants after he went into the bathroom. In addition, Jeffrey was strongly oppositional and did not interact with others. According to one of Jeffrey's teachers, the other students were upset when he interfered with their work.

Program options were limited. One of the more distant high school programs had been tried with little success, and other options, such as junior high school, would not have provided Jeffrey with age-appropriate peers, making the placement contrary to New Hampshire law. Since the more distant program had proved ineffective and since there was some evidence that a mainstreaming program at Jeffrey's neighborhood high school could produce educational benefits, the court rejected any effort to remove Jeffrey from his home school.

The court noted past "segregated" failures, reviewed some of the key mainstreaming cases, and honed in on a core difficulty that many other courts have wrestled with:

> The *Roncker* court rejected a less segregated placement in favor of a superior program in a more segregated setting. The *A.W.* court also chose a superior, although more segregated program over a mainstreaming plan that offered minimal educational benefits. And the *Lachman* court refused to choose between teaching methods.

> Unlike the above cases, the Court in this action is not offered a choice between two appropriate programs. Instead the School District champions a plan that violates state law, and the parents ask that their son receive an education in their neighborhood school, despite the absence of evidence that Jeffrey received any benefit from his program at Memorial, a public high school better equipped to handle handicapped students.[11]

The court concluded that Jeffrey would be better served in his neighborhood school, noting one expert's testimony that Jeffrey would have a better chance of fitting in because there were fewer special education students in the building.

It may have been that Jeffrey's needs were so serious and the options so limited that a neighborhood school was worth a try. Ironically, the court stated that if it "had the authority to impose its views on those who must provide for Jeffrey's schooling, it would seriously consider the option of a specialized residential program. . . ."[12]

In *Hendricks v. Gilhool*,[13] a class of special education students challenged the Pennsylvania method of assigning placement. When severely disabled students were found to need services beyond the scope of the local district, or when districts had only a few students "suffering from a particular type of handicap" (thus making it impractical to set up programs), these children were referred to an intermediate unit, which often assigned them to centralized programs.

The Carbon-Lehigh Intermediate Unit operated 95 classes, and served 14 school districts. Of the 95 classes, 65 were single-district classes consisting of students from one district with "mild" disabilities and 30 were multidistrict classes for students with more severe disabilities. Carbon-Lehigh had inadequate classroom space, which created unequal facilities for disabled children, frequent movement of those children from district to district and school to school, and placement in facilities that were unnecessarily restrictive and separate from those open to non-disabled students.[14]

The district court found that the failure to provide "comparable" facilities and the disruptive relocation of classes violated both IDEA and Section 504 of the Rehabilitation Act. As to more restrictive placement, the court found that for "children with particularly severe mental, emotional, or physical handicaps, education in separate facilities, or separate sections of regular schools, may not only be warranted by logistical exigencies, but may be required for the students' appropriate education."[15]

Regarding those students who are capable of being educated in special classes in regular schools with non-disabled peers, the "mainstreaming objective of EHA is thwarted if disabled youngsters are shunted off to separate facilities, or unnecessarily segregated in isolated classrooms in regular schools, solely because the local school districts refuse to provide adequate classroom space for [those] students."[16]

The court then distinguished between those students who needed separate facilities (or for whom logistical exigencies required such placement) and those who were capable of mainstreaming but were isolated in regular schools. In discussing more severely disabled children, the court, like other judicial panels, found that appropriateness and individual need, along with such other factors as administrative convenience and costs, may preclude integration. As to Section 300.552, the court would not read into the regulation a prohibition against distant schools:

> The plaintiffs seek an order prohibiting the assignment . . . of students to a facility located at a traveling distance of more than one hour from the students' home. The present record does not furnish a sufficient basis for imposing such a blanket requirement, particularly in light of the fact that classes for severely handicapped children are sometimes made up of students from several school districts.[17]

The court concluded, however, that a school district would violate both Section 504 and IDEA if disabled students had to travel extended distances to school because a school district refused to make classroom space available.

In *L.F. v. Greater Egg Harbor High School District*,[18] a bright 14-year-old student using a wheelchair suffered from Werdnig-Hoffmann's disease, a progressive, and in this case fatal, neurological disorder. L.F.'s school district had two high schools— Oakcrest, which was not barrier-free, and Absegami, which was. L.F. would have attended Oakcrest if she were not disabled. The hearing officer ruled that the law did not require placement in the school closest to L.F.'s home because the cost of making that facility accessible was prohibitive and because L.F.'s right to attend a closer school was outweighed by the availability of a barrier-free (albeit more distant) alternative. Since Absegami High School was otherwise appropriate, the close-to-home issue was merely one among many to consider, and in this case it was not determinative.*

In the 1983 California hearing decision *In re Dixie School District*,[19] a 14-year-old deaf child sought placement in her neighborhood school with the provision of a sign-language interpreter. The school district, relying on the first and still most important

---

* In *In re* Royal Oaks Schools, 19 IDELR 194 (Sept. 2, 1992), a 17-year-old student with severe multiple disabilities was offered an intense program in an integrated school. The family sought placement in the home school. The hearing officer ruled against the family, noting that the costs of creating a new program in the home school could not be "justified with [an] argument about home school placement." *Id.* at 197.

Supreme Court analysis of IDEA, *Board of Education v. Rowley*[20] argued that it need only provide an appropriate education. The district offered the neighborhood school without an interpreter, or in the alternative, a special education class in which the teacher signed (approximately five miles from the child's home), or the state school for the deaf (to which Janet Morrison would seek placement some years later).*

In distinguishing the matter from *Rowley*, the hearing officer ruled that although the student was receiving good grades, she could not understand classroom discussion without the use of an interpreter, and "Classroom lectures and discussions are a significant aspect of Petitioner's educational experience. . . . Petitioner needs to receive total communication to understand oral language. Without an interpreter, Petitioner would not understand films, lectures, or classroom discussions. . . . without an interpreter [Petitioner] would feel socially isolated and excluded from classroom participation."[21] The hearing officer specifically found that under Section 300.552 the student was entitled to placement in the school she would have attended if she were not disabled, and that the interpreter was necessary for her to benefit from special education. The decision is worthy of note since it followed *Rowley* and focused on nonacademic factors, which in turn triggered the application of the home school regulation. This decision further illuminates how diverse the special education community is and how individual each child is. The deaf child and her parents in the *Dixie* case, unlike Janet Morrison, sought a mainstreamed program and greater accessibility to her hearing peers.

*    *    *

The right of a child with disabilities to attend his or her neighborhood school touches upon unsettled and unsettling issues. The Section 300.552 entitlement was meant to counter decades of "segregated" education for children with disabilities.

---

* Amy Rowley, a deaf first-grader in a regular class, sought the services of a sign-language interpreter. The Supreme Court ruled against Amy, concluding

It stands in sharp and ironic contrast to the efforts to racially desegregate schools through busing. Section 300.552 ostensibly fosters integration by creating a right to remain in one's home school, while racial desegregation encouraged integration partially through removal of children from their neighborhood schools.

In addition, the home school element of LRE touches upon an equally important and emotional issue—control. Implied in the full inclusion movement is the increased power of parents to determine where their children will be placed. The Association of Retarded Citizens has stated that in the "best tradition" of empowerment efforts, "[p]arents must be trained to be informed consumers in order to advocate for revision in education policy to bring about inclusion. . . ."[22]

IDEA, while not mandating parental choice, does make parents co-decisionmakers through the IEP process. Regulations like Section 300.552 enhance that power. Full inclusion and other efforts based on the inherent wisdom of parents, however, face a significant paradox.* Parental choice *and* power, once accepted, cut both ways. To the extent that full inclusion advocates call for one placement—Gartner and Lipsky, among others, proposed that the "neighborhood school must be viewed as the appropriate place for *all* children"[23]—their position runs counter to the real exercise of parental choice. What of those parents who choose to place their children in nonregular environments: would parental choice apply only to those who pursue neighborhood school placement?

---

that the district need not provide Amy with anything more than those services or programs designed to allow her to pass from grade to grade. The decision is analyzed in detail in Chapter 4 of this book.

* When the Sacramento City School trustees voted in April, 1994 to appeal the Ninth Circuit Court of Appeals' affirmation of *Holland* to the Supreme Court, one of the reasons for the action was the belief that "professionals ought to be in charge of the education system." Carlos Accaln, *District Will Appeal on Disabled Student*, SACRAMENTO BEE, April 14, 1994.

The home school and broader inclusion-exclusion debate moves, perhaps inexorably, toward a difficult internecine conflict between various special education communities. Natural allies—parents—stand on either side of a well-defined dividing line. There may be no middle ground in this struggle between those who seek to integrate all children and those who contend that some children should not be placed in neighborhood schools.

In the 1993 Nebraska report on full inclusion, which recommended that the local school be accountable for *all* students and that a "zero-reject" philosophy be adopted, the State Special Education Advisory Council noted three primary forces driving the full inclusion movement: legal, policy, and research issues.[24] As to the former, the report stated that "[s]tatue, regulation, and case law have increasingly demanded it."[25] There is, in fact, no evidence that the law demands that all children with disabilities be placed in their home schools. The misstatement underscores the determination of the generic philosophy.

Not long before Nebraska issued its full inclusion report, the Iowa Council of Administrators of Special Education wrote to Lamar Alexander, U.S. Department of Education, stating that while it strongly supported home school placement, "the national frenzy to place *all* students back into the regular classroom setting is irresponsible and could result in irreparable harm to many students."[26]

Gartner and Lipsky also wrote of harm, notably the stigma that follows children with disabilities who are removed from a regular school environment. One wonders whether the various sides of the full inclusion-integration debate can reach some mutually acceptable understanding of the role of both the neighborhood *and* more distant school and how each can be potentially harmful or helpful depending on the unique needs of the individual child. *Inclusive Education Programs* reported in early 1994 of the Ontario School District in Oregon, whose goal was to include "all" children. The district developed a site-based management policy and gave each principal control over special education dollars. All of the district's 260 special education children ultimately were included, although the director of special education made it "clear that if [a parent] wanted the segregated system '[w]e would bus one kid if we had to.'"[27]

The Ontario story may reflect all the encouraging and troubling issues involved in changing special education into an inclusive model. The Oregon effort to change the system, alter attitudes, and increase inclusive opportunities should be applauded, but just as school administrators in the past too easily removed children from regular education, the rush to include "all" children involves equally troubling generalizations. The alternative to a regular classroom is viewed as "segregated"— although Ontario was willing to bus one "kid" if they had to— and viable continuum options lose funding, administrative support, and resources necessary to maintain a quality program. In spring of 1994, for example, the San Diego County Coalition for Learning Differences filed a complaint with the United States Office for Civil Rights, noting, among other things, that the local school district had unilaterally eliminated special day classes for learning disabled and language disordered children, offering those students either full inclusion or a special class of "applied" curriculum (which would only offer the student a certificate of attendence, not a diploma).[28]

To the extent that the Ontarios and San Diegos of the special education world seek mainstreaming for all children with disabilities, they become retrogressive. In the name of opening doors, the full inclusion movement would assume control over a child and insist on a placement in direct opposition to the wishes of the child's parents. How much is the movement's philosophy compromised when it demands unilateral decisions? How much does it oddly parallel the attitudes of many school districts that historically excluded children en masse?

The line between full inclusion for the individual child and for all children has become blurred, and as a result confusion over integrating children with disabilities has increased. The movement to include *all* children becomes fundamentalistic in nature and reflects a kind of educational colonialism. This has added irony since, on the face of it, the full inclusion component of the IDEA community appears aligned with other civil rights communities, which have historically been viewed as progressive, change-oriented, and founded upon notions of social inclusion and equality.

Janet Morrison's right to go to a so-called "segregated" school does not necessarily run counter to the larger desegregation ethos, but it does create, at least, some need to justify an exception. Ultimately her desire to be in a communicatively appropriate and accessible environment is a difficult matter to contest. To be fully viable, the full inclusion movement must consider this issue. The remaking of special education and the move to compel IDEA to live up to its promise of home school placement must be judged by how it accommodates Jennifer Remis, Rachel Holland, *and* Janet Morrison.

## Endnotes

1.    Hendrick Hudson Board of Educ. v. Rowley, 458 U.S. 176, 189, 1981-82 EHLR 553:656, 662 (1982).

2.    ALAN GARTNER & DOROTHY KERZNER LIPSKY, NATIONAL CENTER ON EDUCATION AND THE ECONOMY, THE YOKE OF SPECIAL EDUCATION: HOW TO BREAK IT 25-26 (1989) [hereinafter *The Yoke of Special Education*].

3.    *Id.* at 30-31.

4.    *See* Dorothy Kerzner Lipsky, *National Survey Gives Insight into Inclusive Movement*, INCLUSIVE EDUCATION PROGRAMS, March 1994, at 4.

5.    *It means more than mainstreaming*, INCLUSION TIMES, Sept. 1993, at 2.

6.    Sharon Davis, Ph.D., Association for Retarded Citizens of the United States, REPORT CARD TO THE NATION ON INCLUSION IN EDUCATION OF STUDENTS WITH MENTAL RETARDATION (1992), at 22 [hereinafter *ARC Report*].

7.    *Implementation advisory group and sites enhance education in the LRE*, The Special EDge, (California Department of Education), Nov./Dec. 1991.

8.   Joseph P. Shapiro et al., *Separate and Unequal*, U.S. NEWS AND WORLD REP., Dec. 13, 1993 at 57.

9.   Remis v. New Jersey Dep't of Human Serv., 815 F. Supp. 141 (D.N.J. 1993), 19 IDELR 879.

10.  Manchester School Dist. v. Williamson, No. 89-227-D (D.N.H. 1990), 17 EHLR 1.

11.  17 EHLR at 3.

12.  *Id.* at 2.

13.  Hendricks v. Gilhool, 709 F. Supp. 1364 (E.D. 1989), 1988-89 EHLR 441:352.

14.  *Id.*

15.  709 F. Supp. at 1371, 1988-89 EHLR at 358.

16.  *Id.*

17.  709 F. Supp. at 1370, n.7, 1988-89 EHLR at 357, n.7.

18.  L.F. v. Greater Egg Harbor High School District, No. SE 84271 (Cal. State Ed. Agency Hearing Aug. 23, 1984).

19.  *In re* Dixie School District, No. 82-343 (Cal. State Ed. Agency Hearing Jan. 31, 1983), 1982-83 EHLR 504:274.

20.  *Id.* 1982-83 EHLR 504 at 276.

21.  *Id.*

22.  *ARC Report, supra* note 6, at 26-27.

23.  *See The Yoke of Special Education, supra* note 2, at 31.

24.  NEBRASKA SPECIAL EDUC. ADVISORY COUNCIL, AD HOC COMMITTEE ON NEIGHBORHOOD SCHOOLS AND INCLUSION IN NEBRASKA, FINAL REPORT, at 34 (Aug. 6, 1993).

25.  *See The Yoke of Special Education, supra* note 2, at 15.

26.  Letter of Nov. 23, 1992 (from Dr. Thomas A. Jeschke, Iowa Council of Administrators of Special Education).

27.  *Rural High School Rallies Behind Inclusion*, INCLUSIVE EDUCATION PROGRAMS, Jan. 1994, at 5, 11.

28.  Correspondence received publicly on Apr. 8, 1994, by the California Advisory Commission on Special Education.

# Part Two

The Relativity of Least
Restrictive Environment:
Restrictions on the Inclusion
of Children with
Disabilities

# 4

# Individual Need in Conflict with Placement Rights

Janet visited the state school once during the administrative hearing. She alighted from the family car and ran pell-mell through the campus, darting in and out of the pathways between the school buildings. She found her sister and began an instant, rapid-fire conversation. A deaf teacher stopped and said hello, signing easily. Janet had been there many times.

The school, about 30 minutes south of Oakland, is set among shopping centers, new office buildings with expansive lawns, and new housing developments and condominiums. The school had previously been in Berkeley, near the University of California, but had moved to Fremont because of seismic concerns. The school is situated on flat, almost barren land, and is a cluster of one-story buildings. There is a sizeable deaf population in Fremont and the school's presence adds to the sense of community. In his book *Seeing Voices,* Oliver Sachs wrote of Fremont as a place where a "fascinating" bilingual and bicultural environment has flourished.[1]*

---

* The residential schools have historically been among the most important institutions for the deaf community. The passage of IDEA and its LRE component was viewed as a significant problem (if not a full-blown disaster) for these residential schools, where there is a richness of language and community.

At lunchtime Janet joined her sister in an outdoor amphitheater. Dozens of students ate sandwiches while signing rapidly to each other. Communication was intense, ongoing, and visible. When lunch was over, Janet bounded away from the amphitheater. It was another 30 minutes before Raymond Morrison found his daughter in the kindergarten classroom where she sat in the middle of the class, signing to the students who did not know her, but who recognized her at once.

*     *     *

Janet had been reluctantly attending the Midvale program since the fall. There had been difficulties on the bus—a boy had asked her to take down her pants and she was having nightmares. She was increasingly more contentious with her siblings and parents.

The Midvale "hearing-impaired" class had eight students of varying ages and abilities. No one in Janet's neighborhood attended Midvale. The bus ride was approximately one hour each way. There were no other deaf children in the school, nor were there any deaf people in the small hamlet of Midvale.

The program administrator, Jean Francis, was called to testify about the program. She was a slight woman, in her early fifties. There was a severity to her, suggesting mistrust. To the Morrisons' attorney she seemed uncompromising and entirely humorless. When she did smile there was a hint, but nothing more, that some sense of mirth was trying very hard to counter the strain she felt and projected to others.

When pressed, her face turned red and her eyes narrowed. She sat at the small table in the crowded room and seemed barely able to hide her dislike of the Morrisons' attorney and her frustration at the effrontery of a family questioning her expertise.

---

Since 1975 there have been efforts in numerous states to reduce the size of, or close down, many state schools.

Under examination from the school district's attorney she easily explained the details of the Midvale program. It was, she testified, an excellent program with a dedicated teacher. Mr. Johnstone used a variety of sign languages, including ASL. The curriculum and methodology were current, the facility modern and comfortable.

The hearing officer took notes and listened intently, but without any evident reaction. He was a slight man who sat impassively through the five-day hearing. The interpreter signed silently to the Morrisons.

The district's attorney finished her direct examination. Janet's attorney asked Francis perfunctory questions about her training and then turned to the program at Midvale.

"Ms. Francis, there are eight children in the class?"

"Yes."

"Can we discuss each of those children in some detail?"

"Sure."

Janet's attorney had a list of the children, identified by name. Jean Francis had provided the information, which was part of the large book of exhibits introduced into evidence by the school district.

"Let us take the first student on the list and refer to her as student A."

"All right."

"How old is she?"

"She's seven."

"Describe her language level."

"She is mostly oral, she's learning some signs."

"You testified that Janet's language ability was at or above her age. What level is A at?"

"Infant level of signing."

"How many signs does she know?"

"A few."

"What is her age level in terms of language?"

"Two or so."

"Student B."

"About the same as A."

"Student C."

"He's Janet's age."

"And his language?"

"Well, he has had a very deprived life and he has little language, oral or otherwise."

"His signing level?"

"Toddler, when he ... toddler anyway."

"Toddler meaning about two?"

"Yes."

"You were going to add something?"

"Well, yes. C has some difficulty in behaving and this sometimes gets in the way of his ability to communicate."

"Even at the level he's at, to begin with?"

"Yes."

"Student D."

"Same, she's very much oral. Nice child and family."

And so it went with the identification of two students who were close to Janet's level of language proficiency.

"How old are these two girls?"

Francis looked at the list, then at her attorney and answered.

"Nine and ten."

"And Janet is just six?"

"I believe so."

"How many age-appropriate language peers does Janet have?"

"Objection. How do you define 'age-appropriate language peers?'"

"It seems a clear enough concept."

"Maybe to you, but there is no expert testimony on what constitutes 'age-appropriate language peers.'"

"Someone who is approximately the same age and uses the same language and has similar language skills."

"I maintain my objection."

The hearing officer studied the tape recorder and without changing his passive demeanor ruled against the objection.

"Please answer the question."

"Well, I'd say eight, since they all have some communication skills. But certainly two."

"The older girls?"

"Yes."

"If Janet is a first grader, then the nine- and ten-year-old girls are what grade?"

"Oh, that's hard to say, since in these kind of classes there is a blurring of grades, but I'd say fifth, sixth, something like that."

"Let me be clear; Janet has two children who are her communication peers and they are about four years older. The other children have rudimentary skills at best. Seems like a very paltry communication environment?"

"Well, that is a matter of opinion."

"How would you feel if your child were in a class where there were no other age peers with whom she could communicate?"

"Objection."

"I'll withdraw the question."

Janet's attorney paused to read from a report; he stopped reading and continued the cross-examination.

"You indicated, Ms. Francis that you have been with the district for approximately ten years. Has that always been in the position of program manager for the hearing-impaired?"

"Yes."

"So you have been involved in deaf education for some time?"

"Yes."

"Tell me, have your programs contained deaf children who sign and deaf children who are more oral?"

"Yes, I told you that already."

"You have worked with purely oral classes?"

"Yes."

"Total communication classes?"

"Yes."

"Sign language used in those classes?"

"Yes."

"Had children in your programs who relied exclusively on sign language?"

"Yes."

"Do you feel you are an expert in deaf education?"

"Well, I certainly feel I know a good deal about it."

"By the way, do you use sign language?"

"No."

"So you cannot communicate with Janet?"

"I know a few signs."

"Thank you. Your witness."

"Ms. Francis. Is Janet's teacher appropriately trained and able to meet her goals and objectives?" the district's attorney asked.

"Yes. And yes."

"Is the program at Midvale appropriate for Janet?"

"Yes."

"You have reviewed her goals and objectives?"

"I was at the IEP meeting during which the lengthy goals and objectives were written." Jean Francis frowned and then added, "You remember, I called you a half a dozen times about them."

"Yes, thank you. Can her goals and objectives be met at Midvale?"

"Absolutely."

"Can her goals and objectives be met, given the make-up of the class?"

"Yes."

"Is the class at Midvale the least restrictive for Janet?"

"Objection, Ms. Francis is not an attorney, the question calls for a legal conclusion."

"No, it doesn't. Least restrictive is an educational term."

"Overruled. You can answer."

"Midvale is a wonderful program, can and does meet Janet's goals and objectives, and is therefore least restrictive. We would be breaking the law if we did not place her there."

"You believe you are not allowed to place Janet at the state school. You have no choice?"

"We have no choice."

———————

Actually Ms. Francis's school district would not necessarily have been breaking the law if it had placed Janet in the state school. Despite its preference for mainstreaming, its requirement that a child with disabilities be placed in the school he or she would attend if not disabled, and other integrating inducements, IDEA significantly qualifies its inclusionary philosophy. In short, it provides specific direction for the exclusion of children with disabilities from a regular classroom environment. IDEA is, by its very nature, a law of separation.

IDEA distinguishes between children with disabilities and non-disabled children—hence the term "special" education. A child with disabilities is entitled to a free appropriate education that is specially designed to meet his or her unique needs. In the narrow statutory sense, in practical application, and by nomenclature, special education is specialized and can be separate. Whether such separation is right or wrong and whether the full inclusion effort to eliminate special education makes sense or not does not change the fact that the law as written and applied creates separation. Special education classes are those programs designed for and made up of children with disabilities. They are frequently staffed by special education teachers, aides, and other support staff and are sometimes held in special schools.

There are specific regulations that provide for alternative placements and rationales for "removal" from regular classrooms—agent provocateurs at the heart of this integrating law.

The LRE language is relative: placement with non-disabled children to the "maximum extent *appropriate*," with "removal" justified when a child cannot achieve satisfactorily in a regular classroom with the use of supplementary aids and services.[2]

If the child's "disability requires some other arrangement," the child can be removed from the home or "closest" school.[3] In determining LRE, "consideration is given to any potentially harmful effect on the child or on the quality of services that he or she needs."[4] The law requires that every school agency provide alternative placements to a regular classroom, specifically instruction in separate classrooms, the home, a hospital, institutions, and other settings.[5] IDEA carves out a very clear set of nonregular options, referred to in the law as a "continuum" of separate placements.*

Through these statutes, IDEA juxtaposes need and placement rights and therefore essentially accepts and codifies the conflict between the two. By law, the right and need to be integrated may defer to other necessities.

*     *     *

Almost 20 years after IDEA was passed there are, therefore, important cracks in the mainstreaming wall—cracks that have been there from the beginning. At the heart of the conflict is the relationship between need and placement, or, in the language of IDEA, the tension between a "free appropriate" education (FAPE) and a "least restrictive" (LRE) one. The United States Supreme Court was first presented with a special education

---

* In California the continuum includes, from top to bottom, or from side to side, a resource specialist, designated instruction, special classes and centers, nonpublic, nonsectarian schools, and state special schools. CAL EDUC. CODE § 56361 (Deering Supp. 1994). In Pennsylvania the continuum goes from placement in a regular school for the entire day to regular school for part of the day to special programs outside the regular class with some mainstreaming, to special schools with mainstreaming opportunities, to residential placement to out-of-state programs to (finally) home instruction. 22 PA. CODE § 14.42.

dispute in 1982, and 12 years later *Rowley v. Board of Education*[6] remains the seminal Supreme Court analysis of IDEA. In this case the Supreme Court defined what constituted an appropriate education and, by extension, what was required in terms of placement. The *Rowley* court developed a limited view of IDEA— not warmly received by advocates, but frequently quoted by attorneys for school districts. A child was deemed to have been provided an appropriate education when he or she was pro- moted from grade to grade.[7] With such a standard, the impor- tance of the placement segment of IDEA was, by inference, weakened.*

Amy Rowley was a deaf child who sought the related service of a sign-language interpreter in her mainstreamed kindergarten class. Unlike Janet Morrison and her parents, Amy and her deaf parents preferred a mainstreamed environment in which there happened to be no other deaf peers. While there was no debate as to whether Amy should be in a regular class, there was an important disagreement as to what a school district had to do to ease her way into that environment. Amy, deaf since birth, had some residual hearing that was particularly good in the lower frequencies where vowel sounds are distinguished. Hear- ing loss often means the "disappearance" of consonants, and when consonants are removed from words it becomes difficult, if not impossible, to distinguish an oral representation between one word and another. Consider the word "constitution" or "hold" or "word" without consonants.

Since vowels are the most difficult components of speech to lipread, Amy's residual hearing was particularly important. She relied on total communication, a system that employs a variety of communication modes: lipreading, sign language, vi- sual cues, facial expressions. By the time Amy entered school,

---

* Subsequent to *Rowley*, other, lower courts took a more liberal view of what constituted an appropriate education and looked beyond the purely academic analysis (securing adequate grades for class promotion) of the *Rowley* decision.

119

she was an excellent lip-reader and used her residual hearing and her sign language to participate more fully in her environment.

In February of her kindergarten year, a full-time sign-language interpreter was placed in Amy's class for a two-week period. The interpreter concluded that due to the "extraordinary sensitivity" of Amy's teacher and Amy's resistance to interpretive services, a sign-language interpreter was not needed. An administrative hearing was held, after which the hearing officer ruled against the Rowleys, as did the State Commissioner of Education. On appeal, the federal district court ruled in favor of the Rowleys.[8]

The court noted that Amy was a "remarkably well-adjusted" child who interacted and communicated with her classmates, and who had an even more successful interaction with her teacher. The district court also found that by using her hearing aids and lipreading skills Amy could identify 59 percent of the words that were spoken to her, whereas with the use of total communication, which included sign language, she could identify 100 percent of the words spoken to her. The court also took judicial notice that the classroom environment was less controlled than a test setting due to ambient noise and other environmental distractions in the classroom, that more than one person might speak at once, and that people often turn their head partially or completely when they speak.

The district court found that Amy had a high IQ, but while she was doing fairly well in school, she understood considerably less of what was going on in class than she would have if she were not deaf. Therefore, she was not learning as much, nor was she performing as well academically as she would without her "disability." The court also found that while the use of an interpreter was less important in the early grades (where the language

---

Those cases were discussed in Part One of this book. The *Rowley* decision, however, remains the Supreme Court standard on appropriateness.

is less complex), anything missed in the early years would have "far reaching consequences" for Amy.

Without an interpreter Amy was receiving an adequate education—she was performing better than the average child in her class and was advancing easily from grade to grade. It was inappropriate, however, not to compare Amy's performance with non-disabled children of similar intellectual ability, energy, and initiative. Amy expended a great deal of energy on "receiving" communication, energy that could have been better used for classroom performance. She should not, the district court noted, be penalized for her own efforts to remain slightly above the median of her class. In short, the district court found that Amy needed an interpreter to fulfill her potential.

The U. S. Court of Appeals for the Second Circuit affirmed the lower court decision, stating that Amy was entitled to have educational opportunities equal to those of her non-disabled peers.[9] However, the United States Supreme Court reversed the lower court decision, ruling that a sign-language interpreter was not required for Amy Rowley to benefit from special education.[10] The manner in which the Court reviewed IDEA and applied it to Amy Rowley provides, at the very least, a context in which to understand the LRE mandate and also virtually every special education court decision that followed *Rowley*.

Since IDEA had not provided a "substantive standard prescribing the level of education to be accorded disabled children," the Court addressed and then developed such a standard. Rejecting the lower court's ruling that Amy Rowley was entitled to an opportunity equal to that provided her non-disabled peers, the *Rowley* Supreme Court stressed that Congress had not intended a "precise guarantee" or a "basic floor of opportunity" for disabled children. Congress intended equal protection of disabled children, but nothing more than "equal access" and certainly nothing that would "maximize" their potential. Rather the law required that Amy Rowley be provided educational opportunities "sufficient to confer some educational bene-fit. . . ."[11] Whether she could effectively communicate with her peers was not significant, certainly not germane to academic achievement.

The *Rowley* court did not, however, elaborate on what was meant by educational benefit and would not establish a test to determine the adequacy of educational benefits children covered by the Act should receive. The Act requires

> participating States to educate handicapped children with non-handicapped children *whenever possible.* When that "mainstreaming" preference of the Act has been met and a child is being educated in the regular classrooms of a public school system, the system itself monitors the educational progress of the child. Regular examinations are adminis-tered, grades are awarded, and yearly advancement to higher grade levels is permitted for those children who attain an adequate knowledge of the course material. The grading and advancement system thus constitutes an important fac-tor in determining educational benefit.[12]

"Whenever possible" did not sound the same as "to the maximum extent appropriate" and reflected the court's more minimalistic attitude regarding educational appropriateness and placement mandates. The court concluded that children "who graduate from our public school systems are considered by our society to have been 'educated' at least to the grade level they have completed, and access to an 'education' for handicapped children is precisely what Congress sought to provide in the Act."*

---

* In a footnote the Court qualified its rather narrow read on educational benefit:

> We do not hold today that every handicapped child who is advanc-ing from grade to grade in a regular public school system is auto-matically receiving a "free appropriate public education." [Board of Educ. v. Rowley, 458 U.S. 176, 203, n.25 (1982).]

The Court thus left the door slightly ajar for subsequent courts to look beyond grade advancement in determining appropriateness.

The *Rowley* reference to grade-to-grade advancement and "adequate knowledge of course material" implies much about LRE. If the standard is grade advancement, then those social, emotional and otherwise nonacademic components of a school program which are obtained through placement in a regular classroom or other "less restrictive" environments may not constitute viable considerations under *Rowley*.

If mainstreaming means exposure to non-disabled peers and presumably the chance to learn both academic and nonacademic lessons, the *Rowley* court certainly placed a higher value on the former rather than the latter lesson. There are, therefore, certain scenarios that simply will not meet this somewhat difficult standard. Since *Rowley* involved the question of a related service, it stands for a narrow read on the provision of such services for mainstreaming opportunities and thus brings into question the statutory and regulatory charge to remove children with disabilities "only when the nature or severity of the disability is such that education in regular classes with the use of *supplementary aids and services* cannot be achieved satisfactorily."[13]

Those children for whom mainstreaming would provide only socialization opportunities,* or those who do not absolutely need auxiliary services to remain in a regular classroom will face, until *Rowley* is reversed, a somewhat daunting task. Since social opportunities may not directly impact on grade advancement or the acquisition of "adequate knowledge" of course material, the *Rowley* standard would work against a mainstreaming placement. Amy may have been significantly isolated in her class, but as long as she secured adequate grades the law created no right of communication. Even where there is a direct relationship between related services, educational achievement, and

---

* With *Holland* and other so-called full inclusion decisions, the erosion of *Rowley* has begun. There have certainly been a good number of cases in which nonacademic needs have played a central role in determining what constitutes an appropriate education and therefore what a school has to supply to ensure inclusion or mainstreaming opportunities.

placement in a regular classroom, *Rowley* may mean that related services are only necessary in a regular classroom to ensure grade-to-grade advancement, not full comprehension of academic subjects. Amy was entitled to be in the regular classroom but not to have access to its language.

The *Rowley* implications for inclusion are notable. In the Morrison case it came up at mediation, in opening arguments in the due process hearing, and in the closing brief submitted by the school district's attorney. As the district's attorney stated at mediation, a maximum educational opportunity is a wonderful thing, but *Rowley* as the law of the land did not mandate the best or most accessible education to a disabled child. To the extent that the Morrisons sought to prove that Janet's communication needs were fundamental to her well-being, her previous success in school would work against that argument. *Rowley*, by limiting the reach of "appropriateness," made it a more practicable concept and lessened the burden upon Janet's school district. Ultimately *Rowley* restricted placement rights and thus may have played an unintended role in the subsequent and varied movements to increase the inclusionary rights of children with disabilities.

Following *Rowley*, few courts have evaluated LRE, analyzed the need-placement debate more fully, or established a more important standard for weighing the two concepts than *Roncker v. Walter*.[14] *Roncker* provided a judicial acceptance of the notion that need can trump placement. And although subsequent cases such as *Holland* look more forcefully to the placement portion of the equation, placement continues to be framed within the evaluation of need, which dictates much of what a program will look like and even where it will be implemented.

At the time of the litigation, Neill Roncker was nine years old and classified as trainable mentally retarded (TMR), a child with an IQ of 50 or less.* Neill had a mental age of two and

---

* As noted by the court, a TMR child was to be distinguished from a less severely retarded or educable mentally retarded child. At least one state court

suffered from seizures, but was generally docile. He could not recognize dangerous situations and therefore required constant supervision. Neill's school district recommended that he be placed in a county school for mentally retarded children. As a result, Neill would have no contact with non-disabled children, although there was evidence that he could benefit from such contact.

The Ronckers objected to the county school, and after a fair hearing the administrative judge ruled that the school district had not met its burden of showing that its placement "afforded the maximum appropriate contact with non-handicapped children."[15] The hearing officer ordered Neill placed in an appropriate special education class in a regular elementary school setting, a gradation on the statutory mainstreaming mandate (regular classroom to the "maximum extent appropriate"). Further, he was entitled to "needed interaction with non-handicapped children during lunch, recess and transportation to and from school."[16]

The school district appealed to the Ohio State Board of Education, contending that Neill could not benefit significantly from mainstreaming and that any slight benefits from mainstreaming would be outweighed by the academic benefits of the county school. The state board ruled in favor of the school district.

The district court affirmed, concluding that the mainstreaming requirement allowed the district broad discretion in the placement of children. County school placement was affirmed because Neill had apparently made no significant progress after 18 months at a more integrated school.

---

has ruled that a child can be so retarded as to be beyond "educability" and therefore not entitled to a free appropriate public education. The cases of Levine v. State of New Jersey Department of Institutions and Guempel v. State of New Jersey, 418 A.2d 229 (Sup. Ct. N.J. 1980), 1980-81 EHLR 552:163 involved one 19-year-old individual with a mental age of 1 year 8 months and a ten-year-old boy with no evidence of any type of mental awareness or development, an IQ of 1, the motor development of a one-month- old, and no vocalization or language skill. The New Jersey Supreme Court ruled that children who

The court of appeals reversed the district court, and in so doing set out the first and most oft-quoted formula for weighing need against placement (an inherently difficult task as is reflected by the oscillating manner with which the *Roncker* court seemed first to land on the side of need, then placement, and then back to need). Initially the *Roncker* appellate court stated that IDEA "does not require mainstreaming in every case but its requirement that mainstreaming be provided to the *maximum* extent appropriate indicates a very strong congressional preference."[17]

The court acknowledged the need-placement conflict, initially indicating that placement might very well trump need:

> In some cases a placement which may be considered better for academic reasons may not be appropriate because of the failure to provide for mainstreaming. The perception that a segregated institution is academically superior for a handicapped child may reflect no more than a basic disagreement with the mainstreaming concept.[18]

The court's inclinations seemed clear enough here—anything other than a regular classroom is a "segregated" placement, a term not used in the law, but powerful in its implications. The court started on the mainstreamed side of the ledger, but in its ongoing analysis recognized the ever-difficult balancing act between need and placement: "In a case where the segregated facility is considered superior, the court should determine whether the services which make that placement superior could be *feasibly* provided in a non-segregated setting. *If* they can, the placement in the segregated school would be inappropriate under the Act."[19]

If feasibility is the determinant, then there appear to be administrative and even fiscal factors that may guide a decision toward the non-inclusive option. The *Roncker* court added that

---

were not capable of benefitting from an education were not entitled to an education at public expense.

"cost is a proper factor to consider since excessive spending on one handicapped child deprives other handicapped children."[20]

But how is feasibility defined? Is it applicable only in those matters in which individual services might be transferred from the "segregated" to the regular environment? It is ostensibly easier to provide a speech therapist or one-to-one aide for a regular classroom than it is to either create or move a comprehensive, full-time program for children with more severe disabilities into a regular classroom. It is not clear whether the *Roncker* court would require that the entire program be moved or replicated in a "nonsegregated" setting. But in any case, once "feasibility" is a factor, an ongoing debate is guaranteed.

Framing the question as it did, the *Roncker* court moved a little further from the integration preference. The court captured the core problem in weighing need and placement, by giving the

> proper respect for the strong preference in favor of mainstreaming while *still realizing the possibility* that some handicapped children *simply must be educated in segregated* facilities either because the handicapped child would not benefit from mainstreaming, because any marginal benefits received from mainstreaming are far outweighed by the benefits gained from services which could not feasibly be provided in the non-segregated setting, or because the handicapped child is a destructive force in the non-segregated setting.[21]

Perhaps the *Roncker* court may have realized that its initial weighing of provision of services versus "segregation" might simplify a rather complicated matter. Practical issues appear to be and are compelling. The question is no longer a matter of shifting services from a superior academic but "segregated" setting to an academically inferior but less restrictive environment. Now it may just be that children with disabilities will simply do better in separate settings. Now mainstreaming benefits may be marginal. "Feasibility" takes on a slightly different meaning, and with it the integration burden in these matters shifts from the school to the child.*

The court went back and forth because the inherent tension of the law is not easily resolved. The court, having indicated that cost is a factor, added that there is "no defense" if a school district has failed to use its funds to provide a proper continuum of alternative placements for children with disabilities.

The *Roncker* majority concluded its argument, qualified yet again:

> In the present case, the district court must determine whether Neill's educational, physical or emotional needs require some service which could *not feasibly* be provided in a class for handicapped children within a regular school or in the type of split program advocated by the State Board of Education. Although Neill's progress, or lack thereof, at Pleasant Ridge is a relevant factor in determining the maximum extent to which he can be mainstreamed, it is not dispositive since the district court must determine whether Neill could have been provided with additional services, such as those provided at the county schools, which would have improved his performance at Pleasant Ridge.[22]

In a strongly worded dissenting opinion, Judge Kennedy noted the lack of progress for Neill Roncker and his minimal ("at best") interaction with non-disabled children. According to

---

* Recently in Northern California one county office of education attempted to save money by moving a good number of county programs back to the home school districts, all of which had previously relied on the county to serve certain low-incidence populations. Several "state-of-the-art" centralized programs were closed. Whereas the county program could bring together a staff of experienced and well-qualified teachers with sufficient administrative support from specialists, each local district would either have to hire new staff or make do. Many parents fought the move to bring their children back to the neighborhood school because it meant reliance on "regular" principals serving as coordinators and administrative specialists (without the training or expertise required), and regular teachers taking on often complex cases for which they, too, had little or no training or expertise. In short, the parents did not believe the more integrated option was educationally "feasible."

Judge Kennedy, the only "benefit" of placing Neill in a regular school environment was to avoid the stigma attached to attending a special school. Whether such a benefit is minimal is debatable.

Although the *Roncker* court ruled against a "segregated" placement, its analysis provided language to justify separation. Ultimately the court recognized that the need for an appropriate education, with its attendant cost questions, may conflict with integration mandates and, under certain circumstances, integration must give way to appropriateness.

The LRE cup is not full; there is no absolute mainstreaming right under IDEA. While the full inclusion movement may ultimately mean the triumph of placement over need (or perhaps, as the movement may see it, the melding of need and LRE into the regular environment), for now *Roncker* and subsequent decisions—*Holland* included—represent the law's balancing effort. Like the *Rowley* court's reference to mainstreaming "whenever possible," the *Roncker* focus on feasibility is a clear acceptance that there is a limit to the right to integration. And while *Holland* and other cases that follow *Roncker* may have recalibrated the need-placement scale and may have done so in significant ways, need can still qualify placement, underscoring the law's unwillingness to create an absolute rule for placing children with disabilities.

\*    \*    \*

There is little doubt that *Rowley, Roncker,* and their progeny stand for the qualified nature of the integration right. Eight years after *Roncker,* the paradox of appropriateness and placement was again debated in *Greer v. Rome City School District,*[23] and while the court ruled in favor of an inclusive placement, it acknowledged that FAPE and LRE are often at odds in mainstreaming cases and that the former does limit and qualify the latter.[24]

Christy Greer was a ten-year-old child with Down's syndrome. She functioned like a moderately mentally handicapped child and lacked substantial language and articulation skills. When she was five, her parents sought to enroll her in her neighborhood kindergarten class. The school district recommended placement in a self-contained special education class attended only by peers with mental disabilities and located at Southeast Elementary School (where there were also classes for non-disabled children). The family rejected the offer, contending that placement in a "segregated" class would deny Christy "peer models to imitate" and deny her the "opportunity to cognitively stretch herself to the limits."[25] The district refused to change its offer.

An administrative hearing officer ruled in favor of the district. The federal district court ruled that Christy could be educated in the regular classroom with the use of supplemental aids and services and while the court recognized that the proposed school district IEP represented an "adequate" free appropriate public education (FAPE), the school district was "not in compliance with the Act because it does not provide placement for Christy in the 'least restrictive environment.' "[26]

The court of appeals affirmed this decision but recognized the inherent tension between IDEA's two goals of "mainstreaming and meeting each child's unique needs," and the fact that the " 'regular classroom[] simply would *not* be a suitable setting . . . for many handicapped children.' "[27] The *Greer* court acknowledged that the Supreme Court had not yet articulated a standard for mainstreaming, and thus for now the provision of an "appropriate" education *may overcome* the " 'presumption in favor of mainstreaming. . . .' "[28] In those situations, the school need not place the child in regular education.

Make no mistake that *Greer* encouraged "removal" or that it took lightly the mainstreaming preference. It after all affirmed the lower court's ruling in favor of a regular classroom:

> a determination by the school district that a handicapped child will make academic progress more quickly in a self-contained special education environment may *not* justify

educating the child in that environment if the child would receive considerable non-academic benefit, such as language and role modeling, from association with his or her non-handicapped peers.[29]

One must pause mid-quote, for the *Greer* court, while focusing on a purely "mainstreaming" issue, altered to some degree the *Rowley* restriction on what a child should really be "entitled" to and the *Roncker* standard of "feasibility." The *Greer* court weighed academic progress in a segregated setting with nonacademic benefit from a regular classroom and found that a child with disabilities was entitled to more than just academics. Mainstreaming had value "in and of itself."

The *Greer* court continued, stirring another ingredient into the placement pot:

If . . . the school board determines that the handicapped child will make significantly *more* progress in a self-contained special education environment and that education in a regular classroom may cause the child to fall behind his or her handicapped peers who are being educated in the self-contained environment, mainstreaming may not be appropriate.[30]

The court concluded that in such a case mainstreaming might actually be detrimental to the child, and therefore would not provide the child with a free appropriate public education as mandated by the Act.* The lower court recognized that while an "appropriate" education is not mere "surplusage" and goes to the "very heart of the Act's requirement that handicapped children be educated in the least restrictive environment," the

---

* The Commission on Education of the Deaf reported in 1988 that "parents, deaf consumers, and professional personnel of all persuasions have, with almost total unanimity, cited LRE as the issue that most *thwarts* their attempts to provide an appropriate education for children who are deaf." (Emphasis in the original.) THE COMMISSION ON EDUCATION OF THE DEAF, TOWARD EQUALITY, (A Report to the President and Congress), at 25 (Feb. 1988).

school district is, however, under no "obligation to place a handicapped child *exclusively* in the regular classroom."[31] There simply may be situations where an appropriate education is in a regular classroom and others when it will be in a special class. The "removal" language guards against precipitous "segregation." The *Greer* Court, all in the same decision, acknowledged the law's preference for mainstreaming and the importance of "need" over placement.

\*     \*     \*

Michael DeVries was a 17-year-old autistic student who needed "considerable special treatment to . . . function in *any* educational environment."[32] He exhibited many "childlike" behaviors—his mannerisms and speech were rigid, and he often became anxious when there were changes in his routine. He was a "fragile" child who required a stable, predictable environment.

Michael had a measured IQ of 72 and depressed academic cognitive skills; his math and reading skills were at the fourth-grade level. Michael participated effectively within small controlled social environments, but he was immature and demanding. He had difficulty with interpersonal communication and relationships.

The DeVries requested placement at Annandale High School, a large general education school serving approximately 2,300 students (but very few disabled students) near his home. The school district contended that Michael could only receive the "statutorily" required appropriate public education at the more distant South County Vocational Center in West Potomac High School.

The court, while "empathiz[ing] with DeVries' desire to be placed in a public high school with his sister and other non-handicapped children, did not agree that he would receive an 'appropriate public education' at that institution."[33] The court of appeals affirmed the district court's decision, ruling that Michael could not be educated in regular classes even with the use of supplementary aids and services.

Noting the *Roncker* logic that any "marginal" benefits of mainstreaming were outweighed by benefits to be gained from special education (not feasibly available in "nonsegregated" settings), the court agreed that placement at Annandale would mean that Michael would " 'simply be monitoring classes' with non-handicapped students," while his disability would "make it difficult for him to bridge the 'disparity in cognitive levels' between him and the other students. . . ."[34] He would learn little, and his work would be at a much lower level than that of his classmates.

Michael's needs were broad, requiring significant programmatic and services components, and so this was not merely a case of shifting one service from a separate environment to an integrated one. The more distant program would provide structure, one-to-one support and instruction in academic subjects, vocational and social skills, community-based work experiences, and access to all programs and facilities of the public high school.

The court concluded that the separate program was appropriate *and* least restrictive. It is interesting that the *DeVries* court did not state that the placement was appropriate and therefore it was LRE, although it may have meant that. The statement was in the conjunctive, suggesting that LRE is a process and that the determination of placement is fluid. LRE is not absolute; individual needs and programmatic responses to them define what is LRE.*

---

* Paul Miller was a 19-year-old student in Fairfax County, Virginia, with complex and pervasive disabling conditions. He functioned at the third-grade level. His parents sought full-day placement at Annandale High School, his community school. The school district proposed part-day placement at Annandale and part-day placement at South County, where Miller would have an intensive vocational program. The South County program was located at a regular high school where there were 48 students with disabilities and 20 staff members.

While the court recognized that the South County classes did not involve contact with the non-disabled, the Annandale High School program would

Nonetheless the continuum of existing law creates a linear, cascading model; spots along the continuum are more or less restrictive, not because of what they offer, but because they are on an arbitrary line. Some educators, in questioning the law's existing tendency to view LRE as a linear concept—the regular class is "least" restrictive, the special class "more" restrictive, and the institution "most" restrictive—turn to the *DeVries* notion that need should truly define restrictiveness. Accordingly, the child is in the center of a circle, with all placement options on the circumference, no one option placed abstractly superior to another.[35] The circle concept is viewed by many as the best way to balance need and placement rights, but it is neither part of existing law nor is it very frequently, if ever, applied to specific children. The appeal of the circle concept is that there is no preordained notion of where something fits on a descending (or ascending) continuum of placement options. The argument against a circle approach is that with all placement spots on the circle having equal value, it is likely that children would be mainstreamed less frequently.

*   *   *

IDEA is a fascinating law and a difficult federal mandate that touches on an American problem—the successful integration of historically excluded and disparate groups. IDEA attempts to provide for individual needs in a least restrictive environment and in so doing generates a fundamental question: Does appropriateness drive placement or is placement the starting point for

---

not benefit the plaintiff, who was an "educational 'isolate' ", and his presence would inpede the progress of other students because he would consume too great a percentage of the teacher's attention.

The court concluded that Miller's community school would be preferable if he could benefit from its program and his needs could be met there, but the preponderance of the evidence "clearly persuade[d]" the judge that "removal from his community school to the extent proposed by the school system is the only way that the plaintiff's needs can be met." Miller v. Fairfax County School Board, (E.D. Va. 1989), 1988-89 EHLR 441:333.

any consideration of an appropriate education? The notions of "appropriateness/need" and mainstreaming mix and match, leavened it seems by other factors, including cost, disruptiveness, de minimus benefit, or even a different concept of LRE, until the components can play against each other as often as they are complementary. IDEA's preference is clear, but there is no doubt that the law allows for separation; statutory language and case law specifically provide a rationale for the removal of children with disabilities from regular or home schools.

Since the tension between need and placement is at the core of IDEA's paradox, some argue that given enough resources any child can be mainstreamed. The gulf between appropriateness and placement is to be bridged by money. But others argue that it is the special education environment itself, including the totality of services and assistance, that constitutes appropriateness. Such an environment is not so easily transferred to a regular classroom.

The complexities involved in shifting special education to a "unitary system," as Gartner and Lipsky recommend, are therefore significant. Consider a teenager with severe emotional difficulties, who has periodic bouts of irrational behavior and hallucinations, and who requires an academic-psychiatric approach to his education. Or what of the child with significant physical disabilities who requires ongoing medical attention and specialized staff and machinery? Consider the logistics in moving the emotionally disturbed and the severely physically disabled students' programs to neighborhood schools. Assume there are two or four or ten other children with the same difficulties, and the same right to attend their home school. There is a fundamental question concerning whether the kind of treatment-environment needed can be provided in a regular class. The more extensive and costly the services are, the greater tendency there is to find that educational needs and fiscal limitations outweigh integration goals. It is easier to shift a service from one program to another; it is more difficult to move or replicate full programs.

Even in less complicated matters, LRE has "deferred" to appropriateness. While it would appear that children with mild disabilities would be more readily mainstreamed, the appropriateness-LRE conflict applies even there. In December 1992, the U.S. Court of Appeals for the First Circuit ruled that for a student with learning disabilities it was proper to weigh the " 'desirability of mainstreaming . . . in concert with the Act's mandate for educational improvement.' "[36] What is to be done when educational improvement is not possible in a regular classroom, or when it is, but only with the outlay of substantial resources? Conversely, isn't it fair to question whether certain fundamental matters, such as the inclusion of individual children, should be beyond budgetary limitations? As currently constituted, IDEA allows for cost and other matters to be weighed against placement rights.

\*     \*     \*

The integration/separate schooling paradox of IDEA is making a lot of people unhappy. The failure of IDEA to live up to its integration promise prompted the full inclusion movement. The effort to weigh need and placement is often delicate; there is no simple formula to apply.

The Undersecretary of Education calls "segregated" education immoral and parents and educators react immediately. The American Federation of Teachers, which represents 830,000 teachers, warns that the full inclusion of five million children with disabilities would "threaten the academic achievement of all students" and would "encourage inappropriate inclusion of disabled students in regular classrooms regardless of their medical, emotional or behavioral disability."[37]

At the December 1993 meeting of Action for Children to Insure Options Now (ACTION), a parent of a child with cerebral palsy and other profound physical disabilities explained to Undersecretary Heumann that her child's placement in a special, "separate" school had been nothing less than a miracle, and asked how highly specialized equipment and personnel could be transferred for one student to her home school. Another parent testified at the same meeting that two of her autistic children had been denied specialized, separate programs. The parent believed that her children's attempts at suicide were a direct consequence of the mistaken placement decision.[38]

The full inclusion movement sees the debate in clear moral tones; the mother of the autistic children had a much different vantage point from which to consider the pluses and minuses of integrated education. The fervor with which the full inclusion movement seeks systemic integration and the fervor with which a parent begs for the continuation of separate options suggest how difficult it may be to resolve the inherent paradox of IDEA.

## Endnotes

1. OLIVER SACHS, SEEING VOICES 33-34 (1989).

2. 20 U.S.C. § 1412(5)(B) (West Supp. 1994); 34 C.F.R. § 300.550 (1993).

3. 20 U.S.C. § 1412(5)(B) (West Supp. 1994); 34 C.F.R. § 300.552 (1993).

4. 34 C.F.R. § 300.552(d) (1993).

5. 20 U.S.C. § 1401(a)(16), 1412(5)(B) (West Supp. 1994); 34 C.F.R. § 300.17(i)(1993).

6. Rowley v. Bd. of Educ., 483 F. Supp. 528 (S.D.N.Y. 1980), 1979-80 EHLR 551:506.

7. 483 F. Supp. at 534, 1979-80 EHLR at 510.

8. 483 F. Supp. at 529, 1979-80 EHLR at 508.

9. Rowley v. Bd. of Educ., 632 F.2d 945, 948 (2d Cir. 1980), 1980-81 EHLR 552:101, 103.

10. Board of Educ. v. Rowley, 458 U.S. 176 (1982).

11. *Id.* at 200.

12. *Id.* at 203.

13.    20 U.S.C. § 1412(5)(B) (West Supp. 1994); 34 C.F.R. § 300.550(b)(2) (1993) (emphasis added).

14.    700 F.2d. 1058 (6th Cir. 1983), 1982-83 EHLR 554:381.

15.    *Id.* at 1061.

16.    *Id.*

17.    *Id.* at 1063 (emphasis in original).

18.    700 F.2d at 1053 (emphasis added).

19.    *Id.* (emphasis added).

20.    *Id.*

21.    *Id.* (emphasis added).

22.    *Id.* (emphasis added).

23.    950 F.2d 688 (11th Cir. 1991), 18 IDELR 412.

24.    950 F.2d at 695, 18 IDELR at 415.

25.    950 F.2d at 692, 18 IDELR at 414.

26.    950 F.2d at 693, 18 IDELR at 415.

27.    950 F.2d at 695, 18 IDELR at 415 (emphasis added).

28.    950 F.2d at 696, 18 IDELR at 416 (emphasis added).

29.    950 F.2d at 697, 18 IDELR at 416 (emphasis added).

30.    *Id.*

31.    Greer v. Rome City School District, 762 F. Supp. 936, 941 (N.D. Ga. 1990).

32.    DeVries v. Fairfax County Sch. Board, 882 F.2d 876, 877 (4th Cir. 1989), 1988-89 EHLR 441:555, 556 (emphasis added).

33.    882 F.2d at 878, 1988-89 EHLR 441 at 557.

34.    882 F.2d at 879, 1988-89 EHLR 441 at 558.

35.    *See* TOWARD EQUALITY, A REPORT BY THE COMMISSION ON EDUCATION OF THE DEAF TO THE PRESIDENT AND CONGRESS, Feb. 1988, at 32.

36.    Amann v. Stow School System, 982 F.2d 644, 650 (1st Cir. 1992), 19 IDELR 618, 621 (quoting Roland M. v. Concord School Committee, 910 F.2d 983, 993 (1st Cir. 1991)).

37.   AFT Calls for Pause In Full Inclusion Push, *Special Education Report*, Dec. 15, 1993, at 2-3. (American Federation of Teachers).

38.   ACTION meeting attended by the author.

# 5

---

# The Case for Removal

---

The Morrisons' attorney considered the case factually difficult and ethically clear. He also understood that it might be
better for Janet if it were the other way around. If the Morrisons
did not want Janet to attend the local neighborhood school with
an interpreter, he would have to show that the state school was
the only appropriate placement; it was a daunting prospect.
Taking a six-year-old child out of her home is not the goal one
wants to build a case on, and yet he understood too clearly the
Morrisons' viewpoint. If there was no absolute legal right to a
mainstreamed class under IDEA, then what did the law offer
when it came to comparing two nonmainstreamed options?

The attorney had, during his visit to the Midvale school,
chatted with the county administrator responsible for the case.
He was a compact, energetic man, with no experience working
with deaf children. He believed emphatically that the Morrisons
were wrong and that the Midvale program was not only appropriate but crucially important for Janet.

He smiled at the Morrisons' attorney. "Tell me, how do your
clients think Janet will be able to adjust to the hearing world if
she goes to the state school? Tell me, do you think the hearing
world is always going to be a cozy classroom in which every-
body signs?"

They watched as one of the regular classes came into Janet's room. The children mingled superficially, while most of the hearing pupils gravitated toward those "hearing-impaired" students who were oral. Janet carefully added up single-digit numbers on a work-sheet. She paid no attention to the hearing children.

"My own feeling is that placing Janet in the Midvale class has nothing to do with whether she will be better able to function in the hearing world. She needs to develop her own language to be prepared for the larger hearing world. Her parents believe the state school is the only place for that."

The administrator smiled more formally and shook his head. "Someone has to watch out for Janet and we gladly accept that responsibility."

"Tell me, do you ever wonder why in the world Janet's parents are so willing to have her leave home. Doesn't that tell you something?"

"I am sure they have their opinion and we have ours. We have a legal responsibility to Janet and tonight when she goes home to her parents, I'll rest easier." He smiled again and went off to watch the interaction between the hearing and deaf children more closely. Throughout the visit, Janet worked alone.

*     *     *

Every night during the administrative hearing, the attorney went back to his motel, a 1950s place of two stories, with the textured walls, the small plastic window over the shower, and the slightly seedy feeling of a part of town that has seen better days. He was several hundred miles from home, the case was a difficult one, and payment was uncertain. He reviewed things, reread his exhibits, restudied his notes for the next day's witnesses, and felt the fatigue of distance factored in with the real possibility of a bad decision. He could go over to the Morrisons, but it was not always easy facing clients who assumed unquestionably that the attorney would solve all their problems. The television was on, but he paid little attention to it.

The district's case was solid, direct, and perhaps inexorable. He looked at the pile of notes and papers, hoping some new tactic would materialize, like Morley's ghost, to give him a clear, if perhaps difficult blueprint for the next four days.

He took a walk to the nearby market for juice and cookies. He walked back, somewhat refreshed by the clear and warm night. The inner yard of the motel had recently been re-covered with a fresh layer of asphalt. There were several dozen older oak trees, sprinkled throughout the property. They gave the motel a softer feel and the attorney was thankful for them.

Back in the room, the pile remained inanimate. There were no other strategies to conjure up, no way to change the evidence, no apparent way to convey to the hearing officer why a deaf child like Janet needed to be placed, in spite of LRE, in the state school. The television droned on, and he turned to watch. The lead story of the day filled much of the public television news hour. He sorted through his notes, jotted down questions, worried over what he had no control over. Three thousand miles away the only deaf university, Gallaudet, was closed down. Gallaudet, founded in 1864 under the Lincoln administration, had always had a hearing president; the latest appointee was Elizabeth Zinser. In 1842 Notre Dame had its first Catholic president. In 1875 a woman became president of Wellesley College. In 1886 a Jewish man became president of Yeshiva College. In 1926 an African-American became president of Howard. Gallaudet was about to have its seventh hearing president.

The students at Gallaudet had responded instantaneously, fully, and unreservedly. The University was shut down. The president of the school's board of directors issued a statement that Dr. Zinser would begin her work and that the students had better go back to class or face the consequences. Police were called; barricades established. What would be called the "Selma" of the deaf had begun.

United States senators spoke of paternalistic attitudes. Jesse Jackson noted that "the problem is not that the students do not hear. The problem is that the hearing world does not listen." The television showed crowds gathering on campus, and students and teachers watching as the student leaders reported a breakthrough. Alumni from all over the country had flown to Gallaudet—this one university for the deaf was almost holy ground. Old friends embraced, 70- and 80-year-old alumni wearing baseball caps signed rapidly to each other. Many addressed the students; neither age, nor gender, nor political or philosophical attitudes affected this sea of Gallaudet people.

The television reported a significant change in the deadlock. Elizabeth Zinser had resigned gracefully as had the president of the board. Jesse Jackson called the change a "victory for all of us . . . a victory for all people who ever felt the pain of being stereotyped, devalued, and unrepresented." On the television I. King Jordan, the newly appointed, and first "hearing-impaired" president of Gallaudet stood smiling and exultant among the students of his university.

Some of the news reports on the television were not captioned, which meant that deaf viewers could not witness the reporting of the events at Gallaudet. The message, however, would go through the deaf community like wildfire. One hundred and twenty-four years after the founding of Gallaudet a deaf person was finally in charge of the institution.[1]

The Morrisons' attorney watched the events on television; the pile of notes and exhibits was unchanged by the drama on the screen. The administrative hearing would continue the next day, with most of its players untouched and unaware of what was happening 3,000 miles to the east.

*     *     *

The struggle between the Morrisons and school authorities was bitter. For a variety of reasons the administration had determined that a line was to be drawn in front of Janet Morrison and all those behind her, even though others before her had been placed by the district at the state school. Between the mediation and the start of the fair hearing there had been an ongoing and often acrimonious debate between the district's and the Morrisons' attorneys. The district had sent some of its staff and expert witnesses to observe the program at the state school, but had been less willing to have state school employees visit the Midvale program. This had greatly affected the Morrisons' case. The school district's expert witnesses testified about what they saw at the state school. State school teachers and administrators were allowed to testify, but were not permitted to visit Midvale for observation.

The county superintendent, who had attended the mediation, was a vigorous proponent of mainstreaming and had been a member of a state commission studying the ways mainstreaming might be more quickly and thoroughly implemented in California. He, like many other local administrators in the state, viewed the state school with some misgivings and even disdain. There was some feeling that the state school only wanted to educate the "normal" deaf children and did not willingly take those deaf children with secondary "conditions" like emotional disturbances or learning disabilities. The state school was also perceived as being expensive and, in addition, as the center of a kind of radical sign-language movement that seemed contrary to the modest world view that some administrators had.

The state school, on the other hand, often felt that local districts did not understand deaf children and felt that the districts saw the state facility as primarily a repository for the most troubled children. The state school perception was that it was the only place where deaf children could be in a full and rich language environment, the only place where the faculty understood deaf children, and the only place where deaf children truly felt at home. It was the only "normal" environment for many deaf children, primarily because there was that somewhat rare but necessary "critical mass" of peers, teachers trained in deaf education and even deaf teachers.

Since the deaf population is small—"low incidence"—there are few regions with sufficient population for classes with a "critical mass" of age and language peers. Hearing parents of hearing children may question the quality of education in general, the dedication or skills of a particular teacher and even the kind of students in a program. Rarely, however, will they even pause to wonder if their child will have dozens if not hundreds of age peers with whom they will communicate.

The issue of peer availability is an intriguing one—there is nothing in the law about it. There is no requirement to provide a child with language or age peers. The IEP does not require that peer or language needs be specifically addressed. That is not to say that the question should not be asked; it is simply not mandated. Arthur Schildroth reported in 1988 that approximately 75 percent of all deaf children attend schools in which there are between zero and two other deaf peers.[2] The linguistic, social, emotional, and even academic isolation can therefore be significant. The state school viewed itself as providing a viable and logical alternative. The school district viewed the state school as an anachronism.

The county superintendent was determined that the Morrison case would not be used to strengthen the role of the state schools, but would be used to show that deaf children could and should be educated locally, for, as an old cliche went, how could they adjust to the hearing world if they were only exposed to a deaf one?*

---

\* This is a curious, if frequently repeated, argument. A good number of academicians recognize that a deaf child must first establish his or her native language (and also roots to his or her native culture or community) to be able to effectively function in the hearing world. In his book *Seeing Voices*, Dr. Oliver Sachs noted that by acquiring sign language from infancy and being able to use that primary mode of communication through the school years, the deaf child "never know[s] the tragedy of noncommunication." (*Seeing Voices*, 59) Dr. Sachs wrote that he saw much "less isolation" at residential schools than in other programs for deaf children. At the same time Dr. Sachs and others have studied, with growing concern, those deaf children who are not exposed

The superintendent was also concerned about money, although the cost of using private counsel exceeded the district's liability for state school placement, which was approximately $27,000. Placing Janet in the hearing-impaired class at Midvale was less expensive. Such comparisons are somewhat misleading. Since IDEA encourages home school placement and the provision of services to facilitate such placement, the actual cost of mainstreaming a deaf child can be considerable. Assume that the "two children" in the Schildroth study are different ages—it may very well be that their school district would be required to provide a full-time sign-language interpreter and other one-to-one services (such as speech therapy) for each individual child. If the core mandate of IDEA was followed, the cost of placing a child locally might match or exceed the cost of state school placement.

Not surprisingly, then, the superintendent took a hard line and employed a clever strategy to prevent state school personnel from visiting Midvale. The employees at the state school came under the aegis of the California Department of Education, and the district distinguished between state school personnel and local district employees, the former's involvement requiring "approval" by the state superintendent responsible for the state school for the deaf. The Morrison attorney contacted the state superintendent who, unwilling to take a "position" in an increasingly political case, stated that his employees could visit the local program if "invited."

The county superintendent, through his attorney, responded that the state school observers could visit the local program if the state school superintendent formally "asked" to observe. The state superintendent then reiterated the need for an invitation. And so it went back and forth, the state superintendent never willing to ask for a visit, but always willing to send his teachers

---

to a native language and who grow up with a foot in both the hearing and deaf worlds, comfortable in neither, isolated from both. *Id.*

once a local request was made. The local superintendent had won—no such invitation would be tendered, but a request to visit would be honored.

Since the state hearing office would not intervene (it infrequently issued pre-hearing orders), the only option for the Morrison family was to go into court for an order compelling the visit, or at least the invitation. This was problematic because it was not entirely clear on what grounds the family would base its action, and unrealistic because the family had no resources for such an interlocutory action.

The importance of this case to the school district and the superintendent was clear—he would take what he thought was the moral high ground and stand four-square with the inclusionary spirit (only partially applied for Janet) of the law.

The state school employees, including deaf and hearing teachers and a state school principal and psychologist, never visited Midvale. They never observed Janet, did not see her in class or on the playground and therefore could not attest to the "appropriateness" of the Midvale program. The day that a deaf teacher from the state school testified generally about the state school program (but could say nothing about the local hearing-impaired program and Janet), the new deaf president at Gallaudet was sworn in.

---

By its very language, IDEA, the integrating law, codifies separation of children with disabilities from children who do not have disabilities: "special classes, separate schooling or other *removal* of handicapped children from the regular educational environment occurs. . . ."[3] We recoil at the thought of statutory "segregation," but there it is. Parents, educators, and judges have viewed the removal language as a narrow exception to the integrative spirit of IDEA—others see it as a viable and reasonable part of the law.

The continuum of placement options, as well as the removal law, confirms the complex nature of IDEA. The *Roncker* court concluded that separation was justified if the child was placed in a superior program and if it was not feasible to replicate that program in a mainstreamed class. Separate but equal.

This notion, canonized in *Plessey v. Ferguson*[4] (which ultimately led to *Brown v. Board of Education*[5]), was based on the belief and policy that segregated schools for African-American children were "equal to" those for white children. They weren't equal, but it was a fiction necessary to maintain the system. The *Brown* Supreme Court ruled that separate could never be equal. U.S. Undersecretary of Education Judith Heumann spoke of regular and special education as two distinct systems, "[s]eparate, but . . . not equal."[6] Whether it is true that separate is never equal and that the provision of superior separate programs for children with disabilities is a kind of current analog to the racism that characterized pre (and post) *Brown* America is another matter. The *Plessey* concept is abhorrent, but then there is Janet Morrison. For Janet, separate was more than equal.

The numbers certainly bear out the separating nature of IDEA. The U.S. Department of Education reported in 1992 that 1,496,964 children with disabilities were in regular classes, while 2,123,122 were in other programs, including 11,998 in correctional facilities and 32,981 either homebound or in hospitals.[7]

As noted, numerous states and school districts have begun inclusionary efforts. Nebraska, for example, looked to a high performance learning (HPL) inclusionary educational system in which there is a "zero reject philosophy" (no student excluded based on type or extent of disability).[8] One school system, Johnson City (NY) Central School District, created the "Outcome Driven Developmental Model," which was

> a school where the systems of "special" and "regular" education have been fully merged into one collaborative, well supported responsible system that is able to meet the needs of children with a wide range of needs without labeling,

sorting or exclusive programs. . . . the right of each student to be educated in his/her neighborhood school or a school in the district. Special and Regular Educational resources must *merge* to achieve the vision for full inclusion.[9]

In order to accomplish these goals, the Johnson City School District began to actively "bring back" students to local programs from special education programs outside the district.

Meanwhile, the effort to integrate all children has turned to alternative language to make the case for finally folding need into placement and eliminating the removal option:

> The *separate* program maintains a range of separate & specialized services and settings. . . . The Separate Program Identity option assumes that special education maintains a separate identity, including separate staff within central administration who oversee the specialized placements and procedures, as well as separate staffs at the local school sites.
>
> *Inclusive* education represents the philosophy that all students, regardless of the challenges presented by their educational needs, should be educated with their peers in neighborhood schools. This type of school does not require or assume a blending of programs—it can exist within a separate categorical special education program administration.
>
> A *unified* educational system is based on the principle that each student represents a unique combination of abilities and educational needs and may require individual assistance at varying times during the school year. . . . Schools are organized around services, not programs. . . . [10]

The terms used to distinguish the three options—"separate," "inclusive," and "unified"—imply different values and qualities.* Michael Peterson of the Developmental Disabilities Institute

---

* The California Department of Education, Special Education Division, in a draft analysis distinguished between "LRE, Mainstreaming, Integration, Supported Education, Inclusion, Full Inclusion, and Inclusive Education" as variations on the placement theme.

has written that "inclusion" implies welcoming and valuing people with disabilities as you would non-disabled people, as well as a system of mutual support between disabled and non-disabled individuals. This contrasts with previous approaches to the disabled: banishment and death, institutionalization and segregated services, institutional reform, and community placement, all of which have finally lead to "community membership."[11] Peterson further defined "inclusion" as a goal in which all "individuals with disabilities will have the opportunity of participating and belonging in typical school and community settings," because the inclusion movement is part of a larger "community building" and "communitarian movement."[12] The removal language of IDEA would hardly be compatible with the evolution that Peterson and others describe.

The push-pull nature of the debate is ever apparent. Not long after Johnson City and other districts began to restructure their programs to facilitate "inclusion," representatives of the blind, learning disabled and deaf communities appeared in Congress to warn about overly zealous inclusionary practices. Phil Hatlen of the Joint Action Committee of Organizations and of Serving the Visually Handicapped told the House of Representatives' Committee on Education and Labor about a "crisis" over misapplication of placement mandates:

> Many blind and visually impaired pupils will need at least a short amount of time in a *disability-specific setting* in order to master both the skills necessary for accessing the regular curriculum and for specialized instruction in areas of the curriculum unique to them.

> What is desperately needed for blind and visually impaired children is a full array of placement options ranging from total mainstreaming to placement in settings with other blind and visually impaired children.[13]

Dr. Hatlen further noted the threat posed by well-meaning, but ignorant full inclusion advocates:

A large but not representative group of professionals and parents are dictating implementation policy relating to LRE. These people are not professionals in education of blind and visually impaired children, nor are they parents of these children.

Rather, they are individuals who have come to certain conclusions about appropriate education of some populations of disabled children, and they have unwisely generalized their position to all disabled children. Professionals in special education who have no knowledge concerning the needs of blind and visually impaired students are making decisions as to how LRE is to be implemented for this very special population.[14]

Hatlen has written that the educational system must "celebrate" the differences in students and reflect the heterogeneity of society; full inclusion is one of many appropriate educational settings.[15] For blind and visually impaired students, there may be many reasons for "removal," including the provision of an expert staff, adapted curriculum, materials, and technology, and the development of social skills that are not learned through imitation.[16] Hatlen, sharing the sentiment of others, criticized the full inclusion movement's effort to eliminate the removal portion of IDEA by generalizing for all students with disabilities what applies only to certain segments of that population.[17]

While the full inclusion movement condemns the reliance on labels (which reinforces separatism), the counterrevolution condemns IDEA's (and the movement's) focus on physical locations such as regular classrooms, separate classrooms, separate schools, and institutions. Dr. Michael Bienenstock of the Convention of American Instructors of the Deaf (CAID) testified before a March 1993 U.S. House Sub-Committee that the real intent of IDEA was to educate children, "not to physically place them."[18]

As the full inclusion movement seeks change in the removal nature of IDEA, others seek protection against a diminution of nonregular class options. In March 1993 South Dakota became the first state to enact a deaf child's educational bill of rights, which recognized the unique communication needs of deaf children, required consideration of those needs in determining the least restrictive environment, and provided that the state school for the deaf "may be the least restrictive environment for a deaf or hard-of-hearing child."[19] Louisiana passed a similar law in June, 1993, and other states are considering similar legislation. Other groups are looking to deaf legislation as a model for their constituents, who are demanding alternative, nonregular programs. In addition to the language of IDEA, case law has confirmed the removal portion of the law and supports the growing movement to pass legislation that protects children against generic full inclusion.

*　　*　　*

In *St. Louis Developmental Disabilities Treatment Center v. Mallory*,[20] the entire special education program for Missouri was challenged. The plaintiffs in *St. Louis* contended that LRE "mandated" placement in either regular classes or, in the alternative, separate classrooms in regular schools; the entire removal structure for Missouri was, according to the plaintiffs, illegal. Five advocacy groups and 13 individuals alleged that Missouri's system of providing separate schooling for severely disabled students violated IDEA, the Rehabilitation Act, federal civil rights legislation, and the Constitutional guarantees of Equal Protection and Due Process. Plaintiffs called for the closure of all special schools (except those serving medically fragile and physically abusive children and the state schools for the blind and deaf), and the full "integration" of children with disabilities into "local schools," where there would be no more than three classes of profoundly disabled children in any one particular school.

Missouri's special education system provided services for approximately 116,000 students, served by 547 local school districts and 52 state schools for the severely disabled. Of the 116,000 disabled students, 111,000 attended local schools. The law suit was brought on behalf of the 2,450 students who attended the schools for the severely disabled.

The court addressed the underlying philosophical struggle:

> The issue for resolution here, however, is not whether it is feasible to transfer *all* the handicapped children in the separate schools to regular schools, but *whether the separate schools and facilities are an appropriate part of a special education system and whether systemically the defendants have procedures that seek to assign the children to the least restrictive educational setting appropriate.*[21]

The court rejected all of plaintiffs' arguments and found ample support in federal regulations and a variety of federal decisions that the continuum was an inherent part of the law, and was indeed prima facie evidence of congressional belief that separate alternatives are required:

> Neither Section 1412(5)(B) nor any other provision of the Education Act indicates a congressional intent to eliminate separate or other facilities for the handicapped children who need them to benefit educationally. . . . The section acknowledges that some handicapped children will not be able to receive a satisfactory education in a "regular educational environment" and will need to be placed in *"special classes, separate schooling"* or otherwise removed from the regular school setting. Unless Congress intended to repeat itself, special classes and separate schooling must mean two distinct education placements.[22]

Plaintiffs argued that even if the "continuum may be valid . . . its use is invalid if the children are not placed in the least restrictive educational placement appropriate for them," and that the LRE for the "'vast majority' of 'severely handicapped' children currently attending separate schools is a self-contained classroom in a regular public school."[23]

The plaintiff children represented about .0062 percent of the total school-age population, a figure that actually proved, according to the court, the individual, nonsegregated approach to placement decisionmaking in Missouri. The court concluded that "separate" schooling was appropriate and consistent with the law, for if the court did as the plaintiffs asked and ordered the wholesale transfer of all children it would be committing the same wrong the plaintiffs alleged against the defendants and also further endorsing a process that did not treat each child as a unique individual. The court's view illuminated the central paradox of a systemic full inclusion approach—to the extent that advocates and parents argue for integrating all children with disabilities, they must ignore the rights of some individual children.

To the plaintiffs' argument that separate programs were inappropriate because there were insufficient opportunities to interact with non-disabled children, the court noted that:

1. Mere placement of a severely handicapped child in a regular classroom does not ensure appropriate social interaction with non-disabled children.

2. As the severity of the disability increases, so does the tendency for non-disabled children to ignore the child.

3. Even if there are interactions, there is no guarantee they will be beneficial.

4. No data exists that shows that mere placement in a regular school leads to positive interactions.

5. Positive interactions are not necessary for the provision of an appropriate education.

6. Placement in a regular environment may in fact arrest social and educational development.

The court was aware of the significant underlying issue of the case, which it believed came "down to a clash between two schools of educational thought on the question of whether interactions with non-handicapped youngsters in a regular school environment are necessary for an adequate education."[24] The court refused to substitute, contrary to congressional intent, one education theory for another. To do so would require a "showing that the theory is completely out of step with present educational thought and with no likelihood of benefiting the children served"[25] Only Hawaii has "fully integrated its handicapped children into its regular schools," but it has only one school district.[26]

The court rejected the contention that the continuum, which includes separate schools, was invalid. It rejected the notion that separate schooling was prima facie inappropriate. Limited opportunities or no opportunity for interaction with non-disabled children did not prove an educational program inappropriate. Removal was justified under the law.

In *Geis v. Board of Education*[27] the parents of a severely disabled student opposed efforts to move their son from residential placement.* S.G. was a 16-year-old, mentally retarded student, with a neurological dysfunction, communication disorders, chronic illness, and secondary emotional difficulties. S.G. also experienced motor and psychomotor seizures.

The school district recommended placement in a class for trainably mentally retarded students in Brooklawn Junior High School, a "regular" junior high school in Parsippany. An administrative hearing officer ruled that placement at Brooklawn was appropriate. During the appeal to the federal district court, the assigned judge visited both placement options.

The court ruled that S.G. was to remain in the residential program because it would "allow [him] to 'best achieve success in learning and that placing S.G. in his home and in local schools would have an adverse effect on his ability to learn and develop to the maximum possible extent.'"[28]

---

* 34 C.F.R. § 300.302 provides that if residential placement is "necessary to provide special education and related services to a child ... the program, including non-medical care and room and board, must be at no cost to the parents of the child."

The U.S. Court of Appeals for the Third Circuit affirmed the lower court decision. On appeal, the school district argued that *Rowley* required only that it provide a suitable education, which happened to be closer to S.G.'s home. The court of appeals rejected the argument, ruling that the New Jersey legislature determined that school children should be provided the fullest possible opportunity to develop their intellectual capacities, which in this case was a more "segregated" program.

The school district also contended that the state standard could always be used to rationalize a private school placement since there will always be some private program somewhere that can offer more facilities, more instructional personnel and more services than a given public school district can offer. The court was not prepared to go down that "slippery slope," since it believed that the residential program was both feasible and appropriate:

> As to the requirement that handicapped children be placed in the least restrictive environment possible, we believe that this determination must include consideration of the particular handicap a student has. . . . Current regulations make it even more clear that the goal of placing children in the least restrictive environment *does not trump all other considerations.* . . . For some pupils a residential placement may very well be the least restrictive.[29]

In the case of *Ash v. Lake Oswego*,[30] the parameters of "removal" were set out in bold relief. The case involved extensive use of district resources and expensive placement options far removed from the regular classroom.

Christopher Ash, at the time of the litigation, was a 13-year-old child with mental retardation, developmental delays and infantile autism. As with many autistic children, Christopher had difficulty responding to sensory stimuli and communicating and relating to other human beings. As a result of its own evaluation, Lake Oswego concluded that Christopher had virtually no language, the adaptive behavior of a two-year-old, poor motor skills, and a very short visual attention span. Christopher had a five-word vocabulary. He also had severe tantrums at home, which greatly affected the family and his mother in particular, who felt she would have a nervous breakdown if he remained at home. The family therapist recommended residential treatment for Christopher.

In September 1985, and before an IEP meeting, the Ashes placed their son in the Tokyo Higashi School, a residential school for autistic children. In 1987 a Higashi school was opened in Boston and Christopher was transferred there, where he lived at the time the U.S. District Court for Oregon issued its order in this dispute. The Higashi program was based on "Daily Life Therapy," a program emphasizing physical strength and daily skill development through group and intense individual work.

After Christopher was placed at Higashi, but before the ultimate litigation, the parties met in an IEP meeting. The school district offered a local self-contained classroom with between 8 and 12 students and one teacher and two aides. Christopher was to be with regular students during lunch, recess, assemblies, and other school activities.

The Ashes rejected the placement offer and, at the subsequent fair hearing, asked for reimbursement for placement at Higashi from 1985 through January 1990. Thirteen witnesses testified at the fair hearing, including Gary Mesibov, an expert on the education of autistic children and a professor at the University of North Carolina. Mesibov observed two classes in the Lake Oswego-Clackamas County region and noted that their strong curriculum was consistent with current educational practices. Mesibov testified that the IEP was appropriate, that Christopher could benefit from the proposed school placement and that residential placement was therefore unnecessary.

The hearing officer ruled in March 1990 that Lake Oswego had the burden of proving its IEP was appropriate and had done so, denying the family's request for reimbursement for residential placement. The hearing officer adopted Professor

Mesibov's opinion and ruled that the Ashes had failed to prove the need for residential placement because "The evidence shows that residential placement for [Christopher] may well be necessary to maintain . . . harmony in his family. But [he] does not require residential placement in order to gain *meaningful benefit* from his education."[31]

A judicial hearing was held in April 1991 at which time Dr. Mary Cerreto, Director of Psychology at the Franciscan Children's Hospital in Boston, testified that Christopher needed a 7-days-a-week, 24-hour program because consistency was crucial to any educational growth:

> Chris is not going to be the type of child that's going to learn how to brush his teeth in a classroom. He is not going to learn how to buy things in a classroom store. . . . He's not going to know how to go to bed. . . . Chris needs to be taught in a natural environment because his cognitive abilities are so low he can't generalize from one environment to the next. . . . the things he needs to learn range the entire 24 hour day.[32]

The federal district court concluded that Dr. Cerreto's testimony was compelling and that Christopher needed a 24-hour, 7-days-a-week environment because "While residential placement for a handicapped child is only appropriate in very limited circumstances, Christopher's medical, social and emotional problems are so severe that they are not segregable from his learning process, and therefore residential placement is required for educational purposes."[33] The court noted that daily living skills, such as toileting and eating and dressing, could only be taught and reinforced in a residential setting, underscoring the particular reasons why removal was in fact justified for some children:

> Handicapped students are normally enrolled in regular public schools, with the public schools providing the necessary services and making the necessary modifications to their environments and programs in order to ensure the continued enrollment of handicapped students and to ensure educational benefits for them. If, however, a local public school

159

district cannot educate a handicapped child in regular or special classes, the Act authorizes placement in a residential program.[34]

There was no debate as to Christopher's removal from a regular classroom—it was never a viable option. Christopher's needs were so complex as to trump virtually all home or regular school considerations. His needs could not have sent him further "down" the continuum or further from home. That he was judged to be appropriately served in Boston reveals, at the very least, that a court of law considered need vastly superior to location of placement. Further, it suggests that LRE is not merely a physical consideration. Christopher was in the LRE, according to the federal court, even if it was 3,000 miles from his home and home school.

In *Drew P. v. Clarke County School District*,[35] the 16-year-old plaintiff was an autistic student who could not speak and who communicated:

> primarily with limited sign language or by pointing to objects. Drew seems to be very distant in his relationships with people. In addition, he "toe walks" when he is under stress, flaps his hands when excited and laughs inappropriately. Drew is fascinated by the spinning of mechanical things, has little comprehension of fear . . . and has difficulty coping with changes in his routine and environment. The evidence also shows that Drew has become increasingly aggressive at home, throws objects when angered, and cannot be left by himself for any significant period of time.[36]

Drew had been in a variety of placements; his school district recommended "foster-type" placement and an in-home trainer until "funding was exhausted." Eventually Drew was placed in a residential program in Valdosta, Georgia, for a trial period. The hearing officer and state appeal officer ruled that residential placement was not necessary for Drew. On appeal the federal court ruled that failure to place Drew in a residential program denied him a free appropriate public education.

During the administrative dispute, Drew's mother placed him in the same school that Christopher Ash was placed: the Higashi school in Tokyo. Drew remained there from 1985 through 1987, at which time he too transferred to the Higashi school in Boston.

Once the court ruled that residential placement was necessary, it tackled the more difficult issues of what and where:

> The court . . . is troubled by the fact that Drew's parent chose a residential facility 8,000 miles from home. . . . Although the State of Georgia may not have an appropriate residential facility for autistic children, certainly one should not need to traverse the Pacific Ocean to find an adequate residential facility for children with disabilities similar to Drew's.[37]

The court stated that the Boston school was not necessarily an appropriate one for Drew, since there were group homes for autistic children in North Carolina. The court noted that Drew's parents were willing to place him in one of those schools and was therefore "reluctant to expand the scope of the EAHCA 'simply because they honestly and very properly feel sorry for the claimants.'"[38]

While the court left open the question of whether payment would be ordered for the Tokyo or Boston placements, it was particularly clear that residential placement was necessary, certainly out of state in North Carolina.

\*     \*     \*

Emily Thomas was a severely retarded, multi-handicapped eleven-year-old who was confined to a wheelchair.[39] Emily functioned at the one-month level developmentally, had severe psychomotor retardation, had no self-help skills, was legally blind, and had borderline hearing loss, but did respond to some auditory and tactile stimuli. Emily also had severe feeding problems, used a gastrostomy tube, and breathed through a tracheostomy, which required constant monitoring and suctioning.

Emily's parent preferred placement in a small special day class where there was intensive stimulation of motor and sensory development, while the school system offered one hour per day of home instruction. A hearing officer ordered Emily placed in the school-based program, concluding that home instruction was not appropriate or legal. A state level review officer reversed, ordering home instruction. The district federal court reversed again, concluding that home instruction was not an option because Emily could be safely transported to school. The applicable state statute provided that home instruction was to be available for children who, even with the help of special transportation, were unable to attend school.

The court of appeals reversed the lower court decision, returning Emily to her home for five one-hour sessions each week, ruling with direct and unmistakable language that while

> federal law does establish a "mainstreaming" policy under which handicapped children are to be educated with non-handicapped children to the maximum extent appropriate, reliance on this policy is misplaced here. There is no doubt that Emily cannot be educated in a regular classroom—her handicaps are simply too severe. Nor is it contested that Emily is unable to benefit from the social contact that a school setting provides.[40]

Whether one views the *Thomas* court as taking an unnecessarily narrow view of placement rights, it is clear that the court believed that IDEA allowed for removal to a socially restrictive, legally permissible placement at home.

In a 1992 case from western Washington, *Pamela B. v. Longview School District*,[41] the issues of removal and restrictiveness as analyzed by the *Ash* and *Christopher* courts were taken a step further. Chris B. was a 20-year-old student suffering from a variety of physiological and psychological disabilities, including Tourette's syndrome and a pervasive developmental disorder. Chris was educable mentally retarded. He had speech problems and a variety of compulsive tics, all of which made educating him a difficult task.

His mother, Pamela B., sought residential placement. A hearing officer determined that Chris required residential placement for medical, not educational reasons, and thus the school district was not responsible for such placement. The hearing officer concluded that the district program was "reasonably calculated to provide the student educational benefits in the least restrictive environment."[42]

The district court ruled that Chris had not made progress in his school program but had in fact regressed, and needed a more structured environment. Therefore a "residential placement is not only the least restrictive environment, but it is the *only* appropriate alternative."[43] The gradation of LRE ends; here need and placement mesh, the former fully defined by the latter.

*     *     *

The *Ash, Drew P., Pamela B.,* and *Thomas* cases all underscore the very clear separating capability of IDEA and in so doing highlight the significant cost of special education. What family prefers to see a child sent across country or across the globe? Should there be a limit to public funding of expensive and distant (or local) programs? Is there a point past which benefit to the child no longer justifies the cost? Since some placements, with travel, can cost in the tens, if not hundreds of thousands of dollars, the issue is a practical one. This may be particularly true where the child's needs are extensive and the "return" may be limited. How is that "point" assessed and judged? And if such a point can be located on the commonweal map, should it be 25, but not 26 thousand dollars for Christopher Ash? Is Boston far, but not too far from Oregon? Is Tokyo simply too distant and too costly?

Is it better to spend "x" amount of money helping Christopher Ash develop appropriate skills, or better to use the money for some other purpose? In an age when many believe that government's role should be narrowed, what of national values and a historic commitment to serving those who cannot always serve themselves? When exclusionary educational policies are criticized based on historic but inaccurate stereotypes of children with disabilities, it is neither easy nor necessarily fair to offer resources as a defense.*

Proponents of full inclusion contend that "separate" programming is based on a medical model ("there is something wrong with children with disabilities") and does not work; using a unitary system in which all children with disabilities are served at local sites will mean better results and ultimately better use of resources.[44] Opponents argue that the inclusion of those children with severe disabilities would result in significant additional costs above the current "high" level of expenditures for special education. Ten children with similar severe disabilities can be provided significant one-to-one services in a central class of one teacher and several aides. Moving each of those children into a local program would often mean a separate one-to-one aide for each child—ten aides as opposed to two or three.

To further complicate the matter, what of the family that can afford such a placement? Will some ask, as others do of the Social Security or Medicare systems, that "coverage" should be restricted to those who cannot pay for the services?

However the funding formula will be changed and cost questions more properly assessed, IDEA stands, if not squarely

---

* There is a certain futility in trying to compare need. How does one determine whether it is better to spend money on Christopher or on, for example, the after-school football program? Perhaps the question should be broadened. Some years ago there was discussion of building a new freeway to ease transport of people to Disneyland. Even if the new freeway made the commute easier for a certain percentage of taxpayers (and created jobs), there was a real question as to whether it was an appropriate use of tax monies, particularly given the value the new freeway had for a private business enterprise. Perhaps the question should be, do we choose a special education program over an after-school football program or a Disneyland freeway over both? Some will ask, of course, why these choices have to be made in the first place.

in the middle, somewhere between an integration and noninte-gration model. The pressure to create a unitary system may eventually lead to a reworking of IDEA. For now the law and many of the court decisions about IDEA continue to provide a significant rationale for separation.

## Endnotes

1. For an account of the Gallaudet Revolution, *see* Jack R. Gannon, The Week The World Heard Gallaudet (Gallaudet University Press 1989).

2. Arthur Schildroth, *Recent Changes in the Educational Placement of Deaf Students*, American Annals of the Deaf 61-62 (1988).

3. 34 C.F.R. § 300.550(b)(2) (1993) (emphasis added).

4. 163 U.S. 537 (1896).

5. 347 U.S. 483 (1954).

6. *Heumann: Oberti Decision Is Core of the ED's Inclusion Position*, The Special Educator 85, 86, (1993).

7. U.S. Dep't of Educ., Fourteenth Ann. Rep. to Congress on the Implementation of IDEA, at A-53 (1992).

8. Nebraska Special Educ. Advisory Council, Ad Hoc Committee on Neighborhood Schools and Inclusion in Nebraska, Final Report, at 2 (Aug. 6, 1993).

9. *One System's Vision*, Inclusion Times, Sept. 1993, at 7.

10. M. McLaughlin and S. Warren, Options In Restructuring Schools and Special Education Programs, (as adapted from Issues and Options in Restructuring Schools and Special Education Programs, Center for Policy Studies in Special Education,) Special Edge, 1992, at 8-9.

11. Michael Peterson, Inclusion and Inclusive Communities, (Developmental Disabilities Institute, University of Michigan 1993), at 1-2.

12. *Id.* at 2, 10.

13. *Hearing before the Subcommittee on Select Education*, No. 101-3, 101st Cong., 1st Sess., Mar. 7, 1989, (comments of Dr. Philip Hatlen), at 190-91.

14. *Id.*

15.  Phil Hatlen, Position Statement on Educational Placement, (provided to author by Dr. Hatlen).

16.  *Id.*

17.  *Id.*

18.  Depts. of Labor, Health & Human Services, Education and Related Agencies Appropriations for 1994: Hearing before the Subcomm. on Depts. Labor, Health & Human Services, Education and Related Services of the House Comm. on Appropriations, 103d Cong., 2d Sess. (1993) (statement of Dr. Michael Bienstock, CAID).

19.  South Dakota, SB 219, signed into law on Mar. 23, 1993.

20.  591 F. Supp. 1416 (W.D. Mo. 1984), 1984-85 EHLR 556:117, *aff'd,* 767 F.2d 518 (8th Cir. 1985), 1985-86 EHLR 557:104.

21.  591 F. Supp. at 1454-56, 1984-85 EHLR at 132 (emphasis added).

22.  591 F. Supp. at 1442, 1984-85 EHLR at 128 (emphasis added).

23.  591 F. Supp. at 1446, 1984-85 EHLR at 130.

24.  591 F. Supp. at 1463, 1984-85 EHLR at 136.

25.  *Id.*

26.  *Id.* at 1464.

27.  774 F.2d 575 (3d 1985), 1985-86 EHLR 557:135.

28.  774 F.2d at 579, 1985-86 EHLR at 137-38.

29.  774 F.2d at 583, 1985-86 EHLR at 140 (emphasis added).

30.  766 F. Supp. 852 (D. Or. 1991), 18 IDELR 3.

31.  766 F. Supp. at 859, 18 IDELR at 7.

32.  *Id.*

33.  766 F. Supp. at 863, 18 IDELR at 10.

34.  766 F. Supp. at 862, 18 IDELR at 9.

35.  676 F. Supp. 1559 (M.D. Ga. 1987), 1987-88 EHLR 559:323.

36.  676 F. Supp. at 1561, 1987-88 EHLR at 324.

37.  676 F. Supp. at 1570, 1987-88 EHLR at 331.

38.  *Id.* (quoting Stacy G. v. Pasadena Unified School Dist., 695 F.2d 949, 956 (5th Cir. 1983)).

39.   Thomas v. Cincinnati Bd. of Educ., 918 F.2d 618 (6th Cir. 1990), 17 IDELR 113.

40.   918 F.2d at 627, 17 IDELR at 118.

41.   No. C90-5256B (W.D. Wash. 1992), 18 IDELR 514.

42.   18 IDELR at 515.

43.   *Id.* at 516.

44.   *See* ALAN GARTNER & DOROTHY KERZNER LIPSKY, NATIONAL CENTER ON EDUCATION AND THE ECONOMY, THE YOKE OF SPECIAL EDUCATION— HOW TO BREAK IT 25-28 (1989).

# 6

## The Continuum of Placement Options

When Ishi came down from the hills he was threadbare, emaciated, beaten. At least the photograph of the "wild Indian" who walked down from the hills appeared that way. He was jailed, but soon university anthropologists came from San Francisco. They represented science, rationality, protection, and the mainstream. Ishi lived at the university and the pictures from that brief period show him smiling, his dark hair pulled back from his face. The heavy suit he wore in the picture seemed a poor fit, wrong for him somehow. The anthropologists eventually took Ishi back to his hills—photographs of that brief repatriation show Ishi swimming and fishing the old way, smiling, his stomach paunchy. He returned to the university, where he died from tuberculosis.

Ishi had quickly assimilated the ways of civilization and was communicative about almost all topics except the fate of his kinsmen and his life in the hills. With his death the Yahi tribe passed away.[1]

Seventy-eight years after Ishi went to San Francisco, Janet Morrison made the trip there to be tested, questioned, and assessed by University of California scientists. The Center on Deafness was located in a residence on campus, probably no more than a hundred yards from where Ishi had lived. The university was built into the hills of San Francisco, above and slightly south of Golden Gate Park. From this vista, one could see east to downtown San Francisco, north to the Golden Gate Bridge, west to the park and beyond to the ocean. The wind came off the ocean, sometimes pouring east through the park and the groves of eucalyptus trees dotting the medical campus.

Dr. Earl Thomas was a quiet man with extensive experience working with deaf children. He had sign language skills and could communicate directly with Janet. Dr. Thomas administered numerous tests, issued a written report, and testified at the due process hearing. Reports from school psychologists and teachers indicated that Janet was shy and reserved; she tended not to mix, preferring to play alone. Dr. Thomas' findings suggested a more severe profile. The battle over goals and objectives had been partially successful, but the district had been prepared and cautious—the language was so general it could support a variety of conclusions.

The debate over Janet's communication needs was not going as the family had hoped. The district had agreed that the state school was arguably a better program, but there was no legal duty to provide the "best" education possible. The district was right and therefore it appeared necessary to prove some malfunctioning. During one of the breaks in testimony the Morrisons and their attorney walked in the modest, tree-lined residential area where the school offices were located. Raymond Morrison, determined, frustrated, asked in precise signs, "Why don't they understand that Janet should go to the state school because it is right for her? Why do we have to show that she is sick? She isn't sick."

Well she is and she isn't, the attorney thought, but upon such thoughts a legal argument begins the slide down a too-slippery slope. The attorney answered as he could, but chose not to discuss what LRE was doing to Janet's case. Like the tuberculosis strain that may have killed Ishi, the LRE preference seemed to be working inexorably to preclude Janet from "going back into the hills."

Dr. Thomas was a quiet witness; he was not like those who testify with fervor and appear to have more to say because of their intensity. He was a thin, small man in his thirties, clear in his own beliefs, but not particularly forceful in hammering them out. He spoke slowly, occasionally highlighting his testimony with half-signs, as though he were more comfortable conversing in both languages.

"I believe that Janet is developing psychological rigidity, a feeling of being hemmed in."

"Could you elaborate on what you mean by 'hemmed in'?"

"Well, it's difficult to say, but she feels, as indicated in her projective drawings, a sense of restriction, that her options are closing down. I believe this is directly related to the communicatively narrow educational environment."

"How so?"

"Children need a variety of language peers, they need a number of children who are about their age and who can communicate directly with them in their native language. The Commission on Education of the Deaf spoke of a 'critical mass.' Janet does not have that and is beginning to feel enclosed."

"How else is this restrictive environment manifesting itself?"

"She seems to gain more satisfaction from her internal world than her external world. She is more engaged with her internal communication and fantasies than with peer interaction. She also feels, I might add, that her language—sign language—is devalued by the world."

"Does she feel a part of the Midvale classroom?"

"She feels like an outsider and as a result she is avoiding emotional matters. She needs an environment in which she can be fluent in her language, can feel free to develop interpersonal relationships with her peers. That can only be done in a language-appropriate environment."

"Does this language deprivation impact on her cognitive development?"

"Yes. Peer interaction is a significant source of cognitive and social skill growth, particularly at Janet's age."

"How important is it that she be in a rich sign language environment?"

"Very important. The stronger the signing environment, the less communicatively disordered she becomes. Her present placement appears to be the opposite of what one would want to provide her, given her communication abilities."

"Did you visit her in the Midvale class?"

"Yes."

The district's attorney took copious notes as Dr. Thomas testified. She had carefully studied the testing protocol and the numbers Dr. Thomas came up with. Janet's attorney continued the direct examination.

"Is Midvale appropriate?"

"Considerating all of Janet's needs, including her communication needs, no."

"Thank you. Your witness."

The district's attorney looked up without emotion. She addressed Dr. Thomas in even tones.

"Tell me, Dr. Thomas, is Janet emotionally disturbed?"

"No."

"Is she linguistically behind?"

"What do you mean?"

"Sorry, is she able to communicate at an age-appropriate level?"

"Yes, she is an excellent signer."

"Have you reviewed her grades?"

"Yes."

"Is she progressing from grade to grade?"

"Yes, although. . . ."

"Thank you. Now let me get back to her emotional state. You indicated she felt hemmed in and that it related to the educational environment. How do you know that?"

"Well first I visited the class. I also spoke at length with Janet and her family. The tests I gave her suggested as much."

"Are some of those tests not adjusted for deaf children, that is, not normed?"

"That is true."

"Isn't it true that several of those tests provide no standard against which to determine whether the results are accurate?"

"Yes, but. . . ."

"Thank you. And it is your testimony that Janet is not emotionally disturbed?"

"Yes."

"Thank you."

The hearing officer took notes, checked the tape recorder. "Any further testimony from petitioners?" Janet's attorney nodded that he had more questions.

"Just a few more questions on re-direct. Dr. Thomas, you testified that Janet was not emotionally disturbed. How do you mean, emotionally disturbed?"

"Well I took the term as used by the district's attorney as normally understood by the layperson."

"I see. Could you elaborate on what you think Janet's emotional state is."

"She is not emotionally disturbed, but she is definitely showing signs that there may be real problems, and sooner than anybody thinks."

"How important is that she go to the state school?"

"Objection, that is a leading question."

"I'll rephrase. You indicated that you are concerned about a deterioration in her emotional state. What would you recommend to arrest that deterioration?"

"She needs placement, probably immediate, in a richer language environment. It is my understanding that the state school is the only place with such an environment."

"Thank you."

The district's attorney smiled and nodded toward Dr. Thomas. "Dr. Thomas, a few more questions on re-cross. Is Janet too young to go to the state school, to be separated from her family?"

"That is a hard question. One must weigh her significant language and cognitive and emotional needs against the obvious importance of remaining at home. I would add here that because the state school is a tradition in the deaf community and in particular here where the Morrisons themselves went to state schools, the separation would be different than for a hearing child."

"Are you saying that deaf children have different familial needs than hearing children?"

"Of course not."

"It sounds like it."

"It may sound like it, but the experiences of the deaf community in general and of the Morrisons in particular do play a role in lessening the negative effects of separation."

"There will be some negative effects then?"

"Yes, but I believe they are outweighed by the positive and necessary reasons."

"You believe. Thank you."

"Could I add one more thing?"

"No, I'm finished." The district's attorney turned and whispered something to the district's administrator.

Janet's attorney realized that Dr. Thomas' testimony was a mixed blessing, and even though he hated to ask a question for which he did not know the answer, he felt there was no choice. "What did you want to say, Dr. Thomas?"

"Objection."

"Yes, we seem through with this witness, counsel."

174

"I have just one more question."

"All right, but make it brief."

"Dr. Thomas, was there anything you wanted to add?"

The district's attorney frowned, but made no further objection.

"Yes I do. I find this all a bit confusing. Every child needs other children and teachers to communicate with. What could be more basic? There can be no education without it. Just think of the rich communication that floats about a classroom, the wonderful and myriad exchanges between students, the ongoing asides, the gossip, the arguments. Language is everywhere for a hearing child. It can be everywhere for a deaf child, but often we must look in different places. For Janet that place is the state school. You are truly restricting her at Midvale."

The district's attorney smiled at the answer. "That is a nice statement, Dr. Thomas, but I must bring you back to the core issue here. Is Janet emotionally disturbed?"

"No."

"Thank you."

---

The starkest proof that IDEA provides for and justifies exclusionary placement is at the "end" of the placement continuum—residential placement and hospitalization for children with severe physical or psychological problems. Each school district has an active duty to provide "alternative placements," including instruction at home, in hospitals and institutions.[2] By regulation, school districts are responsible for educational services and non-medical room and board for children placed in residential programs.[3]

In 1989-90, for example, approximately 70,000 students with disabilities were placed in some form of residential or hospital program. Another 240,000 were in other separate facilities. While a significant portion (25,000) of the residential-hospital population were children with "serious emotional" disturbances, there were many children with other disabilities who were removed and placed in so-called more restrictive environments. Approximately 26,000 children with learning disabilities were in separate facilities, while 4,600 were in residential, hospital, or homebound programs. Approximately 14,000 speech or language-impaired children were in separate facilities, while 1,873 were in residential, hospital, or homebound programs. Approximately 58,000 mentally retarded children were in separate facilities, while 9,921 were in residential, hospital, or homebound programs. One-third of the 9,254 visually impaired children were in separate facilities, including 2,600 in residential, hospital, or homebound programs.[4]

Residential and hospital placements often involve complex educational and psychiatric issues. The difficulties of applying the LRE mandate and analyzing the full inclusion and other similar movements are particularly illuminated when medical or psychiatric issues are involved, for as one judge noted early in the life of IDEA, the "social, emotional, medical, or educational" factors are "so intimately intertwined that realistically it is not possible for the Court to perform the Solomon-like task of separating them."[5]

Services that have a decidedly medical quality to them and which are required to maintain a child in a particular placement can raise nettlesome problems. Although IDEA does not require the provision of purely medical services, it does require "diagnostic" medical services and, more than that, medical services that can be provided by someone other than a doctor.[6] The United States Supreme Court in *Irving Independent School District v. Tatro*,[7] established the medical-nonmedical test to be used in special education matters. Amber Tatro had spina bifida, orthopedic and speech impairments, and a neurogenic bladder, which prevented her from voluntarily emptying her bladder. She could not attend school without the provision of an "accepted" medical practice, clean intermittent catheterization (CIC).

The court ruled that CIC was not subject to exclusion as a medical service as long as it was not provided by a licensed physician and could be administered by a layperson or nurse. The decision was significant for two reasons: First, it clarified an important related services issue and, by implication, stretched the requirements for assisting a child into a regular classroom. Second and conversely, it underscored the inherent complexities of placing a child with severe disabilities, and therefore the importance of alternative programs and placements.

A number of courts have addressed this issue, restricting or enlarging upon the *Tatro* rule and, as a result, LRE. In *Detsel v.Board of Education*,[8] intensive life support services necessary to maintain a child in school were ruled to be outside the related services mandate of IDEA even though they could be provided by a practical nurse rather than a physician. The court concluded that the provision of "extensive, therapeutic health services" was contrary to the medical services exclusion portion of IDEA. On the other hand, in *Max M. v. Thompson*,[9] the court ruled that simply because psychotherapy was provided by a psychiatrist (a physician), it was not necessarily an excluded service.

In *In the Matter of "A" Family*, "A" was schizophrenic, functionally retarded (with an intelligence quotient between 58 and 80), socially insecure, combative, and nervous.[10] In times of stress, "A" became disoriented, was regressive and self-destructive—he once cut himself with a razor blade and stood under a hot shower. His parents sought placement at Devereux Foundation in Santa Barbara, California, a private residential program. The central issue was whether "A's" schizophrenic condition required the provision of psychotherapy, a service that is not specifically mentioned in IDEA and *was* specifically prohibited by Montana law. The Montana Supreme Court ruled that while medical services were limited to purely diagnostic practices, "psychological" services were required and could include psychotherapy.

The court ruled that the federal regulations providing for psychological services, including psychotherapy, override state

177

regulations that exclude psychotherapy. "A" was therefore justifiably placed in a psychiatric treatment center in California. Services that certainly had a medical quality to them were required, and once required could mean that a school district had to place a child with disabilities in a distant and expensive program.

\*　　\*　　\*

The implications of psychiatric/medical special education cases for full inlcusion are evident. Can a psychotic student with violent tendencies who needs 24-hour psychiatric intervention be placed in a regular classroom? What of the child who relies on unique and complicated life support systems and professionals with highly specialized expertise? Even if money were not an issue, can such programs be duplicated in regular neighborhood schools?

In late 1991, a Massachusetts hearing officer ruled that a disabled child should be, as argued by his parents, placed in a hospital.[11] The school district proposed a less restrictive environment, in particular a 24-hour residential program.

Christopher K., 16 at the time of the dispute, was paralyzed from the chin down as the result of an automobile accident. He required frequent tracheal suctioning and monitoring and a positive pressure ventilator and diaphragmatic pacers so he could breathe. He used a sip and puff wheelchair for movement, had a history of seizures, and relied on others for virtually all life activities.

Christopher was a bright, friendly student who was emotionally stable. His academic skills were consistent with his age and grade level; he was bright and wanted to attend college. In many ways, Christopher represented the ultimate IDEA placement dilemma. He was not learning disabled, emotionally unstable, or communicatively restricted. He needed a "more restrictive" environment because of purely physical limitations.

The parties agreed that he required a 24-hour, integrated educational and "rehabilitative" program in which there were similarly situated age peers and life-sustaining medical intervention, including professionals who would recognize the signs of air hunger, hypothermia, and other distress. A registered nurse or respiratory therapist would have to be available at all times in case of equipment malfunction or other unforeseen difficulties. Christopher also needed a physician to be on call and able to perform emergency pneumothorax procedures.

The parties further agreed that the program at Massachusetts Hospital School (MHS) program met all of Christopher's needs, except for that of an on-site, 24-hour-a-day physician. MHS had been created to provide care and education for physically disabled children and was located on a large campus that served approximately 100 residential students and 30 day students, all of whom had physical disabilities requiring multiple therapies and environmental or technological adaptations. One hundred of the 104 students were in wheelchairs, approximately 15 were quadriplegic and several required mechanical ventilators. Each residential unit had a nurse's station. None of the students except Christopher required a positive pressure ventilator.

While MHS had use of three pediatric nurses and 3.5 full-time physicians, a special respiratory unit (with a 24-hour, seven-days-a-week physician), other nurses, respiratory therapists, technicians, and additional equipment were needed. The entire budget of MHS was $9.9 million; the new respiratory unit would cost about $1 million.

The hearing officer noted the "compassion, vigor and good humor" of all the parties, but correctly understood that the case "raised the difficult issues forming the sharp edge where the medical and educational models serving severely–disabled youngsters meet: resource management, medical ethics, personal responsibility, national health care regulation, the scope of educational services."[12]

The hearing officer concluded that MHS offered the least restrictive environment, as well as an appropriate educational placement for Christopher. Since the provision of related services, notably an on-duty physician, was crucial to MHS's appropriateness for Christopher, these services were not considered medical and were therefore necessary to provide Christopher with a FAPE. The hearing officer ruled that they all had a "rare opportunity to hold our government and our principles to close scrutiny, and to 'do the right thing.'"[13]

Although *Tewksbury* was an administrative case, it is important for many reasons, not the least of which is its ruling that an on-duty physician did not constitute a medical service. More to the point of the placement complexities of the law, it raised the question of removal to a fine degree. Nothing in the mainstreaming portion of the law trumped the need for Christopher to have an intense, nonintegrated placement.

While it seems untenable, given the professional staff and technology needed to serve Christopher, to suggest that sufficient funding could be shifted from MHS to the local program to "allow" for mainstreaming, one might ask, if full inclusion is intended to give all children with disabilities access to regular education, why not place Christopher into a mainstreamed program with all of the attendant support services, including the technology and pneumothorax doctors required?* Christopher had the necessary cognitive and intellectual skills to function in a regular classroom. He appeared to be at grade level and so his substantial needs involved "access" rather than educational remediation. While the cost of providing his needs was substantially greater than it was in the case of Raul Espino, the underlying issue was no different. Christopher needed to "get into" the classroom. But mainstreaming was not considered, and thus

---

* The question of exactly what is required in order to allow access to a regular classroom may not have a simple answer. As one federal court that ruled in favor of mainstreaming said, "A school district cannot be required to provide a handicapped child with his or her own full-time teacher, even if this would permit the child to be satisfactorily educated in a regular classroom." Greer v. Rome City School District, 950 F.2d 688, 697 (11th Cir. 1991).

*Tewksbury* stands for a viable hospital placement (and regular classroom removal) under IDEA's placement rules.

The medical-nonmedical debate and its relationship to placement is no easier for the *Tewksbury* decision than it is for any other. Two California hospitalization decisions reveal both the "segregating" portion of IDEA and the manner in which arbitrary distinctions are made regarding severely troubled children. In *Clovis Unified School District v. California Office of Administrative Hearings*,[14] Michelle Shorey was placed in Kings View, an acute care psychiatric hospital in Central California. Michelle had a long history of mental health problems, including destructive and deteriorating behaviors, which directly affected her ability to benefit from her education. Michelle's school district proposed placement in a diagnostic school at a cost of $50,000 a year. The family sought placement at Kings View at a cost of $150,000 a year.

The legal debate in *Clovis* centered on whether intensive psychiatric services were medical or nonmedical in nature and whether these services were needed to facilitate Michelle's education. Clearly the issue was not whether Michelle should be included in a regular class, but exactly how "restrictive" her program would be.

The Ninth Circuit ruled that since Michelle was hospitalized for primarily medical (psychiatric) reasons and was provided with services by licensed physicians, the institution was noneducational in nature and therefore the school district was not responsible for the cost of such a "medical" placement. The diagnostic school was sufficient. Since Michelle was being treated for an underlying medical crisis, she did not qualify for placement at Kings View under IDEA. The court rejected the notion that the medical services at Kings View were "supportive" of Michelle's education and therefore related services under IDEA:

> If a child requires, for example, ear surgery to improve his hearing, he may learn better after a successful operation and therefore in some respects his surgery is "supportive" of his

181

education, but a school district is certainly not responsible for his treatment. Similarly, a child who must be maintained on kidney dialysis certainly cannot physically benefit from education to the extent that such services are necessary to keep him alive, but again, it is not the responsibility of the school district to provide such maintenance care.... 'If [a schizophrenic child] had not been medically treated, she would have been unable to take advantage of and receive any benefit from her education, but the same would apply to any illness'.... All medical services are arguably 'supportive' of a handicapped child's education; therefore mere 'supportiveness' is too broad a criterion to be the test for whether a specific service is necessary under the Act to assist a child to benefit from special education.[15]

The court also rejected the notion that the intertwining of medical and educational problems requiring hospitalization created a mandate to place and pay. The key question, according to the *Clovis* court, was whether placement was primarily educational or medical.

The *Clovis* decision involved an interesting distinction between psychiatric illnesses and psychological disabilities. Is schizophrenia inherently different from autism or depression or moodiness or learning disabilities or blindness or physical disabilities? Did it really matter *why* Michelle was placed when she had significant emotional problems that affected her educational experience? Is the line between "psychiatric" and "psychological" justified? While there may be a philosophical or even scientific distinction, it may be that cost is the ultimate concern; courts are reluctant to require schools to pay for costly psychiatric or medical services. Perhaps the *Clovis* case turned on the $100,000 difference between the Kings View placement and the diagnostic school. After all, the school district offered placement in a restrictive and intense residential program.

The Ninth Circuit took a decidedly different approach to its *Clovis* decision in *Taylor v. Honig*.[16] Todd Taylor was a seriously emotionally disturbed child who required special education services, including psychotherapy and monitoring of his medication. Todd had been arrested for assaulting his family and had spent approximately two months in juvenile hall. His IEP called for long-term residential placement, but specifically ruled out a state hospital program.

The family wanted Todd placed in San Marcos Treatment Center, a comprehensive psychiatric facility located in Texas. A due process hearing officer ruled that because Todd's social, emotional, medical and educational needs were not severable, he needed a 24-hour residential placement in which there was psychotherapy, a psychiatrist on call to prescribe and monitor anti-depressants, and a nurse on the premises to check Todd's somatic complaints.

The Ninth Circuit Court of Appeals, in ruling for placement at San Marcos, distinguished the case from *Clovis* by noting that Todd, unlike Michelle, was considered "medically stable." Michelle's problems were acute, while Todd's were apparently somewhat less severe. In addition, the *Taylor* court concluded that San Marcos, unlike Kings View, was primarily an educational institution. These factors apparently justified the distinction between the needs of the two students and between a condition that justified IDEA responsibility and one that did not.

Nonetheless, the distinction between the *Taylor* and *Clovis* decisions is not entirely clear. What of the differences between institutions? Both Kings View and San Marcos had psychiatric personnel involved in the treatment of the two students. Is it enough that one was psychiatric in nature and the other provided psychiatric support services and personnel? Since state and federal law requires that children in hospitals be provided educational services and programs, the question then becomes, at least for the courts, What is the "sole" or "primary" purpose of placement?

What of the distinction between "disabling" conditions? Does it matter, for example, that Michelle had an acute psychiatric problem that generated the need for placement while Todd appeared to have secondary psychiatric needs? Both needed psychotherapy; Todd secondarily needed a licensed physician to monitor medication, while Michelle needed significant psychiatric assistance. The Ninth Circuit created a quantitative distinction, not necessarily insignificant, but still one of degrees.

Federal law defines a child as being "seriously emotionally disturbed" if that child exhibits, "over a long period of time and to a marked degree," one or more of the following characteristics, to the point that they "adversely affect a child's educational performance:

> An inability to learn, which cannot be explained by intellectual, sensory, or health factors . . .
>
> An inability to build or maintain satisfactory interpersonal relationships with peers and teachers . . .
>
> Inappropriate types of behavior or feelings under normal circumstances . . .
>
> A general pervasive mood of unhappiness or depression; or
>
> A tendency to develop physical symptoms or fears associated with personal or school problems.[17]

This definition not only affects a determination of eligibility, but may directly affect where on the "continuum" the child is placed. How does one determine whether a child's educational performance is adversely affected by emotional characteristics? What of the child who is unable to relate to peers but who receives passing grades? What of the child who is inappropriately aggressive with other students? What of the child who is so deeply depressed that it is difficult to determine exactly how that affects his or her grades or general classroom performance? Should Michelle Shorey even qualify for special education? How should these questions be evaluated in light of the central question of appropriate placement and least restrictive environment?

According to *Rowley,* the mental difficulties experienced by children are irrelevant if those children pass from grade to grade.

Has the *Rowley* decision skewed our analysis of what education should be or is it right on point in requiring a simple focus on grade advancement? If, on the other hand, one accepts the *Daniel R.* and *Holland* rationales that education is more than academics, then a child with psychological difficulties must be served regardless of whether or not the mental illness affects academic advancement.

Other courts have viewed residential placement and serious emotional disturbances with a similar diversity of opinion. In *Ahern v. Board of Education*,[18] for example, a trainably mentally retarded child had congenital heart abnormalities, a hearing loss, and speech and visual problems. While she made educational progress as a young child, by the time she reached adolescence she began to demonstrate significant psychological problems, which were described as "borderline psychotic defenses of withdrawal into fantasy."[19]

The emotional difficulties were traceable to her home environment and the need for more peer interaction and stimulation after school. The psychiatrist in the case concluded that the child needed a constant, safe, supportive environment to maintain her grasp on reality and to even begin to cope with the world around her. The school district contended that such difficulties were common among their students, and that the child was making some academic progress. The district court ruled against residential placement, noting that the child's emotional problems were easily separated from her learning process.

What is the nexus between the "disabling" condition and service or placement mandates? Is the child in the *Ahern* case any different from Amber Tatro or Michelle Shorey? The provision of clean, intermittant catheterization for Amber Tatro was not necessary for her to learn, but for her to be physically in the classroom. Amy Rowley may not have needed the interpreter to achieve adequately (although there was evidence she could achieve more), but simply to be able to be in the classroom. The child who has a physical disability may need physical therapy to improve mobility, but not to be a better student. How is it that the child in *Ahern* had no less a need for access?

Taking the long view, these distinctions become less discernable. It may be that the real question is what specific responsibilities does society have to its children? Drawing the line between *Clovis* and *Taylor* is arbitrary, but may be necessary to staunch the flow of public monies for expensive and complex services, assuming society determines that such expenditures are indeed excessive. It may be that school districts can rightfully say (emotionally, if not legally) that they are not responsible for the psychological problems that they did not create. Perhaps it may simply be best to acknowledge the "determinative" and significant cost factors, rather than rely on a kind of jerry-built distinction between an acutely psychiatric child and one whose psychiatric problems are less severe.

34 C.F.R. § 300.7(a)(g) provides that a "serious emotional disturbance" may include, among other things, pervasive moods of unhappiness and an inability to build friendships. This is certainly language that offers a broad rather than narrow view of the particular disabling condition.[20] Does the law require that school districts provide for all manner of personality disorders? What of the distinction between traditional emotional disturbances and behavioral or antisocial personalities? In [ ] *v. Sequoia Union High School District*,[21] an implusive student who was involved in the punk subculture and who was manipulative, socially maladjusted, and truant, was found not to have a "disability" under Section 300.5(b)(8). The student's parent had placed her at a private residential program at a cost of $36,000 a year, which had proven to be "extremely helpful." The court found the distinction between "depression" and an "identity disorder" significant, the former placing the student outside the eligibility standard. The court also concluded that a decline in grades had to do with truancy and not disability.

Whether falling grades are caused by depression (an eligibility criterion) or an identity disorder (not a criterion), seems less than compelling. Is one a psychological difficulty and the other not? What of the brilliant but psychotic child who earns appropriate grades but is unable to relate socially to the educational experience? Perhaps the line should be drawn between the depressed child and the behaviorally maladjusted. But to the extent that the line is there, it seems to rest on a gut feeling that something like depression is beyond the student's control, while truancy or an antisocial outlook is willful in nature. Whether that justifies the distinction is another matter.

*     *     *

The residential-hospitalization portion of IDEA reveals several things. There are children with disabilities whose needs are so intense that the question is no longer whether additional resources in regular classrooms or schools are needed, but rather that "removal" to a so-called more restrictive placement is appropriate and required by the law. The full inclusion of some children is more than problematic.

When it comes to costly placement issues, it appears that need (and even eligibility) may become decidedly noneducational. Removal and determination of LRE are affected by how school districts and courts view the general responsibility of the system. Some are loathe to see that responsibility go beyond traditional notions of schooling. Removal is no longer at issue; the debate is whether the school system is responsible for that removal.

With removal sanctioned by IDEA and the argument to be made that separate placements are both necessary and LRE, the inclusion paradox is no longer one of simple ethics; it is not possible to reduce the debate to one of immoral "segregation" versus moral inclusion. There is no clear integration/segregation dichotomy.

In *Teague Independent School District v. Todd L.*,[22] the U.S. Court of Appeals for the Fifth Circuit ruled against a residential placement and referred to the "restrictions" placed on the child's "liberty" if removed from the "home environment."[23] The court noted that IDEA was intended to redress a long history of discrimination against disabled children; the "isolation" of a child violated IDEA.

Such an analysis clearly applied to Todd L. and Rachel Holland, as it should to many children, but not to Janet Morrison or Michelle Shorey. For Janet in particular, the closer she came to a legal "less restrictive environment" (home school) the greater her isolation became. Whether Christopher K. could have been mainstreamed is a complex matter; it was not enough to say that sufficient resources would have accomplished it.

The full inclusion plan to integrate all children into regular home schools must address the intense needs of Michelle Shorey and others like her. The unitary system proposed by the full inclusion movement would have "regular education adjusted to meet all students' needs . . . [with] all students educated in the mainstream of regular education."[24] Exactly why and how Michelle Shorey or Christopher K. or Janet Morrison would be placed into a regular program is a question not answered by any of the proponents of generic full inclusion.

# Endnotes

1.   *See* A.L. Kroeber, Handbook of the Indians of California, 343-44 (1953).

2.   34 C.F.R. § 300.551(b)(1) (1993).

3.   34 C.F.R. § 300.302 (1993).

4.   U.S. Dep't of Educ., Fourteenth Annual Report to Congress on the Implementation of IDEA, at A-54-77 (1992).

5.   North v. District of Columbia Bd. of Educ., 471 F. Supp. 136 (D.D.C. 1979), 1979-80 EHLR 551:157, 160.

6.   20 U.S.C. § 1401(a)(17) (West Supp. 1994).

7.   468 U.S. 883 (1984), 1983-84 EHLR 555:511.

8.   637 F. Supp. 1022, 1027 (N.D.N.Y. 1986), *aff'd*, 820 F.2d 587 (2d Cir. 1986).

9.   592 F. Supp. 1437, 1444 (N.D. Ill. 1984).

10.  1979-80 EHLR 551:345 (Mont. 1979).

11.  Tewksbury Public Schools, No. 89-1843 (Mass. State Ed. Agency Hearing, Aug. 7, 1991), 17 IDELR 1221.

12.  17 IDELR at 1226.

13.  17 IDELR at 1232.

14.  903 F.2d 635 (9th Cir. 1990).

15.  *Id.* at 643.

16.  910 F.2d 627 (9th Cir. 1990).

17.  34 C.F.R. § 300.7(a)(9) (1993)

18.  593 F. Supp. 902, 906 (D. Del. 1984), 1984-85 EHLR 556:175.

19.  593 F. Supp. at 906, 1984-85 EHLR at 177.

20.  34 C.F.R. § 300.7(a)(9) (1993).

21.  No. C.85-4426 EFL (N.D. Cal. 1987), 1987-88 EHLR 559:133.

22.  999 F.2d 127, 132 (5th Cir. Aug. 31, 1993), 20 IDELR 259, 262.

23.  *Id.*

24.  Alan Gartner & Dorothy Kerzner Lipsky, National Center on Education and the Economy, The Yoke of Special Education—How to Break It 26 (1989).

189

# 7

---

# Centralized Programs

---

Janet Morrison, her father, and their attorney walked east from the Morrison home to a small shopping center. Janet and her father signed quickly about the day's events, about minor matters of the home, about the possibility of buying candy at the store, and about how that might work if it were true that Janet did not have any cash.

They occasionally stopped along the way, slowed down their walking pace as a way of slowing down their signing so the attorney might be more involved. He was reluctant to ask them to repeat what they signed. Janet would stop and ask him whether he knew the name of the family dog, whether his car was new or old, and finally whether he had any opinion about candy. She was already seeking out free legal advice.

As they walked, those around them—other pedestrians, drivers, children—paused to watch a deaf man and a deaf child. Janet and her father were in their own natural language environment and quite comfortable; the attorney, on the other hand, thought the staring rude. Later, Raymond would tell the attorney a story about a time when his family had been in a local restaurant. It was Betty's birthday and they had enjoyed themselves, signing rapidly about everything and only partially aware of the frowning hearing couple near them. A deaf friend had come in, and when she noticed the Morrisons she came over and greeted them warmly and with great animation. This was apparently too much for the couple; one of them stood and called the manager over and demanded that the Morrisons be removed. They were, she said, invading her privacy, ruining her dinner with her husband. The manager tried to calm the woman, but she was angry and the manager asked the Morrisons if they were done. Raymond knew this scenario too well. He told the manager that they were not done, and he asked that the waiter come over for a dessert order. The couple demanded a refund and when the manager refused, the woman took the bill, threw it on the Morrisons' table, and left.

The shopping center was worn and debris flew about in tiny wind swirls. Few cars were parked in the small lot—the center had been built long before covered malls defined collective shopping practices. Janet and her father seemed not to notice. There was milk, coffee, beer, and perhaps even candy to secure for the night.

The convenience store was empty and Janet went straight to the candy counter. The clerk was an older, beefy man. The attorney stood nearby as Raymond Morrison gathered up the supplies. Janet weighed a Snickers bar against jelly beans. The clerk coughed.

"Honey, you gotta make a big decision here."

There was no emotion to the man, it was hard to tell whether Janet irritated or amused him, whether he saw in her an innocent, or a potential shoplifter, or just one more child who would squeeze a candy bar that she would not pay for. Janet did not look up.

"What do you say, honey?"

Janet continued to study the candy. The attorney watched uncomfortably.

"Sweetie, you deaf?"

The attorney nodded.

"No shit?"

"Yes, she's deaf. She wasn't being rude."

"She's cute. How's she talk?"

At that moment Raymond came to the counter, tapped Janet on the shoulder. She looked up at her father and then signed, "Please?" He frowned and signed, "Not now, later." A father's futile effort at avoidance. She signed, "Please?" again. He signed, "No," and for a moment they argued.

"Say, that's sign language?"

"Yes."

"Tell him to let her have one piece of candy."

Raymond looked up at the man and then over to the attorney.

"He said that Janet should have a piece of candy," the attorney signed slowly.

Raymond signed to the counter man, "Why?"

"Huh?"

Before the attorney could answer, Raymond spoke in a husky, strained voice, "No candy for her now." The counter man looked to the attorney, not entirely sure what Raymond had said.

"He doesn't want her to have any candy."

"Oh hell, here honey, take the candy. It's on me."

Janet took the candy, while Raymond frowned and then added, in a louder voice, "No candy for her."

"What did he say?"

"NO CANDY. NO." Raymond's voice was flat, a contrast to the fluid beauty of his signing.

Raymond paid for the milk, beer, and coffee. He caught Janet outside and pushed her back into the store. He signed to her rapidly. She handed the man the candy and turned and left. The counter man began to speak to Raymond, but he did not hear and left the store to chase Janet home.

*   *   *

The county superintendent answered the district's attorney's questions without affect. He was a man in his sixties, serious and distant. There was nothing lighthearted about this conflict. He had a clear understanding of what was right and what was wrong.

"I am co-chair of the statewide LRE task force. We have studied the issue in great detail."

"What has the task force concluded about LRE?"

"That we have a legal and moral duty to mainstream disabled children; that federal and state law require placing these children in the least restrictive environment."

"Are you familiar with the state school for the deaf?"

"Yes."

"Has your task force drawn any conclusions about the state school for the deaf?"

"Well, yes we have. I might add that there are two state schools for the deaf, one in southern California and one here in the northern portion of the state. A representative from the state school was on the task force. We recognized the state school as a viable option, but also acknowledged that it is a restrictive environment."

"How so?"

"Objection."

The Morrisons' attorney paused. He had studied the superintendent and concluded that he would not likely be budged; this was a man who knew what he believed, believed it without reservation, and viewed questioning of his beliefs as a waste of time. The Morrisons' attorney thought about the man at the convenience store, about the restaurant story Raymond had recounted, how hearing people viewed people who could not hear, what they thought when they saw people using their hands to communicate and doing so with energy and pleasure. The attorney decided, without proof, that the superintendent had no more understanding of Janet Morrison than the convenience store clerk.

"What is the basis of your objection, counselor?"

"This witness is not a lawyer or a legal expert and therefore cannot testify as to what the law says."

The district's attorney interjected, "Of course he can. He administers these laws and understands them as an administrator, not as a lawyer. I'm willing to acknowledge that."

"Thank you both. I'll overrule the objection. Continue."

"The question was, how is the state school restrictive?"

"It is farthest from the home, it has the fewest opportunities for interaction between deaf and nondeaf. State law also requires, I might add, that we cannot place a child in the state school unless the IEP team finds that the local school cannot provide an 'appropriate' program. We have an appropriate program for this child and so the state school is most restrictive."

"Why is it important that a student be in a local program and exposed to non-disabled children?"

"The task force believes, and I support this point of view, that disabled children need to be in normal environments, need to be exposed to normal children. They learn normal behaviors, they model and develop this way. Deaf children will become part of the hearing world. They cannot become part of the hearing world unless they have this exposure. Thus the law and good sense dovetail. We insist that our children have this opportunity and are sent to the state school only when no other options exist."

"Thank you. Your witness."

The Morrisons' attorney stood and faced the witness.

"Superintendent, do you know Janet Morrison?"

"By name only."

"Do you know sign language?"

"No."

"Have you ever taught deaf children?"

"No."

"On what do you base your conclusion that deaf children can become part of the hearing world only if they are exposed to it at this age?"

"Well, first I would say common sense. Second, I would point out that this is a hearing world, with a small percentage of the population having a hearing loss. It is not the other way around. Finally, one cannot live his or her life forever in the safety of an insular existence. We do a disservice to deaf children if we do not prepare them for that majority world."

"I see. Do you view deaf children as having pathological characteristics?"

"Objection. What is the point here?"

"Let me rephrase. Is there something wrong with deaf children?"

"They can't hear."

"Are they unable to communicate?"

"Well, some cannot."

"But as a general proposition?"

"They have alternatives; whether those alternatives are viable or not is the question."

"Is that the question?"

"There is no reason to soft-pedal this issue. These children are not able to communicate with the hearing world and this is to their detriment."

"Is it they who cannot communicate, or is it the hearing world."

"That is specious."

"Is it?"

"Of course it is. They are the minority. The hearing world is the norm and, at the very least, sets the standards."

"Would you agree, though, that both worlds are able to communicate, they simply cannot always communicate with each other?"

"Yes, and at the same time I would say you are missing the point. Janet Morrison must live in the hearing world."

"If that is so, how is it that exposure to a rich, continuously accessible communication environment in which she has peers to communicate with will prevent her from living in the hearing world?"

"Common sense."

"Common sense?"

"Of course. Consider this, counselor. For a long time we were criticized for not educating our disabled children, and if we did educate them, it was not in the regular environment. We took a beating for that. And now we are trying earnestly to meet our responsibilities and then you come along and suggest that this goal of openness and inclusion is not right. Make up your mind."

"Do you feel that the goal of inclusion is incompatible with the goal of appropriateness?"

"You can't include and exclude at the same time."

"Can you offer different options for different children?"

"Yes, but the law wants us to put these children in less restrictive environments. That's what we're doing, and that's what we will continue to do."

"Whether they can communicate in those environments or not?"

"I won't answer that. We took heat for keeping these kids at home or in dilapidated buildings, or off in some hospital, and now when we try something else, that is a good thing."

"Superintendent, I am not sure we are going to see eye to eye on this. We may simply have different perspectives. Janet Morrison does not need a hospital placement, but a school where she can communicate with her friends."

"Well, as far as I'm concerned, placement in the state school for the deaf is like placement in a hospital."

"Thank you."

"One more thing counselor." The superintendent was not finished.

"I have no more questions."

"I'll re-direct," the district's attorney said.

"This has gone on long enough counselor, just one more question." The hearing officer motioned to the district's attorney to be brief.

"You had a final comment, superintendent?"

"Yes, we have hundreds of disabled children in this county. They range from learning disabled to deaf to emotionally disturbed to autistic, to those in wheelchairs, to anorexic, to behaviorally troubled. Within each group are odd mixtures of age and ability levels. We have large *and* small school districts—in remote parts of the county, there may be one disabled child. We can't individualize for each child. Sometimes they must be placed in central programs that better serve a large number of children. I can't guarantee a perfect, individual program for each child. Sometimes the emotionally disturbed child must be with the retarded child. Sometimes the language-delayed class must include a wider variety of kids. Sometimes Janet Morrison can't go to the state school but must attend a central program. We can't be all things to all people."

Janet's attorney interrupted, "Superintendent, isn't the whole purpose of IDEA to provide 'individualized' attention—the program must fit the child, not the other way around?"

"Not that individual, counselor. Janet Morrison is going to have to adjust. That's the way the world works."

The superintendent gathered up his papers, stood, and then strode out of the hearing without further comment or pause.

---

IDEA, with its "FAPE," "removal" and "continuum" requirements, encourages nonintegrated programs for reasons of mere practicality. Not infrequently children with disabilities are placed in centrally located, homogenous programs to save resources and make better use of budget dollars, as well as for reasons of convenience and educational purpose. It is better, the argument goes, to bring 10 children from 10 separate school districts where 10 special aides would be necessary, to one program where only one aide would be necessary. If the special education structure is changed and the continuum ended, the structural and financial consequences will be far-reaching.

In October 1992, Judith Heumann's predecessor, Robert Davila, issued policy guidelines regarding the placement of deaf children in the United States.[1] The U.S. Department of Education concluded that central programs had distinct advantages for some deaf children, that communication needs should define placement (not the other way around), and that what might be ostensibly less restrictive for some (the regular classroom), might be more restrictive than a central program. Full inclusion turned on its head; the appropriateness of removal becomes the imperative to centralize. Rachel Holland and Janet Morrison passing each other as one returns to and the other leaves the neighborhood school.

\*　　\*　　\*

Michael Barnett, a profoundly deaf high school student, had been in special education since the first grade and used cued speech to communicate.[2] Cued speech is a method for clarifying phonetic uncertainties in spoken language by using eight hand shapes held in four positions close to the mouth.\* Fairfax County School Board—Michael's school district—offered three "hearing-impaired" programs in the jurisdiction, including a cued speech program at Annandale High School. There was no cued speech program or class in his home school.

During his freshman and sophomore years at Annandale, Michael was fully mainstreamed with the assistance of a cued speech interpreter. He also received daily support from a certified teacher of the hearing impaired and speech and language therapy several times a week. Michael excelled both academically and athletically at Annandale.

---

\* A good portion of the deaf community opposes systemic integration, while a large segment of the cued speech community is philosophically aligned with the full inclusion movement. Michael Barnett and Janet Morrison were both profoundly deaf, but that may be the only thing they had in common. Their parents' views on how and where to educate them could not have been more in opposition.

Michael's family agreed that the cued speech program at Annandale was appropriate but contended that he was entitled to attend his home school, West Springfield High School, which was five miles closer to his home than Annandale. After losing an administrative hearing, Michael's parents appealed to court, seeking placement at West Springfield with the requisite support services, and $100,000 in compensatory damages. The district court ruled in favor of the board (and therefore the Annandale program) and granted a motion to strike the family's claim for monetary damages. The court of appeals affirmed.

The placement implications of the case were significant as reflected in the list of amici curiae: Association for Retarded Citizens of the United States (ARC),* the Paralyzed Veterans of America, United Cerebral Palsy Associations, the National Council of Independent Living, the Disability Rights Education and Defense Fund (DREDF), Schools Are For Everyone (SAFE) and the Association for Persons with Severe Handicaps (TASH).

Plaintiffs (and amici curiae) contended that the board's "unspoken" policy of "categorically placing at Annandale all high school handicapped students using the cued speech method violates" the law's requirement that each IEP be individually designed.[3] The school district contended that there were educational, financial, and resource allocation factors justifying the centralization of programs. The "low incidence" nature of deafness and the stress on the system to individualize the program for every deaf cued-speech student was a telling factor. The district court stated and the court of appeals agreed that:

> The Cued Speech program is . . . utilized by a small number of students drawn not merely from Fairfax County, but from the entire Northern Virginia area.

---

* ARC issued the "Report Card to the Nation on Inclusion in Education of Students with Mental Retardation," which revealed the statistically dismal national inclusive effort. *See* Chapter 2.

The program has been established at a network of centrally-located elementary, intermediate, and high schools in order to maximize scarce economic and human resources, particularly qualified interpreters.[4]

In addition, the court noted that:

The school system can and must consider the effect of providing a specialized program to one student at his base school upon the rights of other similarly-situated students to demand the same treatment. There are presently at least 78 other hearing impaired students who have or will use interpreters. Were an exception made for Michael, these other students would also expect that they be provided with their own interpreter at their respective base schools. The school system could not provide individual interpreters for each student at his or her base school.[5]

The district court added that having all interpreters, teachers, therapists, and students together in an ongoing program allows staff interaction, accessibility, and provides much greater cohesiveness.[6]

For both courts, the availability of one comprehensive program that served 78 students, as opposed to the possibility of individually serving and paying for those students in 78 different settings, was crucial. But theoretically, at least, should the cost of providing 78 individual interpreters be a factor? What constitutes an excessive expenditure? For the parent of a child with disabilities, is there any cost too prohibitive for that child to attend the school he or she would attend if not "disabled?" What matter that there are other 77 other children who might assert an individual right to a cued speech interpreter at each of their home schools?

But theory rarely ventures where budgets live. And so, not surprisingly, the *Barnett* courts were persuaded that cost justified centralization; the right to regular-home school placement was trumped by service-resource factors.*

Interestingly enough, the law does not provide an explicit budgetary "out." IDEA requires the provision of a "free" education, at "public expense . . . and without charge. . . ."[7] Related services are those "developmental, corrective, and other supportive services" as "may be required to assist a child with a disability [to] benefit from special education. . . ."[8] The LRE mandate precludes "removal" unless it is shown that the child cannot achieve satisfactorily in the regular classroom even with the use of supplementary aids and services.[9] Michael Barnett excelled with cued speech assistance—there was no evidence that he could not achieve satisfactorily at West Springfield with the provision of supplementary aids and services.

Nonetheless, the *Barnett* courts concluded that the Annandale program met mainstreaming requirements. The court of appeals found that the laudable mainstreaming "requirement" of the law was satisfied, since Michael was mainstreamed, and particularly because Section 300.552 did not impose "upon a school board an absolute obligation to place a child in his base school."[10]

The court ruled that IDEA did not require a duplication of the cued speech program for one student merely because there existed a high school that was slightly closer to his house, or one he would rather attend. A five-mile difference was not significant to the court, especially when weighed against the potential cost of providing 77 other individual home programs. Rather, the school board was required only to evaluate geographical proximity as one factor in making placement decisions. The special needs of a child must be balanced against the "competing interests of economic necessity."[11]

---

* It also considered the dispute to be one of methodology, a matter courts are usually reluctant to address. The court was unwilling to adopt the plaintiffs' position, which would require the court to intrude upon educational policy choices that Congress consciously left to state and local school officials. Where

Whether Section 300.552 is as flexible as the *Barnett* courts concluded is another matter. Section 300.552 does include qualifying language: the child will be educated "as close as possible" to the child's home and in the school that he or she would attend if not disabled unless "some other arrangement" is required. But IDEA, when providing leeway to school districts, tends to be much more expansive than Section 300.552. Consider Section 300.532, which provides that evaluation materials shall be administered in the child's native language "unless it is clearly not *feasible* to do so," or Section 300.17, which defines special education as "specially designed education" to meet the "unique" needs of the child. Terms like "feasible," "specially designed," and "unique" provide school districts with a great deal of room in which to move.

Of the two Section 300.552 directives, the "close as possible" requirement is softer—it gives a school district a world of room to operate in. The mere five miles separating Annandale and West Springfield may have greatly affected the way the judges viewed the reach of Section 300.552. The qualifier could be two blocks, two miles, or 20 miles; either one could be "as close to home *as possible*."

The requirement to place a student in the "school which he or she would attend if not handicapped" is a bit trickier for the court—there doesn't seem to be as much wiggle room there. A school either is or is not the "home" school. West Springfield was the home school, Annandale was not. What then would be the "other arrangement" justifying removal to Annandale: cost, centralization, comprehensive programs? Michael was achieving satisfactorily, and thus what other "removal" factors apply? Perhaps Michael's IEP could have been read to mean that the need for cued speech was the "other arrangement" that trumped the home school requirement, but the regulatory language does not

---

a particular service will be or how a method of teaching is used should be determined by school officials, not judges.

say that. It appears that it was the school district that required some other arrangement; there is no evidence that Michael did. The law provides rights for the student, not the school district.

Ultimately the court could not justify forcing a school district to replicate one program at West Springfield and establish a rationale for 77 other individual programs. What if the home school was two blocks from Michael's home and the centralized program was 18 miles away? Is actual distance irrelevant since there is only one school the child would attend if not disabled? Is the importance of attending one's home school any less important or even different than the right to attend a mainstreamed program?* Whether the distinctions and rulings are fair or statutorily justified, it is clear that the *Barnett* decision stands squarely for the proposition that there are administrative and resource justifications for denying placement at one's home school.

\*    \*    \*

The United States Court of Appeals for the Seventh Circuit in *Lachman v. Illinois State Board of Education*,[12] concluded, as the *Barnett* courts did, that the mainstreaming preference was not an unqualified right and that administrative needs could be factored into the consideration of placement decisions.

Seven-year-old Benjamin Lachman, like Amy Rowley, Michael Barnett, and Janet Morrison, was an intelligent, profoundly deaf student who did not need extensive additional services. The family wanted Benjamin placed in his neighborhood school

---

* Peer availability often comes up in disputes over centralized programs. For Janet Morrison, the centrally located Midvale program pulled in most of the deaf children in the large county. That the age, ability and language ranges were wide reflects how difficult it is to provide what the Commission on Education of the Deaf called the important "critical mass." To the extent that it was important, there was no way Michael's district could provide a full peer group (all of whom used cued speech) in his home school, unless of course the other cued speech children were willing to move to Michael's home school. The availability of other cued speech peers was apparently not significant for Michael. He was very oral and thus most of his peers were "non-disabled."

in a regular classroom and provided with a full-time cued speech instructor. The school district proposed to place Benjamin in a self-contained classroom with other hearing-impaired children in a school outside of his neighborhood. The district's program used total communication, a combination of sign language, speech reading and reliance on other visual clues. Cued speech was not part of the total communication process, although the district did propose that cued speech be used as necessary to help Benjamin move into the total communication program.

The fair hearing state review officer ruled that the district's proposal was appropriate. The federal district court dismissed the *Lachman* appeal and the federal court of appeals affirmed that dismissal. The courts found that the more "segregated" placement, the regional program that provided total communication, was sufficient to meet Benjamin Lachman's needs; the district had no responsibility to provide a cued speech or total communication program in Benjamin's home school. The need to centralize and save resources trumped inclusion.

The *Lachman* court referred to the more narrow *Rowley* vision of IDEA:

> The purpose of the Act was to open the doors of public education to handicapped children ... rather than to guarantee any particular substantive level of education once the child was enrolled. The Act does not require a state to maximize the potential of each child commensurate with the opportunity provided non-handicapped children.[13]

A review of case law revealed, according to the *Lachman* judges, that the "mainstreaming preference was not meant by Congress to be implemented in an unqualified manner."[14] Rather, Congress intended that the mainstreaming preference is to "be given effect *only* when it is clear that the education of the particular handicapped child can be achieved satisfactorily in the type of mainstream environment sought by the *challengers* to the IEP proposed for that child."[15]

This was one of the strongest judicial statements limiting placement rights under IDEA. It was a double blow; the *Lachman* court seemed neither inclined toward mainstreaming as an important option nor much concerned with a child's right to "start" in a regular class. The *Lachman* court turned the mainstreaming mandate on its head—the parent must prove the need for such placement. The removal burden was no longer on the district.

The *Lachman* court did not view placement rights expansively:

> we must establish the nature of the mainstreaming obligation created by section 1412(5)(B) and clarify the *relationship of that statutory language to the general section 1412(1) requirement that handicapped children be provided with a free appropriate public education.*

> The degree to which a challenged IEP satisfies the mainstreaming goal of EAHCA simply cannot be evaluated in the abstract. Rather, that laudable policy objective must be weighed in tandem with the Act's principle goal of ensuring that the public schools provide handicapped children with a free appropriate education.[16]

This was a provocative read on the law. The first and perhaps most defensible notion offered by the *Lachman* court was that the mainstreaming goal was considered in tandem with the Act's principle aim—providing an appropriate education. The *Roncker* decision with more ballast on the "appropriateness" side; appropriateness as equal to regular education placement.

For the court, placement was merely a matter of disputed methodology: the primary justification for a mainstreamed placement in this case rested squarely on the plaintiffs' belief in and preference for cued speech. The issue of mainstreaming was encompassed within the parties dispute over methodology. And under *Rowley* determination of methodology was left to the school authorities.

Despite the court's strong focus on methodology, it is not entirely clear that IDEA supported the court's conclusion. The

Lachmans thought their child should attend a regular class in his neighborhood school and needed cued speech to facilitate that placement. The issue then was not one of disputed methodology, but rather a question of whether he needed cued speech (or, for that matter, total communication) as a support service in order to achieve satisfactorily in the regular environment. Notwithstanding the court's ruling, the law places the burden on the school district to show that even with such services he could not so achieve and therefore was not entitled to placement with non-disabled children to the maximum extent appropriate. The *Lachman* court made regular placement a privilege to be earned, rather than a right to be protected. In creating this kind of restricted legal overview, the *Lachman* court seemed to have gone beyond the core purpose of IDEA. And while *Holland* neutralized some of *Lachman*, the latter, along with *Barnett*, reflects the legally viable and legally endorsed notion that administrative need is part of the placement decision.

\*    \*    \*

In *Troutman v. School District of Greenville County*,[17] Laney Troutman, a blind child, required one 50-minute special education period per day (taught by an itinerant special education teacher) and two 50-minute periods of Orientation and Mobility training per week. Eventually she was assigned to Sara Collins Elementary School, which was 11 miles from her home. Her parents preferred placement at Armstrong Elementary, one mile from Laney's home.

The Greenville County School District served 52,000 students at 67 individual elementary schools, with three schools, Sara Collins among them, designated as "satellite schools" for special education. Twenty-four percent of the Sara Collins and 20 percent of the Armstrong population were students with disabilities. The court noted that although

> [Section] 300.552 requires that unless a handicapped child's individual education program requires some other arrangement, the child must be educated in the school which he or

she would attend if not handicapped. .... the school district has determined that *other arrangements* in connection with her school assignment are necessary in order to provide the special training required by her IEP. Even with the designation of Sara Collins Elementary as a satellite school, all handicapped children attending it are still mainstreamed. .... The designation of Sara Collins ... was made to concentrate and conserve personnel and financial resources.[18] (emphasis added).

The court acknowledged the appeal of Section 300.552, in that it "would personally prefer to see the parents' wishes granted and that Laney be assigned to the elementary school closest to her home and that at the neighborhood school she receive the special education for the visually handicapped she needs. I am sure that all parents would prefer that."[19]

But the Section 300.552 requirement was trumped by "other arrangement[s]," particularly the budgetary restrictions of the school system. The court added that without the designation of a satellite program at Sara Collins, the district would need a minimum of eight additional teachers trained to teach the visually disabled.

When exactly do fiscal matters trigger the "other arrangement" portion of the home school mandate? Here the need for eight additional teachers was enough to translate "other arrangements" into a non-home school for Laney. In *Barnett,* it was the potential of having to establish 78 separate and individual programs.* There is no easy way, of course, to calculate the cost *and* benefit of teaching a child in a regular classroom, especially when individual need is weighed against distribution of limited resources. IDEA requires the provision of a "free" appropriate education "at no cost to the parents," but "free" has never been read to mean "unlimited."

---

* As noted, the "other arrangement" language of the regulations seems to apply to the child's needs, not the district's.

As school districts centralized programs and provided comprehensive options by utilizing many professionals on one campus, corresponding pressure was building on the LRE faultline. That is not to say that the centralized programs were or were not appropriate, but merely that efficiency had become a factor. The *Roncker* court, which primarily focused on the relationship of appropriateness to placement, considered cost an element in the general equation—was it "feasible" to provide the specialized program in a less restrictive environment.

The Barnetts, the Lachmans, and the Troutmans all opposed centralization because it precluded regular or home school placement; the Morrisons' core contention was that the centralized program at Midvale was inappropriate not because it was intended to approximate a regular class, but because in essence it was too "close to home" given the paucity of language opportunities for Janet in either her home school or the Midvale class. Others sought more distant programs because those highly specialized options simply could not be readily duplicated on an individual basis in home schools.

Courts have not always used a "common good" approach in comparing the cost or complications of educating a child locally as opposed to placement in a more distant centralized program. Paul Devericks, Jr. (who was profoundly deaf and communicated only by homemade gestures without syntax), and his sister Barbara (who was also deaf and who communicated orally), were placed in the Lewis County public schools.[20] They were the only deaf students there.

At ages 16 and 14, respectively, they exhibited behavioral problems, significant academic delays, and inadequate communication skills. Eventually it became clear that the Lewis County schools lacked the resources necessary to provide adequate educations for Paul Jr. and Barbara. The school board concluded that a deaf educator was not the children's primary need, but rather placement in an institution, specifically the School for the Deaf and Blind, to compensate for their deficiencies in sign language. Their father refused to give permission for such "removal."

Pending resolution of the disagreement, the children were placed in an alternative learning center, where they received individual tutoring and mainstreaming opportunities. At first Paul Jr. continued to have behavioral problems and was "sent home" for instruction with a teacher provided by the district. Eventually both children were removed from the alternative program due to attendance problems. Between 1982 and 1985 no educational services were provided to the children by the school district.

In fall 1985 Paul Jr. and Barbara were reenrolled in county schools with the provision of an educator of the deaf. At the time of the administrative hearing both children were making progress. The hearing officer concluded that Paul Jr. and Barbara were entitled to placement in a local program (the "least restrictive environment"), incidental damages of $5,000 each, and compensatory education until they were 24 (federal law provides for special education through the age of 22).

The circuit court reversed this decision, but the West Virginia Supreme Court of Appeals held for the family regarding the placement and compensatory education issues (the incidental damages were reduced to $2,500 each).

The Supreme Court noted West Virginia law on LRE, which makes use of phrases different from federal law:

> Provisions shall be made for educating exceptional children ... who differ from the average or normal in physical, mental, or emotional characteristics, or in communicative or intellectual deviation characteristics ... to the extent that they cannot be educated safely or profitably in the regular classes of the public schools ... to educate them in accordance with their capacities, limitations, and needs.[21]

Although terms such as "safely" or "profitably" are quite different from federal removal language, the West Virginia Supreme Court of Appeals stated that the school district "failed to consider the 'least restrictive environment' placement provisions for the Devericks children, by offering to send them out of Lewis County. . . ."[22] Accordingly, Paul Jr. and Barbara were denied an appropriate education.

It is the dissent in this decision that most dramatically illuminates the complex cost versus placement-right debate. Justice Neely's assessment was blunt:

> This decision sets a terrible precedent. It values the irresponsible demands of parents above the clear interest of their handicapped children. It requires *exorbitant* expenditures by local school boards in rural counties in what will ultimately amount to utterly futile efforts to offer an approximation of the education available at good specialized schools for handicapped children.[23]

Neely continued, "[u]nder the majority's view, local school boards must divert money from conducting their usual classes—a task they do well—to setting up special local schools for a few handicapped children—a task they cannot do well."[24]

Noting that the School for the Deaf and Blind was an excellent school with a long record of serving students with disabilities, Justice Neely stated that "Commanding Lewis County to educate these children does not make it possible for Lewis County to do so. If the world could be made a better place simply by entering an order, the Russians would have achieved utopia long ago!"[25]

As to a child's right to an integrated setting, Judge Neely concluded that the majority "has enshrined an unhealthy fetish for local schooling of handicapped children," and found that the "only legitimate end of these anti-discrimination statutes: the best education for handicapped children" was trumped by an "accident of geography."[26]

Judge Neely gave passing notice to the dictates of LRE, saying "there is a loss when children must be removed from regular classes and their home environment," but "once that point is passed, the school board must not tarry in finding the best possible education for the child." He continued his take-no-prisoners approach to the cost/need assessment:

> Having a handicapped child is a grievous misfortune for parents, but it is an even greater misfortune for the child. A child who is handicapped must be taught at an early age to compensate. . . . and learning other compensatory skills at an early age is the difference between a potentially successful life and mere vegetable existence. Parents, however, must also bear a responsibility for their children; if parents are entirely reluctant to be separate from their children so that they can be educated in good schools, it is appropriate for the state to expect the parents to move to where such good schools are located. Ours is a world of finite resources—a consideration of which courts as well as legislatures and executives should be constantly mindful.[27]

Like Justice Holmes, who believed the state could ask the retarded to give up their right to procreate, Justice Neely believed the state could ask parents of disabled children to move if it were a matter of choosing location over quality. Whether a parent could afford such a move or should have to make it in the first place did not seem a concern of the dissenting judge.*

*   *   *

The law does not give us a standard by which to weigh cost concerns against placement rights. For example, while the price of Raul Espino's air-conditioning unit was $5,700 and therefore represented only .0001461 of the total budget for the school system, it did represent approximately one-half percent of the total special education budget. Should that difference matter? Is there

---

* Some years ago the author sat next to a parent who testified before a House Subcommittee on IDEA. Her deaf son had been in a variety of programs, none of which had provided him with teachers or peers with whom he could communicate. Finally she and her family had to sell their home, move to another part of the state, and find new jobs so her son could attend the state school for the deaf.

a budgetary line past which no special education cost can possibly go? Did it extend the school district too far to require Christopher Ash to be sent to Japan, but not Boston? The statutory requirements that a child's education be "free," at "no cost" to the parent, and crafted to meet individual needs will likely be weighed against daily budgetary factors.

Within the placement context, the right to be in a regular class or one's home school represents a strong congressional preference but has been assigned no particular value, so that cost becomes a countervailing component without clear calibration of the scales. The courts give us no clear answer, no standard as to either when or how the weighing is to be done.*

In *A.W. v. Northwest R-1 School District,*[28] parents sought placement in a local program, while the school district offered a state school placement. A.W. was severely retarded and required close supervision at all times. Adopting the *Roncker* "feasibility-segregation" test, the Eighth Circuit affirmed the so-called more "restrictive" placement and acknowledged that "both cost to the local school district and benefit to the child" can be considered, since "available financial resources must be equitably distributed among all handicapped children."[29] Accordingly, the Eighth Circuit "decline[d] to construe" the law so as to "tie the hands of

---

* The *Roncker* court noted, perhaps underscoring unwittingly the difficulties regarding placement and cost of placement, that "[c]ost is a proper factor to consider since excessive spending on one handicapped child deprives other handicapped children" although "cost is no defense . . . if the school district has failed to use its funds to provide a proper continuum of alternative placements for handicapped children." Roncker v. Walter, 700 F.2d 1058, 1063 (6th Cir. 1983). *See also* David D. v. Dartmouth School Committee, 775 F.2d 411 (1st Cir. 1985), *cert. denied,* 475 U.S. 1140; Doe v. Anrig, 692 F.2d 800 (lst Cir. 1982), *aff'd in pertinent part, sub nom.* Burlington School Comm. v. Dept. of Education, 471 U.S. 359; Geis v. Board of Education, 774 F.2d 575 (3d Cir. 1985); Kruelle v. New Castle Co. School District, 642 F.2d 687 (3d Cir.1981); Christopher T. v. San Francisco Unified School Dist., 553 F. Supp. 1107 (N.D.Cal. 1982); Papacoda v. State, 528 F. Supp. 68 (D. Conn. 1981); North v. D.C. Board of Education, 471 F. Supp. 136 (D.D.C. 1979); Pinkerton v. Moye, 509 F. Supp. 107 (W.D. Va. 1981) (in which, the cost of placing a child in a neighborhood school, six miles

local and state educational authorities who must balance the reality of limited public funds against the exceptional needs of handicapped children."[30]

In *Department of Education v. Katherine D.*,[31] the court ruled that budgetary limitations preclude providing a child the best possible education "[b]ecause budgetary constraints limit resources that realistically can be committed to . . . special programs, the [Department of Education] is required to make only those efforts to accommodate Katherine's needs that are 'within reason.'"[32] And, in *Greer v. Rome City School District*,[33] the court noted that a "school district may consider the cost of the supplemental aids and services that are necessary to achieve a satisfactory education . . . in a regular classroom."[34] The *Greer* court captured the conflict between cost concerns and non-removal rights:

> This is not to say that a school district may decline to educate a handicapped child in a regular classroom because the cost of doing so, with the appropriate supplemental aids and services, would be incrementally more expensive than educating the child in a self-contained special education classroom. On the other hand, a school district cannot be required to provide a handicapped child with his or her own full-time teacher, even if this would permit the child to be satisfactorily educated in a regular classroom. . . . If the cost of educating a handicapped child in a regular classroom is so great that it would significantly impact upon the education of other children in the district, then education in a regular classroom is not appropriate.[35]

\*      \*      \*

Cost then has been a significant factor in removing children from regular or neighborhood schools. Even when programs have been centralized, the fiscal impact can be significant; some

---

closer than a centralized program, was deemed sufficient to justify denying the home school placement).

placements, with travel, can cost in the tens, if not hundreds of thousands of dollars.* Should society fully integrate children with disabilities regardless of the cost? Put another way, can cost consideration be used to preclude what for many children is a significant childhood opportunity? According to the *U.S. News & World Report,* by late 1993, 23 states funded special education by rewarding schools districts with more tax dollars if they placed more students in special education programs.[36]

The implication is that since much of special education is "separate," there is a monetary incentive to keep children excluded from regular education. Some in the full inclusion movement argue that a change to a unitary system will save money and precious school resources. Others, including the American Federation of Teachers, view full inclusion as a threat to already weakened school budgets.[37]

However society chooses to tackle the difficult question of the cost-to-benefit ratio, it is clear that the law allows for removal, and in so doing may ask a great deal of service-providers to facilitate that removal. It is also clear that cost and administrative convenience are acceptable countervailing forces against the integrative rights of children with disabilities.

## Endnotes

1.    Deaf Students Education Services: Policy Guidance, 57 Fed. Reg. 49,274 (1992).

---

* There have been a number of cases where the secondary travel costs of the family have become part of the "free appropriate public education" the child is entitled to: in Cohen v. Dade County School Board, 450 So.2d 1238 (Fla. App. 3d Dist. 1984), 1984-85 EHLR 556:162, the provision of three round trips per year for the Florida family of a child placed in a residential program in Georgia was upheld. In a California administrative hearing, the school district was ordered to pay lodging at $895.00 (rent and utilities) per month for the San Jose mother of a child placed in a clinic in Los Angeles. Union Elementary School District, No. 404-89H (Ca. State Ed. Agency Hearing, June 18, 1990), 16 EHLR 978.

2. Barnett v. Fairfax County School Board, 927 F.2d 146, 148 (4th Cir. 1991), 17 IDELR 350.

3. 927 F.2d at 151, 17 IDELR at 352.

4. *Id.*

5. *Id.*

6. *Id.*

7. 20 U.S.C. § 1401(a)(18) (1990).

8. 20 U.S.C. § 1401(a)(17) (West Supp. 1994).

9. 34 C.F.R. § 300.550 (1993).

10. Barnett v. Fairfax County School Board, 927 F.2d 146, 153 (4th Cir. 1991), 17 IDELR 350, 353.

11. 927 F.2d at 154, 17 IDELR at 353.

12. 852 F.2d 290 (7th Cir. 1988).

13. *Id.* at 292.

14. *Id.* at 295.

15. *Id.* (emphasis added).

16. *Id.* at 294-96 (emphasis added).

17. No. 82-2759-14 (D.S.C. 1983), 1982-83 EHLR 554:487.

18. 1982-83 EHLR at 489.

19. *Id.* at 490.

20. Board of Educ. of the County of Lewis v. West Virginia Human Rights Comm'n, 385 S.E.2d 637 (W. Va. 1989), 16 EHLR 145.

21. 385 S.E.2d at 641, 16 EHLR at 148.

22. 385 S.E.2d at 642, 16 EHLR at 149.

23. 385 S.E.2d at 644, 16 EHLR at 150 (emphasis added).

24. *Id.*

25. *Id.*

26. 385 S.E.2d at 645, 16 EHLR at 150.

27. *Id.*

28.  813 F.2d 158 (8th Cir. 1987).

29.  *Id.* at 163-64.

30.  *Id.* at 164. Numerous other courts have tackeled the cost problem. *See* Board of Educ. v. Holland, 786 F. Supp. 874 (E.D. Cal. 1992), 18 IDELR 761 (the cost of mainstreaming a retarded child was $109,000 a year, according to the school district, but the court found the right to regular school placement surpassed the cost concerns of the school). *See also* Kerkam v. District of Columbia, 672 F. Supp. 519 (D.D.C. 1987), 1987-88 EHLR 559:210 (a District of Columbia student was ordered placed, at district expense, in a program in Pennsylvania); Tokarcik v. Forest Hills School District, 665 F.2d 443 (3d Cir. 1981), 1980-81 EHLR 552:513 (court ruled that catheterization necessary to keep a child mainstreamed did not adversely affect state finances); Shook v. Gaston County Board of Education, 882 F.2d 119 (4th Cir. 1989) 1988-89 EHLR 441:561 (a North Carolina child was placed in the Brown School in Texas).

31.  727 F.2d 809 (9th Cir. 1984), 1983-84 EHLR 555:276.

32.  *Id. See also* Doe v. Anrig, 692 F.2d 800 (1st Cir. 1982), 1982-83 EHLR 554:271, in which the court found that the reality of limited public monies must be considered in reviewing placement decisions).

33.  Greer v. Rome City School District, 950 F.2d 688 (11th Cir. 1991), 18 IDELR 412.

34.  950 F.2d at 697, 18 IDELR at 417.

35.  *Id.*

36.  Jospeh P. Shapiro et al., *Separate and Unequal,* U.S. WORLD & NEWS REP., Dec. 13, 1993, at 50.

37.  "American Federation of Teachers Resolution Inclusion of Students with Disabilities," Adopted by the AFT Executive Council, October 27, 1993.

# 8

---

# Disruption and Other
# Reasons for Exclusion

---

MLUs. They filled the small hearing room. Witnesses analyzed them and concluded, one way or another, how they affected Janet Morrison's placement. Her case and the right to attend a distant, language-rich environment was turning, at least for one difficult day of testimony, on MLUs.

Outside the administrative building, during a break, the Morrisons stood with their hands in their pockets, a cold March wind whipping leaves about them and their attorney. The Morrisons showed neither interest nor concern about the MLUs. They were bored with that kind of testimony; what, they asked during a break, did this have to do with Janet's right to communicate with her classroom friends? He told them that MLUs were a way for the district to explain their case in quantifiable terms. Mrs. Morrison signed "Why?" The fingers pulled away from the forehead. The attorney shrugged and signed back, "It is easier for them to talk about numbers." They went back into the building.

There is no mention of MLUs in the federal or state laws, nothing in the statutes, regulations or even legislative history. No court had analyzed MLUs or assessed them within the context of IDEA. The Morrisons, who were newly introduced to MLUs, considered them irrelevant. MLUs had no place in Janet's consciousness; one might as well mention a particular article in a

Soviet magazine about a strain of wheat blight. Ishi did not know of MLUs. The hearing officer seemed to frown at their mention. Some witnesses treated them with a certain reverence.

"Janet communicates on an average of three to four signs per utterance."

The district's attorney looked at her notes, whispered something to her client and continued her questioning of one of her expert witnesses.

"So her 'mean length utterance' is about three to four words a sentence?"

"That is correct."

The witness was an affable man, an administrator from a distant school district. He knew the state school and had visited it as well as the Midvale program.

"What did you observe about the other children in Janet's class at Midvale?"

"They appeared to be communicating somewhere near the same MLU level."

"Which would be?"

"Three to four utterances or signs per utterance."

"What is your opinion about Janet's language environment at Midvale School?"

The administrator was not a paid witness. In special education hearings, school employees, especially teachers, are often in a difficult situation. They are well aware that their testimony may be crucial, that the child's well-being is at stake, and that their employer may be affected by their statements. John Phelps was an anomaly, clearly testifying for the district and against Janet, but still by far the most neutral of the district's witnesses.

"I believe Janet is in a language environment that meets her needs. I should also say that I believe the state school has a richer language environment and would provide her with greater opportunity to use and develop her language skills. But that is not to say that her local classroom is not appropriate."

"Thank you. Your witness."

The Morrisons' attorney considered the MLUs; pesky, necessary, something quantifiable, evidence that the school district preferred to assess.

"Tell me Mr. Phelps, would you consider a three-to-four phrase utterance consistent with the language of an intelligent six-year-old?"

"It would depend."

"On?"

"Many things. But let me say that Janet is clearly a smart child with fluency in ASL."

"And given her fluency . . ."

"I was going to say that she was communicating with her peers."

"But not at the level she might be capable of."

"Perhaps. I did not see her in any other environment and I don't know if she communicates at a higher level."

"Aside from the MLUs, did you see Janet interacting with her peers?"

"Objection. That has been asked."

"No it hasn't."

"It's precisely what we have been discussing."

The hearing officer waved to the witness to continue. John Phelps seemed indifferent to the attorneys; he might even have been sympathetic to the Morrisons.

"Communication and mean length utterances are not always the same."

The hearing officer listened without expression.

"Go ahead with your question."

"Mr. Phelps, did you see a lot of communication between Janet and her peers?"

"I saw her communicating with one child, I believe her name was Carol. I also saw her talking with a boy, I think his name was Stan."

"His name was Steve."

The school administrator sitting next to the attorney helped the witness. No one objected.

"Steve. All right."

"There has been testimony that Carol and Steve communicate at the toddler level."

"Well I saw them communicating, but generally there was not a lot of opportunity for the children to interact during the lessons I observed."

"What about at recess and lunch?"

"There was a good deal of activity."

"Between Janet and her classmates?"

"Not a lot. She may be a loner."

"How do you know that?"

"I don't."

"Did you see her communicate in or outside of the classroom with more than three to four signs per utterance?"

"I may have seen her use five or six signs on a few occasions."

"What would be the average MLU for a relatively intelligent six-year-old?"

"With intact language?"

"Yes. In this case age-appropriate sign language."

"An average of six or more."

"And it is your testimony that you only saw an age appropriate MLU a few times?"

"Yes."

"Is the environment in which you saw Janet a language-rich environment?"

"I would not say it was a rich language environment."

"Thank you."

The district's attorney studied her notes, conferred with the school administrator.

"Just a few questions on re-direct, Mr. Phelps. You've testified that you believe the state school has a rich language environment?"

"Yes."

"I believe you also testified that the district's program has an appropriate language environment?"

"Yes."

"Does the fact that the state school has a more varied language environment change your opinion about the appropriateness of the local program?"

"No."

"Thank you."

The witness began to leave, when Raymond Morrison began to sign, slapping his right hand on his left. He did this with such force that everyone in the small room paused to watch. The interpreter studied Raymond carefully, taken aback by his anger, but trying to convey his anger through her oral representation of his sign language.

"Shit! What are you talking about? 'Mean length' what? What does this have to do with Janet. You, Mr. Phelps, you know deaf children, what is this all about?"

The Morrisons' attorney tried to stop Raymond, but Janet's father was a strong and angry man and paid no attention to his counsel.

"Do you have children? You judge, you counselor, you Mr. Phelps, all of you?! Do you waste your time talking about these MLUs in order for your child to talk to her teacher?! Do you measure these MLUs when your child is outside playing with friends?!"

The hearing officer looked at the interpreter and finally stood to silence Mr. Morrison.

"That's enough!"

For a moment everyone paused and then everyone in the room sagged back into their chairs. The district administrators shook their heads as though to emphasize to the hearing officer how difficult they felt this family was.

The hearing officer looked over at the tape machine, recording the hearing. "Let's take a ten minute break. I am going off tape now."

Raymond Morrison sat without expression. His attorney patted him on the shoulder and signed for him and Betty to come outside. In the parking lot the attorney signed, "I understand your frustration, but you must try to hold back your anger. The hearing officer needs to see you two as reasonable people and when you get angry you don't seem reasonable."

Raymond Morrison moved closer to his attorney and signed slowly, carefully.

"Reasonable? What parent would be acting in a reasonable way if they allowed this nonsense to decide whether their child had anybody to communicate with? I do not understand why we have to go through this process so our daughter can talk with her friends."

He shook his head, looked to his wife. She smiled at Raymond and then the attorney.

\*     \*     \*

Carolyn Simpson, a hearing woman and the director of a nonprofit program for deaf infants, testified about the program at Midvale. She was a pleasant woman in her thirties, slightly nervous, but direct and unwavering in her answers. She testified that an English-based sign language was more than appropriate for deaf children, but ASL was equally important, especially for the early development of language skills. She had visited the Midvale class on several occasions and had met with Janet. She had also reviewed Janet's records. She had spoken with Janet's teacher and classroom aide.

"Would you please review the goals and objectives for Janet, exhibit 12, item D. Do you see it? Fine. Would you read that for us?" the Morrisons' attorney began.

"'American Sign Language will be used in conjunction with Signed English to facilitate the acquisition of academic subjects.'"

"What is your professional opinion of that goal?"

"Given Janet's natural ASL ability and usage, it is a good and important goal."

"Did you visit Janet's class at Midvale?"

"Yes, on several occasions."

Carolyn testified that the classroom aide spent between one and two-and-a-half hours with Janet each day, and that although the aide used sign language, she did not use it at all during one of her visits.

"The aide was a weak signer at best and she did not always use ASL."

"Why is it so important that ASL be used?"

"It is Janet's natural language; cognitive growth, particularly early cognitive growth, is directly related to opportunities to develop spontaneous and natural language. It is from this language base that her other language skills, notably English, will develop."

"What else did you observe about the aide?"

"On several occasions she had her back to the students and was speaking without signing. They had no idea what she was communicating."

"You testified her signing skills were weak. Could you give us some examples?"

Carolyn Simpson paused. Her face was fully flushed, although it wasn't clear whether she simply did not like this kind of spotlight or because, as an educator of the deaf, she was troubled by the testimony she had to give.

"Well, she signed 'math' and said 'new.' I heard her say 'much' and saw her sign 'many.' I heard her say 'how many' and saw her sign 'how soft.'"

"Anything else?"

"I heard her say 'all you girls are so smart' but saw her sign 'all you girls are so suspect.'"

"Can you calculate the cost of such mistakes?"

"Objection."

"Never mind, thank you."

Raymond Morrison moved in his seat, but before he could rise, the hearing officer spoke.

"It is four o'clock, we've had a long day. I suggest we stop now. Anything further? Fine, we will resume at 9:30 a.m. tomorrow. I am going off tape."

In the parking lot, the Morrisons spoke briefly with Carolyn Simpson. Nearby the district's attorney spoke to the county superintendent.

"Let me tell you something counselor, I'm ready to let her go. She's disrupting our program, she's disrupting my office. Why should we be in the middle of something where no matter what we do the parents are unhappy?"

Leaves in the parking lot swirled about, and the district's attorney paused for the wind to die down.

"Because you said to me that parents cannot run the school, that sending Janet to the state school involved resources, and because you believe in the least restrictive mandate."

"Well obviously there are times when a kid just doesn't belong. The teacher tells me that Janet and particularly her parents are not making life easy."

"Come on Richard, you and I know what's at stake here. We've got a clear and supportable position; it would do no good to change horses midstream. You'll get all wet."

"And now more of this ASL stuff," the superintendent continued. "Where are they going with that? Do they realize how difficult it is to find interpreters and aides who can sign? We try to find ones who know English sign language and then they want ASL. Tell me what happens when a deaf family from Korea moves here. Do I have to find a teacher who can sign in ASL and speak in Korean? This kind of stuff will bankrupt the system and takes an inordinate amount of time for one child. It disrupts everything."

"Richard, the case is going well—they're not going to win, and when a Korean or French family moves in, we'll deal with that then."

The superintendent shook his head and strode to his car. He pulled out of the parking lot and onto the street, saw the

Morrisons' attorney, and gave a clipped and perfunctory wave. Had the Morrisons' attorney known of the superintendent's frustration, he might not have advised Raymond Morrison to try to keep his emotions to himself.

––––––––––

IDEA provides specific authority for removing a child whose presence will impact on others: "... where a handicapped child is so disruptive in a regular classroom that the education of other students is *significantly impaired,* the needs of the handicapped child cannot be met in that environment. Therefore regular placement would not be appropriate to his or her needs."[1] "Disruptive" children might be those who are dangerous to themselves or others, or those who require enough teacher time to reduce the educational opportunities of other children. Is the disruptive qualifier a legitimate exception to mainstreaming or another artificial barrier to full inclusion?

In June 1993 the U.S. Department of Education issued what it called its "Absolute Priorities" for special education, including its first priority for projects aimed at "Educating Children with Severe Disabilities in Inclusive Settings."[2] But many argue that it is children with more severe disabilities who might be potentially the most disruptive, and so the conflict between the individual right to be included and the rights of others to be spared the complexity of that effort is engaged. In its 1993 report on "inclusion," the New York State United Teachers (NYSUT) noted the tension between integration and disruption: students in "inclusion programs" who interfere with the ability of other students to receive an appropriate program may need to be placed elsewhere.[3]*

––––––––––

* NYSUT also reported that "Inclusion is *not* a mandate of either the federal government or of New York State," and while the "philosophy of inclusion is appealing, the present structure of our educational system may be essentially incompatible with inclusion." *One Teachers Union Report,* INCLUSION TIMES, Sept. 1993, at 6.

IDEA also provides that in determining the LRE for a child, "consideration is given to any potential harmful effect on the child."[4] In its written opposition to full inclusion, the American Federation of Teachers noted that "insufficient medical personnel are employed by school districts for medically fragile children ...and inclusion would place these students in medical danger...."[5]

The process of removing disruptive or medically fragile children raises numerous questions. What constitutes sufficiently disruptive behavior to justify removal? While it may be easier to assess a situation in which the child acts out, what of the child who is well-behaved but requires a great deal of teacher time? Are the LRE rights of the children with disabilities (who have historically been excluded) superior to those of the other children in the classroom? Yet, what is gained for one is not necessarily lost for another. Would the provision of sufficient related services allow for the needs of both children to be met and would additional resources ultimately eliminate the concern about disruption? Those courts that have analyzed this question have frequently found that removal under Section 300.552 was justified.

*     *     *

A number of courts have upheld removal of children with disabilities from regular or neighborhood schools because the children were either unruly, or because they required, according to the schools, an inordinate amount of staff time.

In *Miller v. School Board*,[6] the parents of a 19-year-old student who functioned at the third-grade level sought placement for him in a learning disabilities class in the neighborhood school. In ruling against the parents, the district court noted that the student's presence would impede the progress of other students because he could not keep up and because his need for specialized individual attention would divert the teacher from attending to needs of the other students.

Leonard Liscio was an educable mentally retarded ten-year-old, who was also socially and emotionally disturbed.[7] He had attention deficit disorder, hyperactivity, and mild oppositional behavior, which was manifested by stubbornness, a strong will and a tendency to get into power struggles with adults. The school district offered full-time placement in the seriously emotionally disturbed-mentally retarded program, while his mother sought placement in a regular district school so Leonard could be mainstreamed with his non-disabled peers. The administrative judge ruled that Leonard required a "transition" plan; ultimately the parties reached an interim agreement that Leonard would remain in the seriously emotionally disturbed-mentally retarded program for part of the day and in a class for the educably mentally retarded in a regular elementary school for the other part.

On appeal the court ruled that the amount of time spent on Leonard was "disproportionate to the time . . . spent on the other exceptional children"[8] and concluded that Leonard should be placed in the separate program for academic subjects and in the regular elementary school for nonacademic subjects "to the maximum extent possible without unduly affecting the entire schedule of the 5th grade classes."[9] The court based its findings on the following facts: (1) It was "not fair to the rest of the class to lower the level of the Behavior Modification Plan in place to accommodate Leonard"; (2) Leonard's work deteriorated and he required "much redirection" and he "disturbed other students"; (3) "Leonard's behavior affected [the teacher's] ability to teach the rest of the students. Their train of thought was often interrupted and the lesson had to be restarted several times during the period"; (4) Leonard did not master any of his 17 math goals and objectives and had "made little, if any, academic progress."[10]

The court was particularly concerned about the "low incidence" nature of Leonard's dual disability and therefore the difficulty and "nonfeasibility" of creating a separate class in a regular school. Ultimately the court could not sanction the disruption of many children because of the needs of one: "the court does not believe that the [IDEA] requires the District to totally revamp its schedule of 5th grade classes for the benefit of one student."[11]

Whether the revamping of the program was a matter of money or substantive change in the program is not clear. It is evident, however, that the court would not tolerate mainstreaming at the expense of others.

Daniel R. was a six-year-old boy with Down's syndrome and developmental and language skills at the two- to three-year-old level.[12*] Despite its expansive read on the mainstreaming rights under IDEA, the *Daniel R.* court found Daniel's presence in regular pre-kindergarten to be unfair to the rest of the class, because an inordinate amount of classroom time was apparently spent on Daniel R. to the detriment of the other students.

In *Chris D. and Cory M. v. Montgomery County Board of Education*,[13] the parent of an emotionally disturbed student sought residential placement after the school district offered home instruction. Chris fought with other students, used profanity, stole money, beat on the walls, and generally disrupted his classes. His behavior grew worse—he had severe outbursts and was finally removed from school by the local police.

The county board offered placement in a learning center, at home or in an administrative building separate from all other children. The court concluded that Chris needed behavior modification and that his problems could not be redressed in an isolated environment. Even as the court ruled for residential placement it recognized that the school district could not hide Chris away to avoid his behavior problems or to prevent him from disrupting the ongoing education of the other students. The court also found that home instruction and education in the

---

* It was the *Daniel R.* court that crafted a lengthy and multi-layered analysis of LRE focusing on the nonacademic reasons—the "in and of itself" value—of a mainstreamed education. *See* Chapter 1.

administrative building would offer Chris "no opportunity to return to the regular class setting, which, of course, would be the least restrictive environment for *any* student."[14]

In any case, the nature of Chris's behavior seemed to have convinced his mother and the court that a more intensive placement was necessary. Hiding him away at school was more restrictive than taking him out of his home and putting him in a residential program. It is clear that continued placement in a local program was not in the cards; his disruptive behavior was simply too much.

In *Board of Education v. Illinois State Board of Education*,[15] placement in a private day-school program was upheld for a student who was disruptive and violent in class. This case offers an odd twist on disruption since both the student and his parents' behavior played a part in determining whether removal was necessary. Apparently the family refused support services for their son, would not give the district his medical history, and in general was "involved on a continuous basis in second-guessing ... the disciplinary efforts of the educators."[16] The parents had made derogatory remarks about school staff members in their son's presence and in general seemed to have irreconcilable differences with the school district. Evidence of the family's "hostility" was introduced at the fair hearing.

The court of appeals upheld the private placement decision and also tackled the difficult question of parental hostility. The school district had taken the position that the parents had sabotaged the process and therefore, by acting in an "aberrant" and "distasteful" way, had forced placement in a more restrictive environment. The Seventh Circuit stated that "A child whose parents oppose an IEP so vehemently and vocally as to 'doom' its prospects should not be enrolled in the placement merely to enable educational agencies and federal courts to 'discipline' parents. The [IDEA] makes clear whose interest must be paramount."[17] The court found it permissible to consider parental

231

hostility when assessing placement determination, and in this case it did, in fact, become part of the rationale for removal.*

\*   \*   \*

With the "disruptive" standard we are reminded again that the right to an integrated education is not absolute. There are certain students whose behavior renders mainstreaming less effective for the student or a significant disruption for the rest of the class. Whether additional resources or a change in the attitude of regular educators might resolve the matter is uncertain. Full inclusionists say yes, others counter that the full inclusion point of view is naive and presumptuous: "[The] reformist impulse has been radicalized. . . . in the interest of fairness and scholarship we [must] distinguish between facts and beliefs. . . . Their solution . . . reveals how poorly they understand general education and how shaky the ground is on which their movement is being built."[18]

Ultimately, the issue of fully including students does not appear easily pared down to a simple formula or an evident moral standard. To remove a disruptive child may reveal a certain lack of educational resolve; it may also speak to the needs of the child and his or her peers. The degree to which the movement to change special education can understand how complex those two viewpoints are will be the extent to which appropriate solutions are forthcoming.

# Endnotes

1.   34 C.F.R. § 300.552, cmt.

---

* There is some irony to the way student hostility is viewed by IDEA. A seriously emotionally disturbed (SED) student is eligible under IDEA and may be so because of an inability to make friends. However, IDEA specifically excludes "socially maladjusted" students, who may also have difficulty making friends and who certainly may be disruptive to the educational process. The difference is arbitrary; in some cases the line between social maladjustment and SED may be quite indistinct. 34 C.F.R. § 330.7 (1993).

2. Program for Children with Severe Disabilities, 58 Fed. Reg. 34,188 (1993).

3. *One Teachers Union Report,* INCLUSION TIMES, Sept. 1993, at 6.

4. 34 C.F.R. § 300.552(d) (1993).

5. AFT EXECUTIVE COUNCIL, AFT RESOLUTION INCLUSION OF STUDENTS WITH DISABILITIES, at 2 (adopted Oct. 27, 1993).

6. No. 88-1082-A (E.D. Va 1989), 1988-89 EHLR 441:333.

7. Liscio v. Woodland Hills School District, 734 F. Supp. 689, 690 (W.D. Pa. 1989), 16 EHLR 861.

8. 734 F. Supp. at 695, 16 EHLR at 864.

9. 734 F. Supp. at 699, 16 EHLR at 867.

10. 734 F. Supp. at 696, 16 EHLR at 865.

11. 734 F. Supp. at 702, 16 EHLR at 869.

12. Daniel R. v. State Board of Educ., 874 F.2d 1036, 1039 (5th Cir. 1989), 1988-89 EHLR 441:433.

13. 753 F. Supp. 922 (M.D. Ala. 1990), 16 EHLR 1183.

14. 753 F. Supp. at 934.

15. 938 F.2d 712 (7th Cir. 1991), 18 IDELR 43.

16. 938 F.2d at 714, 18 IDELR at 44.

17. 938 F.2d at 717, 18 IDELR at 46.

18. Douglas Fuchs and Lynn S. Fuchs, *Inclusive Schools Movement and the Radicalization of Special Education Reform,* 60 EXCEPTIONAL CHILDREN 296, 302 (1994).

# 9

---

# When the Most Restrictive Environment Is Inherently Least Restrictive

---

Dinner was chaotic: children sitting, standing, eating, chasing one another around the table. All the while the Morrisons and their attorney discussed Janet's case, which was winding down. There was one more day of testimony. Janet balled up her napkin and threw it at her sister. Both laughed and then signed rapidly to each other about real and perceived slights. Janet threw another napkin at her sister and then tapped the table to get the attorney's attention. She signed in precise, beautiful movements.

"I won't go to my school anymore. When do I go to Fremont?" she asked.

Then she smiled and then sailed out of the kitchen, like the lead ship in a small armada racing to an engagement. Raymond Morrison watched her, stroked his beard, and then also tapped the table to be sure that the attorney understood an important question was coming.

"You should call Janet to testify!"

Betty Morrison shook her head and signed harshly to her husband. "No, that isn't good for Janet. She is not sleeping well now. She won't sleep at all if she has to answer their questions."

"We will lose our case, won't we counselor?" Raymond asked without emotion as though he had already made a decision, no matter what the answer.

"No, but it is not going well. We've discussed why."

"Then call Janet."

The attorney looked for Janet to sail back into the kitchen, but no such relief was forthcoming. He paused to consider his answer to the Morrisons.

"I don't think we should. The officer already knows Janet wants to go to the state school. Janet is just too smart and articulate. . . ." The attorney slowly finger-spelled 'articulate.'

"Whatever chance we still have will be gone once the officer sees how strong and appealing Janet is."

Raymond stroked his beard again, but his eyes burned with anger, frustration, and full knowledge of the high wall he and his daughter had to scale.

"What do these people think? That if you smile you are happy and if you fall you are weak? Janet is strong, but she suffers. She is smart, but she struggles. Janet is happy, but is more and more sad."

"I hope that Bill Hanover can convey Janet's message. I think the officer will understand our message through Bill's testimony," the attorney signed.

"Does this officer send his child to a school where there is no one to talk to?" Raymond leaned back in his chair and studied the ceiling, knowing the answer to his question.

*     *     *

William Hanover sat uncomfortably at the end of the table. It was the fourth day of the hearing. The room seemed to grow smaller each day, and while there continued to be superficial civility among the parties, the early good humor was gone. The Morrisons brought in the morning paper, which continued to tell of the Gallaudet "revolution," but no one noticed the headlines.

236

As William Hanover took the oath before testifying, he looked at the interpreter, not at the hearing officer who read the oath aloud. Hanover was a compact man with dark features. He looked around the small, overheated, and tense room; it was difficult to tell whether he felt apprehension or determination. He signed that he understood and accepted the oath. He was the principal of the secondary program at the state school. There are people in this world whose gentleness is evident in their features; Hanover was such a man. The Morrisons' attorney knew him to be kind and dignified, and hoped that the weight of his decency would convey more powerfully the difficult issues of communication and isolation. Slowly he signed information about the state school, while the interpreter, a word or phrase behind, voiced Hanover's testimony.

"There are approximately 480 students, kindergarten through 12th grade. We have approximately 50 teachers and other professional staff. There are both hearing and deaf teachers and administrators. There are a variety of languages at the school, including ASL and Signed English and total communication. All of the students use some kind of sign language, although there are students who are profoundly deaf and students who have residual hearing and oral skills.

"We have several programs in which our students attend local schools for mainstreaming. We have a very cooperative relationship with the local school district. There is reverse main-streaming—I'm sorry, that's where students from the local school come to our campus for educational services. It's a wonderful way to meet and begin to understand one another.

"There are comprehensive services at the school, our library has extensive resources, including communication-language development programs. We have speech therapists, psychologists, and counselors who are either deaf or have extensive experience working with deaf children.

"We have a full array of sports, after-school and social activities. We compete in the North Bay League of Schools. Our school is really a small community."

"Do you know Janet Morrison?"

"Yes." Hanover smiled.

"How do you know her?"

"I taught her sister, I know her mother and father, and I have seen her many times on campus. I have also reviewed her records. You sent them to me."

"Yes. Do you have any opinion as to where Janet should be placed?"

"Objection. He's not qualified to recommend where Janet should be placed."

"He knows more about Janet than the professor or your county administrator."

The hearing officer waved for both attorneys to be silent.

"The question can be answered."

"I think she belongs at the state school. She's deaf, she needs friends, and she needs to feel proud of her language. Too many deaf children have shriveled up in mainstreamed classrooms."

"Thank you, Mr. Hanover."

The district's attorney looked at her notes, leaned over to whisper something to the district administrator, and addressed William Hanover.

"Tell me, Mr. Hanover, did you attend a state school?"

"Some of the time."

"Did you also attend a school for hearing children?"

"Yes, in the earlier grades."

"You are principal of the high school?"

"Yes."

"You have a graduate degree?"

"Yes."

"Would you consider yourself a success?"

"Objection. This is not relevant."

"It is. Mr. Hanover attended local programs and is evidence that non-state school education works."

"I'll allow that, but briefly."

"Thank you. Are you opposed to keeping deaf children in their homes and local schools?"

William Hanover paused. He had been asked such a question many times. No matter how he answered, it never seemed that the hearing person understood that being deaf was not a bad thing, that a deaf child should not grow up to be like a hearing child, that deaf people were happy and led productive lives and, yes, preferred their world. If only this attorney could see a gathering of deaf people, then she would understand that deaf people are different, not less, not more.*

"I believe that parents should decide what is best for their children. If I can elaborate for a moment?"

Hanover looked at the hearing officer. He smiled slightly.

"Deaf people are not unhappy people. I mean that we are not unusually unhappy or frustrated. We have our own culture and community. We have our language. We get along. We have to deal with the hearing world and at times it is difficult. Ninety percent of deaf children have hearing parents, and that can often mean a delay in the development of an appropriate language. I believe that deaf children do better in a deaf school because there is language, there are friends to talk to. That is my belief. I believe that deaf children are healthier when they grow up in this kind of environment. Statistics back that up."

"Are you a psychologist or have you had training in psychology?"

---

* Lawrence R. Newman, a graduate of Gallaudet and former president of the National Association of the Deaf, has written a wonderful essay entitled "Violins," in which he discusses being deaf in a world of music:

> Most of us probably do not think about it or have relegated it to somewhere in the subconscious. But I often wonder about it. What does it sound like? The world goes round with the play of stringed instruments, the tooting of horns, the beating of the drums, the arias in operettas, the mellifluous songs of nightclub singers. And we, like the postman, rise up at dawn, give a shrug at what we do not hear and go to our appointed assignments.

*Perspectives on Deafness, A Deaf American Monograph* (1991), at 107, 109.

Hanover waited for the interpreter to finish. He seemed more bemused than offended by the question. How many times had he been asked his credentials when talking about what was his life experience?

"No. I am a deaf man with deaf children. I know."

"Do you have any first-hand knowledge of the Midvale program?"

"No. I was not allowed to visit it."

"What is the cost of educating a child at the state school?"

"That may vary depending on whether the child is a day or residential student."

"Residential."

"Approximately $30,000, although that figure. . . ."

"Thank you."

"Could he finish?" the Morrisons' attorney interjected.

The hearing officer agreed and allowed the witness to continue.

"Please go ahead, Mr. Hanover."

"Thank you. One should compare what it would cost to educate a deaf child in a local program, especially when you must add the cost of bus transportation, speech therapy, and other services. Also, for a child who is mainstreamed there may be the cost of the interpreter."

"This is not relevant." The district's attorney turned to the hearing officer, who responded quickly.

"I want him to finish. While this information may be only marginally relevant, I'd like to know more about these issues."

"If Janet were to attend her neighborhood school she would need a full-time interpreter, probably an ASL interpreter. That alone would cost anywhere from $15,000 to $25,000 a year. Does she attend her home school?"

"No!" Raymond Morrison signed the answer.

"Objection."

Hanover quickly signed, "I can explain. . . ."

The hearing officer smiled for the only time during the hearing. "Sustained. Finish your answer, Mr. Hanover, and please no questions."

"Let me add some other statistics. Has anybody given thought to what it costs when a deaf child is not properly educated? Deaf children graduate from high school with third grade reading skills, while their hearing counterparts finish school with 10th grade reading skills. Thirty percent of deaf children leave school functionally illiterate and gain eight months in reading from age 10 through 16, while hearing students gain six years in the same time period.

"This has nothing to do with intelligence or desire or ability," Hanover continued. "Approximately one-third of deaf adults receive some form of governmental assistance, and while the median income of a deaf family in 1987 was $14,000, it was $29,000 for a hearing family. Fifty-four percent of the deaf population had incomes below $15,000. Those statistics are directly related to the failure to develop language in a child, directly related to illiteracy."

"I'm finished with this witness."

"Might I add one thing?"

The hearing officer waited for the interpreter, while the district's attorney began to study her notes for the next witness.

"Please go ahead Mr. Hanover."

"You probably don't give much thought to this, but consider what it would be like for your child or children to go to a school and not have any teachers or friends to communicate with. Your children never have to think about that. Why should our children be removed from an environment where they can communicate? Give our children a chance to develop language and you will see a change in those statistics. We're not asking for expensive programs or extra things. Just what every other child in this country takes for granted. Does the law require you to ignore that?"

Raymond Morrison smiled at the witness, knowing that no one would answer Hanover's question.

---

The full inclusion movement generates much heat and increasingly creates controversy, and it does so because it raises as many moral issues as it does educational ones. And therein lies some of the difficulty of analyzing full inclusion, for to question its educational purpose is to doubt its moral foundation. And to doubt an ostensibly integrating movement can be a daunting proposition.

The counter-arguments to full inclusion have been made: cost, the possibility that need trumps placement, concern over certain disruptive behaviors, and administrative convenience. These ultimately involve resources, and such finite issues are more susceptible to the moral question. If something is important or moral enough, there should be enough willpower and money to do it.

But there is a truer crack in the generic full inclusion movement. The educationally and morally questionable fabric of the movement is no more evident than in (1) its underlying position that "all means all," and (2) those cases in which the so-called most restrictive environment is fundamentally least restrictive for the individual child. Once there is a Janet Morrison—a student for whom a regular classroom cannot be made appropriate even with limitless resources, positive attitude, and systemic realignment—the moral basis for what Nebraska calls a "zero reject" approach is no longer persuasive. If the placement question under IDEA involves a fundamental notion of fairness, then the moral rightness of the full inclusion movement loses its force and becomes, for Janet Morrison, a retrogressive and even dehumanizing threat. It is, according to some, a "change guided by radical . . . blueprints unsubstantiated by research."[1]

> Why are at least some full inclusionists out of step with general education's steady drumbeat? Because as zealot advocates of children with severe intellectual disabilities, they

march to a beat of their own. Despite their slogan of "all children," they are concerned primarily about their own children. Their plan for school reform is driven by the concern, "What type of school will be best for our children?" and by a related presumption that "What's best for our kids is good for all kids." The academic needs of low-, average-, and above-average-achieving students, as well as those with varying disabilities, typically are ignored.[2]

Educators are noting that the movement's "rhetoric has become increasingly strident and its perspective increasingly insular and disassociated" from the larger educational community. Some predict that "if the full inclusionists adhere to their no-optional-placement strategy, opposition to their movement will become increasingly vocal" and if they "cling to a vision of regular education . . . that de-emphasizes curriculum, academic standards, and student and teacher accountability, general education will lose interest in special education as a partner in reform making."[3] The integration movement is viewed as "polariz[ing] a field already agitated."[4] That may be happening because the movement has lost its ability to understand Janet Morrison and to allow her to be "included" as she wishes.

The final exceptions then, to the mainstreaming preference of IDEA and the full inclusion movement, are those children for whom a separate program is as basic and necessary as a regular classroom is for many other students.

\*     \*     \*

The Commission on the Education of the Deaf described to the President and the United States Congress on what constitutes true "restrictiveness":

[t]hat environment [regular school] which may be least restrictive in terms of the integration of other handicapped students becomes the most restrictive in terms of basic communication between deaf children and their hearing peers, setting the stage for drastic retardation in development and

243

> identity, social skills, and maturity. . . . Worse, severely lim-
> iting a deaf child's access to a whole range of experiences
> with other children and adults may also impede the child's
> ability to acquire and develop language, a factor which will
> limit his or her education permanently.[5]

To this end some states have had laws or policies giving parents
a unilateral right to place their children, if they choose, at the
"segregated" end of the continuum. Florida and Indiana, for
example, have given parents the option of placing their deaf
children in state schools. In 1991 California considered legislation
that would have given parents the right to pick among any
number of placements, provided the selected option was appropriate. In August 1991, however, the Indiana State Board of
Education removed the parental choice law. The U.S. Department
of Education had concluded that the Indiana parental choice
option was "inconsistent" with IDEA. In letters between the
Superintendent of the Indiana School for the Blind and Robert
Davila, the Undersecretary of Education in the Bush administration, the issues of parental choice and a true "least restrictive"
environment were addressed.

Much of the text of Michael Bina's letter to Robert Davila
has been reprinted because of the unique and fervent nature of
his view. There is also a sense of how deeply the notion of
absolute inclusion affects the different parts of the special education community. He illuminated the fundamental question as
to what constitutes an inherently appropriate environment—as
opposed to using labels to determine need:

> Many professionals across our country still insist upon the
> neighborhood school as the only option for children with
> disabilities and that specialized schools are an outmoded
> option which should be eliminated. I am not anti-integration.

> By the late 1960's this nation began graduating from high
> school a generation of visually impaired youth who had
> never set foot in a segregated class or a school for the blind.
> We were very proud of these young people—they had spent

every school day of their young lives with sighted class-mates. We naturally assumed that they were well-prepared to be assimilated into the adult community. They would be socially and occupationally integrated. They would have no difficulty living in a sighted community and working in a sighted world.

How wrong we were!! We learned quickly that we had produced a generation of visually impaired young adults, many of whom were "academic automatons." They could solve binomial equations, but couldn't make change for a dollar. They knew all about iambic pentameter, but couldn't dress themselves. They could recite the pythagorean [sic] theorem but did not know the qualifications for working as a computer programmer.

In short we had not prepared these young people for living as adults because we had ignored a broad range of unique needs—needs which were the direct result of vision loss—needs not shared with sighted classmates . . .

Needs, by the way which may be similar in content to children with other disabilities, but needs which require a totally different teaching methodology—a fact which means that these are disability-specific needs!!

. . . .

We, like our colleagues in education of the hearing impaired, are out of step with much of special education today. We are needing to more carefully determine when and for whom mainstreaming is appropriate. We must balance the possibilities for interaction with non-handicapped peers with the realities of educational needs.

. . . .

We must reject the common definition of LRE. It has no relevance to visually impaired children. We must consider every placement option as the LRE . . . for an individual child.

We must consider the following: a blind five-year-old child, in rural California. The IEP team decides that placement in

245

the local neighborhood school is the LRE. An itinerant teacher for the visually impaired is able to serve the child one hour a week. . . . The child? As an adult, she will in all likelihood be illiterate, a social isolate, dependent in daily living skills, and unemployable!!

But, our critics will say, she was mainstreamed! She was placed in the LRE. At what price?

. . . Placement *should never be determined* by a generic philosophic belief.

It is apparent why educators, parents and consumers have been frustrated, sad, and angry. . . . We begged and pleaded to be heard, and we were greeted in arrogance and silence. . . . We were outraged when our colleagues in TASH generalized their feelings about severely handicapped children to *all* children with disabilities. . . . LRE was defined by persons with no knowledge of the effects of sensory impairments. Schools for the blind were threatened, and we were told by uninformed persons that the mainstreamed visually impaired child needed only some instructions in braille and mobility.[6]

In response, Dr. Davila noted the difference between a policy that allowed parents to choose between two placement options that met the LRE requirements of the law and a policy that gave parents a unilateral right of placement—parental preference cannot override the decision of the IEP team.

Moreover, Dr. Davila added that the continuum requires the availability, not the right to, placement options. The U.S. Department of Education would therefore not take any position supporting parental right of placement.*

---

* Not long after these letters were exchanged Dr. Davila wrote that "inclusion is not a place. It transcends the idea of physical location and incorporates basic values that insist on participation, friendship, and interaction in all aspects of education and community life." OSERS NEWS IN PRINT, Spring 1992, at 2. In a June 30, 1992 speech before the National Association of the Deaf, Dr. Davila stated that school officials "may believe they are precluded from considering placements that are viewed by some as 'more restrictive' because of the strong

A number of courts have sided with Dr. Bina's point of view, concluding that IDEA has room in its broad directives for the notion that what may be ostensibly less restrictive is really more restrictive. In *Visco v. School District*,[7] Judge Louis Rosenberg recognized an unmistakable right of a child not to be mainstreamed. Mainstreaming, he concluded, might not only be harmful, but conversely separate placement might be moral and necessary. The problem was not merely a "dispute," but because of "our fundamental concern for tender children . . . symbolic of that which is a national deficiency."[8]

Jennifer Visco, age 13, and Rene Visco, age 11, were deaf and attended a private school, the DePaul Institute. Their school district offered placement in "hearing-impaired" programs at public schools, in which sign language development was encouraged and emphasized. Rita Mae Visco contended that her children needed to develop their oral/aural skills, and therefore only the more restrictive DePaul could provide for those needs.

This case reflected the varied nature of disabilities in general and hearing loss in particular, because the Visco children had entirely different needs from Janet Morrison. The Morrisons and Rita Mae Visco sought wholly incompatible placements, and yet mainstreaming was considered the most restrictive environment in both cases.

Judge Rosenberg saw the dispute as one between placement in an "oral" school exclusively for deaf children and placement in a public program that used sign language but provided mainstreaming opportunities. Judge Rosenberg had significant concerns about mainstreaming deaf children without regard to their individual needs, particularly the inability of the educational system to assist deaf children in acquiring good enough language

---

tilt toward mainstreaming that has been reflected in federal policy." Dr. Davila continued, "The result is that what is determined an appropriate education for a deaf child is too often driven by the location of the placement, rather than by . . . the child's particular needs. *We are more than convinced that this is wrong.*" (Emphasis added.)

skills to be able to function in society. Judge Rosenberg called the problem a "national epidemic."[9]

He concluded that mastery of language skills is vital and thus the benefits of integration were placed in "serious doubt" because mainstreaming was "a means not an end." The law did not mandate, Judge Rosenberg continued, that a disabled child be "required to sink or swim in an ordinary classroom." It is better, the court noted, that children are prepared in special schools, because the purpose of IDEA is to "adequately prepare individuals for the mainstream of life" and thus "[n]escient educational mainstreaming defeats the very purpose for which mainstreaming was conceived."[10] We should not, Judge Rosenberg wrote, produce "an adult who might have to rely on social services later because he or she cannot communicate effectively."[11]

Judge Rosenberg stated that mainstreaming was intended to "prepare a handicapped individual to function as a normal adult in society, it is *not* a goal in and of itself."[12] Accordingly "mainstreaming that interferes with the acquisition of fundamental language skills is foolishness mistaken for wisdom."[13]

The *Visco* decision emphasizes more precisely why need should drive placement and ultimately undercuts generic full inclusion plans. In *Visco* we come full circle from *Thornack, Holland,* and other cases where the courts saw mainstreaming as an inherently valuable experience, standing as the core purpose of the law. *Visco* and *Thornack* reflect two very diverse ways of looking at the placement scheme of IDEA. Ultimately they may also represent why any law regarding the placement of children with disabilities must be flexible and allow for individual and very different placement options.

\*     \*     \*

In *Geis v. Board of Education,*[14] the parents of a severely disabled student opposed efforts to "remove" their son from the Woods School, a residential program. S.G. was a 16-year-old student with mental retardation, a neurological dysfunction, motor and psychomotor seizures, communication disorders, chronic illness, and secondary emotional difficulties.

The school district recommended placement in a less restrictive and public program at Brooklawn Junior High School, a regular junior high school in Parsippany. An administrative hearing officer ruled that placement at Brooklawn was appropriate. On appeal to the federal district court, the district court judge visited both placement options.

The court ruled that S.G. should remain in the residential program at Woods School because it would "allow [him] to 'best achieve success in learning and that placing S.G. in his home and in local schools would have an adverse effect on his ability to learn and develop to the maximum possible extent.'"[15] The district court partially relied on New Jersey law, which required that a "local public school district must provide each handicapped pupil a special education program and services according to how the pupil can *best* achieve educational success."[16] The state standard was higher than the federal one and stood in some contrast to the *Rowley* requirement of mere academic progress as indicative of appropriateness. The use of the "best" standard to justify a separate placement gives particular emphasis to the notion that an ostensibly more restrictive environment may be fundamentally right and therefore truly least restrictive. Given the full inclusion debate, there is no little irony that a higher standard actually cut against full inclusion, at least in the *Geis* case.

The court of appeals for the Third Circuit affirmed the lower court decision and, in so doing, more fully recognized that "need" determined "restrictiveness." It ruled that both "appropriate" and "suitable" were vague terms, and that there was no statutory "impediment to the State Board concluding that an 'appropriate' or 'suitable' educational program is one that *best* helps a pupil to achieve success in learning."[17] The New Jersey legislature determined that school children should be provided "the fullest possible opportunity to develop their intellectual capacities"[18] and nothing in federal law precluded the application of such a standard.

The school district also contended that the state standard could be used to rationalize a private school placement since there would always be some private program with private tuition that would be able to offer more facilities, more instructional personnel and more services than a public school district can offer. The court was not prepared to take judicial notice of such a "dubious" proposition. The court believed Woods was both feasible and reasonably "cost-effective," therefore there was no need to "go down that hypothetical slippery slope."[19]

The court justified "removal" because it would allow S.G. to best achieve educational success. It does not appear that any significant argument was made that S.G. could best achieve educational success by placement in a local program with support services. Perhaps this was either fiscally impossible or programmatically unlikely. In any case, abstract notions of LRE did not enter into the court's equation or act as an impediment to residential placement:

> As to the requirement that handicapped children be placed in the least restrictive environment possible, we believe that this determination must include consideration of the particular handicap a student has. . . . Current regulations make it even more clear that the goal of placing children in the least restrictive environment *does not trump all other considerations.* . . . for some pupils a residential placement may very well be the least restrictive.[20]

The court did not say much more about this notion. It is not clear, for example, whether the court viewed Woods School as the least restrictive because it represented the best balance between cost and service provision and S.G.'s need to be in the most integrated setting. It is not clear whether the court sensed that in the best of all worlds and given some pure notion of integration of disabled children, S.G. might be best served locally.

The subtle message here might be that Woods School is least restrictive because it is the only way to serve S.G. in a world of limitations. And perhaps the court meant exactly what it said—Woods School was least restrictive not because it was the only choice, not because limited resources were best spent there, but because it was, in reality, least restrictive.

*   *   *

In *Grkman v. Scanlon*,[21] parents of a disabled child sought removal to a more restrictive placement, only to be opposed by the school district. Lindy was profoundly deaf, had a high I.Q. and "no mental defects," and had been placed at the private DePaul Institute because it specialized in "training" the deaf. The county school system argued that it had a local program that was appropriate for Lindy. A reluctant district court judge noted initially, with credit to Justice Robert H. Jackson, that "we act in these matters not by authority of our competence but by force of our commissions."[22]

Giving credit to the integrity and intelligence of the school district administrator (who admitted that his "line of work was administration rather than teaching children"), the court noted that the DePaul program, unlike the district's, had children who were the same age as Lindy, whose degree of hearing loss was closer to Lindy's, and whose cognitive abilities were closer to hers. The court concluded that because the DePaul program specialized in training the deaf, her entire school day was oriented toward learning pertinent communication skills.*

---

\* The court sensed the sometimes vacuous nature of IEP goals and objectives, which infrequently touch upon a child's broad social, linguistic, or emotional needs. "Measurability" seems more important than certain basic needs, an issue not missed by the *Grkman* judge:

> The 11 page IEP in the record . . . fully complies with the statute. For practical purposes a skeptic might think it ought to receive the attention of one of the current task-forces seeking to eliminate unnecessary paperwork. Under 'Reading' the 'Annual Goal' is that 'Lindy will acquire and use comprehension strategies and study

While Lindy would be exposed to "normal" pupils in the district's program (which would advance the goal of mainstreaming), the court believed that it would not promote socialization or the development of those skills necessary for "a deaf person." The court saw the development of Lindy's communication skills as a predicate to her successfully functioning in a mainstreamed environment, rather than as crucial to her developing in her own unique deaf environment. It understood that placement required careful consideration of a child's language needs:

> If [socialization is]undertaken prematurely, when the pupil has not sufficiently acquired the necessary communication skills, it might have traumatic consequences or result in regression. . . . Championship prowess will sooner be attained if [Lindy] concentrates on intensive training and learning to swim before she plunges unprepared into the *turbulent mainstream.* When her strokes are stronger she will be able to make better headway in the water.[23]

It appears no argument was made that related services, such as interpreters or other supplementary aids, might have smoothed the way into the district's program. Did the court take the position that DePaul was appropriate because it was inherently least restrictive, or that it was least restrictive because Lindy could not function in any so-called less restrictive environment? The distinction is significant, for the former speaks to an inherent

---

skills needed to understand and enjoy messages communicated in written language.' Does this encourage passing notes in class? Under 'Social Studies' the goal is 'Lindy will demonstrate an awareness of holidays and special event celebrations.' The 'short term objective' to be evaluated by 'teacher observation' is that 'Lindy will demonstrate an awareness that a person's birthday honors the day he or she was born.' Does deafness impede enjoyment of birthday cakes and presents? [528 F. Supp. at 1033, n.4.]

least restrictiveness at DePaul, offering Lindy a positive communication environment, whereas the latter acknowledges the continuum and a strict linear notion of restrictiveness. The *Grkman* court concluded that Lindy should remain at DePaul because the risks of change outweighed potential benefits, suggesting an understanding that DePaul was essentially LRE. To ensure that his audience understood his position, the judge noted at the end of his decision that if anyone thought his ruling arbitrary they should consider that when an antitrust client of Clark Clifford asked why there was such a large bill, the attorney explained (for a further substantial fee), "Because I said so."

\*　　\*　　\*

The future of education in America, including special education, is at one of those frequent crossroads. That it seems to reach them often should not neutralize the importance of this particular stop. With the passage of reform measures such as America 2000, the federal government looks to a new century and therefore a changing educational goal. The full inclusion of children with disabilities is part of that aim. In late, 1992, the "Full Inclusion of Children and Youth with Disabilities in Community Schools" conference was held in Washington, D.C., and specifically called for generic inclusion. The movement to reform special education has been under a full head of steam, but it is not entirely clear whether it has factored in the *Visco* line of cases and the real possibility that non-integrated settings may be inherently least restrictive.

Janet Morrison, Lindy, Jennifer and Rene Visco, and S.G., for whom separate programs were fundamentally appropriate, remain the exceptions that will not go away, the most significant and persuasive challenge to special education reform. While the full inclusion movement is on firmer footing when arguing that a bad attitude or the lack of additional resources should be no excuse for the separation of children with disabilities, it faces a much thornier problem regarding those separate programs that provide essential educational components for the child. A class with a critical mass of peers, or an appropriate language environment, or highly specialized and comprehensive services cannot and, perhaps, should not, be replicated in a regular classroom. Many of the individuals and groups who oppose full inclusion do not view separate programs as an ironic but quasi-evil necessity. Those separate programs embody basic educational components and meet the fundamental human rights of some children with disabilities.

Judge Rosenberg's remark that under certain circumstances mainstreaming is "foolishness mistaken for wisdom," has particular resonance for Janet Morrison and her peers.

## Endnotes

1.    Douglas Fuchs and Lynn S. Fuchs, *Inclusive Schools Movement and the Radicalization of Special Education Reform*, 60 EXCEPTIONAL CHILDREN, 303-04 (1994).

2.    *Id.*

3.    *Id.* at 295, 304.

4.    *Id.* at 305.

5.    THE COMMISSION ON EDUCATION OF THE DEAF, TOWARD EQUALITY, A REPORT TO THE PRESIDENT AND THE CONGRESS OF THE UNITED STATES, at 32 (Feb. 1988).

6.    Letter from Michael Bina to Robert Davila, Nov. 5, 1991, 18 IDELR 582-86.

7.    684 F. Supp. 1310 (W.D. Pa. 1988).

8.    *Id.* at 1311.

9.    *Id.*

10.   *Id.* at 1316.

11.   *Id.*

12.   *Id.* at 1314.

13.   *Id.* at

14. 774 F.2d 575 (3d Cir. 1985), 1985-86 EHLR 557:135.

15. 774 F.2d at 579, 1985-86 EHLR at 137-38.

16. 774 F.2d at 579, 1985-86 EHLR at 137.

17. 774 F.2d at 582, 1985-86 EHLR at 139-40 (emphasis added).

18. 774 F.2d at 582, 1985-86 EHLR at 140.

19. 774 F.2d at 583, 1985-86 EHLR at 140.

20. *Id.* (emphasis added).

21. 528 F. Supp. 1032 (W.D. Pa. 1981).

22. *Id.* (quoting Board of Educ. v. Barnett, 319 U.S. 624, 640 (1943)).

23. *Id.* at 1037.

# Epilogue

Because of a scheduling conflict, the parties met in a shopping center at the southern end of town for the last two days of the Morrisons' hearing. The shopping center was new, with many unoccupied buildings. The interstate freeway running from San Diego to Seattle was just to the west, while immediately to the east were the Sierra foothills, rolling, generally empty and dry, dotted with oak trees, some cows, and moss-covered fencing.

The hearing was held in a modern room, clean and sparse. The active world seemed quite far away. After the final witness, the hearing officer asked whether the parties would make closing arguments. Both sides agreed to submit written briefs on the evidence and the law. The hearing officer then made final, perfunctory remarks for the tape recording he kept. The parties gathered up their notes and exhibits. It was late afternoon, and the parties stood and chatted amiably as the room filled with sharp light. Slowly they all filtered out and away from this dispute.

The hearing officer rendered his decision several weeks later. Noting that Janet Morrison had made progress in school, that there were other deaf children in the Midvale program, and finding that there was no clear evidence that Janet was deteriorating emotionally, the officer ruled that she could not be placed in the "more restrictive" environment of the state school. The Midvale program could meet her academic needs, and therefore the school district had met its legal duty to provide her with a free appropriate public education. The attorney considered explaining to the Morrisons that, given the evidence and law, the decision could be justified, but he knew that would hardly help them tell Janet that her suitcase would remain at the door of her room.

Janet Morrison remained in Midvale for the rest of the school year. Her family discussed the possibility of appealing the decision, but could not afford to take legal action. It wasn't long after the decision was rendered that the school district sent out notice that the IEP meeting for the next school year would be held. The process and dispute would begin anew, although having prevailed at the hearing, the district was confident that the matter was resolved. They offered another year at Midvale and would not consider state school placement.

And so Raymond Morrison began his daily protest, marching up and down in front of the district's administration building. The local paper took his picture and told his story. Day after day he marched. Phone calls and letters on behalf of the Morrisons came into the district. The school attorney assured her clients that the matter was closed, that the Morrisons were on weak ground factually and legally. If they chose to go to another hearing, the facts would be so similar as to render the conflict settled almost before the first witness took the oath and testified.

But not long before the next school year began Janet's teacher, Phillip Johnstone, transferred, and the district suddenly informed the family that they now considered the state school an appropriate placement and would place Janet there for the fall program. One year after the dispute first began and six months after the hearing decision was rendered, Janet took her suitcase and drove with her family to Fremont.

\*     \*     \*

Many years after the Morrison hearing, Janet's attorney ran into one of the county special education administrators at a special education workshop. The administrator had testified at the hearing. They chatted for a moment, each balancing a dish of buffet food and the recollections of an acrimonious dispute, no doubt.

Ultimately Janet's case came up. The administrator, a short fireplug of a woman who had taken an uncompromising position throughout the dispute, asked about the Morrisons. The attorney told her what he knew and then asked the question that had been on his mind throughout the hearing: Why had the district felt so adamant about the state school, especially since the family was deaf, seemed obviously concerned about their daughter, and had made a compelling emotional (if not legal) argument for a rich language environment?

The administrator paused and took a sip from her drink. She discussed the least restrictive environment, the growing desire to integrate students, and the district's commitment to bring children with disabilities into the mainstream. They chatted further, perfunctory questions were asked. The administrator waved to a nearby acquaintance and began to pull away.

"You know something," she said, "someone had to stand up for Janet." She smiled broadly and moved to another part of the room.

---

A judge once wrote that "adequately prepar[ing] individuals for the mainstream of life" was significantly more important than placing children with disabilities into mainstreamed classes.[1] That viewpoint is not universally held. The philosophy statement of Schools Are For Everyone (SAFE) stresses that the "full inclusion" of all children with disabilities into the "same schools and classrooms attended by their brother, sisters, and neighbors" is more than a legal right, it is a "value and the underlying philosophy by which we educate all students."[2]

The integration of children with disabilities is not a simple matter, though. It is not simple because of the inherent conflict of the law. It is not simple because some parents of children with disabilities agree with the judge and some parents agree with SAFE. It is not simple because IDEA requires two sometimes paradoxical considerations—the provision of an appropriate education and placement in the least restrictive environment. It is not simple because other factors come into play: the need to centralize programs, money, disruption.

It is not simple because the notion that all children could be "mainstreamed" if there were only adequate resources and aligned attitudes does not quite fly. It takes to the air and the view seems fine, but Janet Morrison and others come into the picture and suddenly a theoretically unlimited supply of money and the necessary expansive vision of educators does not appear to be enough.

It is not simple because the mainstreaming of children with disabilities is not entirely like other societal efforts at "desegregation." Even if Janet Morrison represented the only child who sought a so-called more restrictive environment, she would still be one viable dissent. Her position should not be seen as a rationale for the "segregation" of children with disabilities or a justification for separation, but as proof that IDEA must serve a great variety of children.

The integration of children with disabilities is not simple because as the full inclusion debate grows more heated and brings into focus the inherent difficulty of IDEA, the individual nature of the law is being challenged by a movement that calls for one option for all students. Ironically, it was the failure of school districts to honor the individual mainstreaming needs of many children with disabilities that inspired the full inclusion movement. Full inclusionists are now described as zealots and ideologues because in seeking one placement for all, they are denying individuals their individual rights in much the same way schools have done in the past.

As written, IDEA cannot move that far and no court has been willing to stretch it beyond its present boundaries. In March

1993 a federal district court in Connecticut was asked to certify, for purposes of a law suit, "all school age children with retardation who have not been or will not be educated with non-disabled children in regular classrooms. . . ."[3] The judge denied class certification, particularly since IDEA prohibited a finding that one placement was appropriate for all the students:

> This court recognizes that mainstreaming is a desirable goal and one which the IDEA seeks to encourage and attain whenever possible. However . . . mainstreaming [must be achieved] on a case by case basis, weighing the individual needs of each child. . . . [T]he very act under which the plaintiffs seek relief . . . emphasizes the individuality of each child.[4]

Whether IDEA will continue to emphasize individual judgments, particularly in light of the effort to change special education into a unitary system, is a significant and difficult question. Ultimately, an effective and humane system must accommodate all children, including Janet Morrison. Determining how and where to educate the five million children with disabilities in this country is particularly daunting when there is such a division about the core issues of integration and separation. The struggle within the educational system and outside among parents, advocates, and reformers is potentially hazardous to all. At the very least those involved in special education should consider the following:

1. An underlying premise of IDEA is that each child's needs are unique, and decisionmaking and program determination must therefore be individually based. The notion of individual determination is contrary to any generic approach to special education. There can be no one program, classroom, philosophy, or placement that applies to all children.

2. Each individual or group involved in the debate must respect and even defend the rights of all other children

to be placed in whatever program meets their unique needs.

3. Advocates for children must realize that they have more in common than in conflict. United they represent a potentially powerful force for children and reduce their own effectiveness by denying the viability of other programmatic options. If the full inclusionists accept that some children *should* be placed in nonregular classes, they may forge a new educational coalition. And before they suggest that such a position would be in violation of their very beliefs, they have to address the issue of Janet Morrison and the many other children who fundamentally require something other than a regular classroom placement. As Douglas and Lynn Fuchs recently recommended to the full inclusion movement, fix your attention on the children you know best and "permit the parents and professional advocates of children with severe behavior problems, hearing impairments, learning disabilities, and so forth to speak on behalf of the children *they* know best."[5]

4. The law must be changed to clarify and underscore the importance of mainstreaming and the right of children to be placed in nonregular classrooms. A stronger burden of proof must be on a school district to prove why a regular or nonregular classroom is inappropriate for a child's individual needs. Current statutes and regulations do not provide enough protection for children who should be fully included. At the same time, the law must be strengthened to protect those children who need alternative placements, particularly for social, linguistic and other reasons.

In the case of Janet Morrison (as just one of many examples), the importance of being in a communicatively appropriate environment should not only be beyond question, but should also represent the most fundamental of educational needs and rights. The IEP process must require specific consideration of and ultimate provision for such needs.

Strengthening the mainstreaming purpose of IDEA and strengthening alternative placements need not be mutually exclusive objectives. Viewing each child individually and eliminating generic concepts "will transform adversaries into allies willing to help secure . . . inclusion . . . [for] those [children] who are the touchstone of [the full inclusion movement's] work and dreams."[6]

5.  Too often abstract notions of inclusion or separation apply. Both in legal and educational terms, the child must be viewed as being in the middle of a circle with all placement options on the circumference of the circle—no one placement is ostensibly more or less restrictive. Need defines LRE. The heavy presumption is that the placement choice of the child's parents is appropriate and that either removal from a regular classroom or systematic insistence that the child be mainstreamed against the wishes of the parents must be discouraged.

6.  Any "push" to refine IDEA to encourage inclusion, with the inevitable "pull" to protect nonregular options, reveals the difficulty of internally resolving the inherent paradox of IDEA. In this regard, it may be that the only practical way to ensure both increased inclusion and individual decisionmaking is to sanction parental choice. Provided that any considered placement option was demonstrably appropriate (could meet the child's needs), the parent would choose placement. In this way arbitrary notions of "restrictiveness" would be eliminated and both inclusion and other options would be truly viable *and* available. This is particularly important since program options are being eliminated as the result of the

appeal of full inclusion. Even a reaffirmation of the continuum's importance may not be enough to protect placement options.

7. Fiscal issues must be addressed by Congress, which has failed to live up to earlier promises to fully or appropriately fund the states. The author acknowledges the ancient and oft-repeated nature of this problem; raising it once more does not reduce its importance.

8. Whether IDEA is changed or jettisoned entirely for a unitary system, the needs of children will not change—in either case the issue of placement, among other issues, will remain and must be addressed by political and educational leaders. If they refuse, the courts will do it for them.

9. Recognition of the paradox of IDEA by the federal government through policy papers, amici briefs, and other efforts is not enough. The placement debate is like no other in the 20-year history of IDEA and, unless it is resolved, the fissures in the special education community will only grow. Federal and state educational agencies must be at the forefront of the placement debate, not merely responding to understandable and historic grievances.

## Endnotes

1. Visco v. School Dist., 684 F. Supp. 1310, 1316 (W.D. Pa. 1988).

2. SAFE philosophy statement, adopted Dec. 1988, revised Dec. 1990.

3. Connecticut Ass'n for Retarded Citizens v. State of Connecticut Board of Educ., No. 2:91CV00180 (JAC) (D. Conn. 1993), 19 IDELR 897.

4. *Id.* at 898.

5.     Douglas Fuchs and Lynn S. Fuchs, *Inclusive Schools Movement and the Radicalization of Special Education Reform*, 60 EXCEPTIONAL CHILDREN, 294, 305 (Feb. 1994).

6.     *Id.*

# Court Decisions Cited

C

## D

# F

Fairfax County School Bd. (see Barnett v. Fairfax County School Bd.)

Fairfax County School Bd. (see DeVries v. Fairfax County School Bd.)

Forest Hills (see Tokarcik v. Forest Hills)

# G

Gaston County Bd. of Educ. (see Shook v. Gaston County Bd. of Educ.)

Geis v. Bd. of Educ., 774 F.2d 575 (3d Cir. 1985), 1985-86 EHLR 557:135, 156-57, 213n, 248-49

Gilhool (see Hendricks v. Gilhool)

Gladys J. v. Pearland Independent School District, 520 F. Supp. 869 (S.D. Texas 1981), 1980-81 EHLR 552:480, 53n

Grace (see Springdale v. Grace)

Greater Egg Harbor High School District (see L.F. v. Greater Egg Harbor High School District)

Greer v. Rome City School District, 950 F.2d 688 (11th Cir. 1991), 18 IDELR 412, 82n, 129-31, 180, 214, 217n

Greer v. Rome City School District, 762 F. Supp. 936 (N.D. Ga. 1990), 132, 138n

Grkman v. Scanlon, 528 F. Supp. 1032 (W.D. Pa. 1981), 251-54, 251n

Group I Defendants (see Parents of Child, Code No. 870901W v. Group I Defendants)

# H

Hairston v. Drosick, 423 F. Supp. 180 (S.D. W. Va. 1976), 1979-80 EHLR 551:143, 83n

Harmon v. Mead School District No. 354, No. CS-90-210-WFN (E.D. Wash. 1991), 17 EHLR 1029, 54n

L.F. v. Greater Egg Harbor High School District, No. SE 84271 (Cal. State Ed. Agency Hearing Aug. 23, 1984), 102, 108n

Lisco v. Woodland Hills School District, 734 F. Supp. 689 (W.D. Pa. 1989), 16 EHLR 861, 233

Longview School District (see Pamela B. v. Longview School District)

## M

Mallory (see St. Louis Developmental Disabilities Treatment Center v. Mallory)

Manchester School District v. Williamson, No. 89-227-D (D.N.H. 1990), 17 EHLR 1, 99, 108n

Martinez v. School Bd., 861 F.2d 1502 (11th Cir. 1988), 1988-89 EHLR 441:257, 83n

Mavis v. Sobol, 839 F. Supp. 968 (N.D.N.Y. 1994), 20 IDELR 1125, 83n

Max M. v. Thompson, 592 F. Supp. 1437 (N.D. Ill. 1984), 177

Mead School District No. 354 (see Harmon v. Mead School District No. 354)

Miller v. School Bd., No. 88-1082-A (E.D. Va. 1989), 1988-89 EHLR 441:333, 228

Mills v. Bd. of Educ., 348 F. Supp. 866 (D.C. 1972), 66

Montgomery County Bd. of Educ. (see Chris D. and Cory M. v. Montgomery County Bd. of Educ.)

Moye (see Pinkerton v. Moye)

## N

New Castle County School District (see Kruelle v. New Castle County School District)

New Jersey Dep't of Human Services (see Remis v. New Jersey Dep't of Human Services)

New York State Ass'n for Retarded Children v. Carey, 466 F. Supp. 487 (E.D.N.Y. 1979), 1979-80 EHLR 551:138, 75-76

Rome City School District (see Greer v. Rome City School District)

Roncker v. Walter, 700 F.2d 1058 (6th Cir. 1983), 1982-83 EHLR 554:381, 100, 124-29, 131, 133, 206, 209, 213, 213n

Rowley (see Board of Educ. v. Rowley)

Rowley v. Bd. of Educ., 483 F. Supp. 528 (S.D.N.Y. 1980), 1979-80 EHLR 551:506, aff'd, 632 F.2d 945 (2d Cir. 1980), 1980-81 EHLR 552:101, 119n, 119-23, 122n, 137n

Royal Oaks Schools, In re, 19 IDELR 194 (Sept. 2, 1992), 102n

Ryan W., In re, No. 225, 1985-86 EHLR 507:239 (Cal. State Ed. Agency Hearing Nov. 25, 1985), 83n

## S

Sacramento City Unified School District v. Rachel H., No. 92-15608 (9th Cir. 1994), 54n

San Francisco Unified School District (see Christopher T. v. San Francisco Unified School District)

Scanlon (see Grkman v. Scanlon)

School Bd. (see Martinez v. School Bd.)

School Bd. (see Miller v. School Bd.)

School District (see Visco v. School District)

School District of Greenville County (see Troutman v. School District of Greenville County)

Sequoia Union High School District (see [ ] v. Sequoia Union High School District)

Sherri A.D. v. Kirby, 975 F.2d 193 (5th Cir. 1992), 19 IDELR 339, 18n

Shook v. Gaston County Bd. of Educ., 882 F.2d 119 (4th Cir. 1989), 1988-89 EHLR 441:561, 217n

Sobol (see Mavis v. Sobol)

Springdale v. Grace, 494 F. Supp. 267 (W.D. Ark. 1980), 1980-81 EHLR 552:191, 37n

Tokarcik v. Forest Hills, 665 F.2d 443 (3d Cir. 1981), 1980-81
    EHLR 552:513, 53n, 217n
Troutman v. School District of Greenville County, No. 82-
    2759-14 (D.S.C. 1983), 1982-83 EHLR 554:487, 207

U

Union Elementary School District, No. 404-89H (Cal. State
    Ed. Agency Hearing, June 18, 1990), 16 EHLR 978, 215n

V

Visco v. School District, 684 F. Supp. 1310 (W.D. Pa. 1988),
    247-48

W

Walter (see Roncker v. Walter)
West Virginia Human Rights Commission (see Board of Educ.
    of the County of Lewis v. West Virginia Human Rights
    Commission)
Williamson (see Manchester School District v. Williamson)
Woodland Hills School District (see Lisco v. Woodland Hills
    School District)

# Index

# G

Gartner, Alan, 29, 96

*Gaston County Bd. of Educ. (see Shook v. Gaston County Bd. of Educ.)*

*Geis v. Bd. of Educ.*, 156-57, 213n, 248-49

*Gilhool (see Hendricks v. Gilhool)*

*Gladys J. v. Pearland Independent School District*, 53n

*Grace (see Springdale v. Grace)*

*Greater Egg Harbor High School District (see L.F. v. Greater Egg Harbor High School District)*

*Greer v. Rome City School District*, 82n, 129-32, 138n, 180, 214, 217n

*Grkman v. Scanlon*, 251-54, 251n

*Group I Defendants (see Parents of Child, Code No. 870901W v. Group I Defendants)*

*Guempel v. State of New Jersey*, 125n

# H

*Hairston v. Drosick*, 83n

*Harmon v. Mead School District No. 354*, 54n

Hatlen, Philip, 151-52

Hearing impaired, 58n

Hehir, Thomas, 98

*Hendricks v. Gilhool*, 100, 108n

Heumann, Judith, 31, 136, 198-215

*Holland (see Board of Educ. v. Holland)*

Holmes, Justice Oliver Wendell, 65

*Honig (see Taylor v. Honig)*

House Subcommittee on Select Education and Civil Rights, 97

# I

*Illinois State Bd. of Educ. (see Board of Educ. v. Illinois State Bd. of Educ.)*

*Illinois State Bd. of Educ. (see Lachman v. Illinois State Bd. of Educ.)*

# T

# U

# V

# W